D0875850

WITHDRAWN

RE: JOYCE'N BECKETT

RE: JOYCE'N BECKETT

edited by
PHYLLIS CAREY AND ED JEWINSKI

FORDHAM UNIVERSITY PRESS
NEW YORK
1992

Library of Congress Cataloging-in-Publication Data

Re: Joyce'n Beckett / edited by Phyllis Carey and Ed Jewinski.
    p.   cm.
    Includes bibliographical references.
    ISBN 0-8232-1340-4 (cloth)   ISBN 0-8232-1341-2 (pbk.)
    1. English literature—Irish authors—History and criticism.
    2. English literature—20th century—History and criticism.
    3. Joyce, James, 1882–1941—Criticism and interpretation.
    4. Beckett, Samuel, 1906–1989—Criticism and interpretation.
    5. Ireland—Intellectual life—20th century.   6. Ireland in
    literature. I. Carey, Phyllis. II. Jewinski, Ed, 1948–   .
    III. Title: Re—Joyce and Beckett.
    PR8754.R4   1991
    820.9′9415′0904—dc20   91–31853
                                                                 CIP

Printed in the United States of America

Contents

Acknowledgments

The editors would like to express their gratitude in particular to Mount Mary College and Wilfrid Laurier University for 1989 mini grants to aid the editors in the preparation of the final copy of this volume.

We would also like to thank all the contributors for their patience, understanding, cooperation, and good suggestions.

Special thanks go to Joanne Buchan for typing and retyping material, to John Harrington for compiling the bibliography, and to Paul Salvini for assisting with the computer at two in the morning.

For the love and support constantly received, Phyllis Carey thanks her husband, Patrick, and her sons, Brian and Michael, and Ed Jewinski thanks his wife, Judi, and his daughters, Nicole and Danielle.

Finally, this book is dedicated to Judi Jewinski and Patrick Carey.

Abbreviations

SAMUEL BECKETT

The Collected Works of Samuel Beckett. New York: Grove, 1970.

Cas	*Cascando and Other Short Dramatic Pieces*
HD	*Happy Days*
HII	*How It Is*
K	*Krapp's Last Tape and Other Dramatic Pieces*
MD	*Malone Dies*
MO	*Molloy*
MPTK	*More Pricks Than Kicks*
MU	*Murphy*
PR	*Proust*
STFN	*Stories and Texts for Nothing*
UN	*The Unnamable*
W	*Watt*
WG	*Waiting for Godot*

The following Beckett texts are not part of the 1970 Collected Works; Grove Press editions, however, have been used for citations.

C	*Company*, 1980
Disjecta	*Disjecta*, 1984
ISIS	*Ill Seen Ill Said*, 1981
LO	*The Lost Ones*, 1972
TN	*Three Novels: Molloy, Malone Dies, The Unnamable*, 1955

JAMES JOYCE

D	*Dubliners*. Ed. Robert Scholes. New York: Viking, 1957.
FW	*Finnegans Wake*. New York: Viking, 1939.
P	*A Portrait of the Artist as a Young Man*. Ed. Richard Ellmann. New York: Viking, 1964.
SH	*Stephen Hero*. Ed. John J. Slocum and Herbert Cahoon. New York: New Directions, 1963.
U	*Ulysses*. Ed. Hans Walter Gabler et al. 3 vols. New York: Garland, 1984.

Introduction

"Thus the unfacts, did we possess them, are too imprecisely few to warrant our certitude. . . ." (FW 57)

I

THE ANNOUNCEMENT OF SAMUEL BECKETT'S DEATH on December 22, 1989, brought tributes from all over the world acknowledging Beckett as a truly original writer of this century. James Joyce was linked with Beckett in the many memorials as an important figure in Beckett's artistic development. Although this manuscript was in its final stages when Beckett died, it serves also as a tribute to both Samuel Beckett and James Joyce, two of the most important authors of the twentieth century.

The personal and literary relationships between James Joyce and Samuel Beckett have long been of interest to critics of both writers. Yet, rather surprisingly, only one book—Barbara Reich Gluck's *Beckett and Joyce: Friendship and Fiction* (1979)—has been dedicated to the subject. Though deserving credit as an ambitious attempt to address the Joyce–Beckett relationship, Gluck's study does not use any of Beckett's works after 1970 or those of his critics after 1974 and, as Melvin J. Friedman puts it in his "Prefatory Note" to the Joyce–Beckett essays in *The Seventh of Joyce*, Gluck's *Beckett and Joyce: Friendship and Fiction* never quite "manages to rid itself of its . . . origins . . . as a Ph.D. dissertation" (28). Besides Gluck's study, however, many other researchers and critics have addressed the Joyce–Beckett relationship; the difficulty is simply that the material is scattered among chapters of books and scholarly journals. Our book, therefore, has three simple purposes. First, it provides an overview of the main trends and dominant problems that typify the discussion of the relationship of Joyce and Beckett. Second, it includes an extensive bibliogra-

phy, "Joyce and Beckett: A Preliminary Checklist of Publications," compiled by John P. Harrington, so that scholars interested
in the topic can begin to study the approaches, findings, and
arguments available. Finally, the book offers eleven new essays—
which, in their various ways, attempt to expand our understanding of the literary relationships between James Joyce and Samuel
Beckett—and a one-act play, which creatively celebrates the Joyce–
Beckett relationship.

Readers should not be surprised by a lack of Johnsonian balance
when reading through the pages of this book. No strictures were
imposed on the essayists beyond the demand that they be lively
and engaging. The complexity of both Joyce and Beckett seemed
to warrant a multi-focused view of the topic, and variety of
approach, critical practice, and theoretical assumptions seemed
the wisest choice when considering what is most worth knowing
about these writers and their relationship. However, to prevent the
book from sprawling, we have imposed an overall order. The first
essay, by Melvin J. Friedman, offers an assessment of the strengths
and weaknesses of the biographies available to readers of Joyce and
Beckett. This essay is placed first because it deals with an issue
that has, until recently, not received enough attention. No biography can claim to be "innocent"; the success of such a book
depends to a great extent on the personality that attempts to offer
a unified vision of a writer's life. Biographies, in other words,
must be read scrupulously, and a reader must always keep in mind
the controlling "voice" of the biographer. By placing emphasis on
this point, Friedman sets the tone for most of the book: some
degree of detachment is necessary so that the "unfacts" do not
woo a reader into a false "certitude." The next two essays, those
by John Fletcher and John P. Harrington, explore Beckett's and
Joyce's handling of Irish materials in the short story form. John
Fletcher carefully measures Beckett's success with the form by
offering a detailed comparison of the treatment of humor in
Beckett's "Fingal" and Joyce's "Ivy Day in the Committee
Room." John P. Harrington offers a complementary essay. He
points out that Beckett's 1934 short story "A Case in a Thousand"
(never republished) closely parallels Joyce's "A Painful Case." The
notion that Beckett was predominantly influenced by *Finnegans
Wake* seems unfounded. Beckett knew his Joyce and his Ireland

well, and the handling of the material in "A Case in a Thousand" leads Harrington into exploring Beckett's consciousness of being an Irish writer.

In the fourth and fifth essays, the horizon expands beyond the short story, although the techniques of the writers are still the issue. David Cohen and James Acheson focus their attention on the allusive links Joyce and Beckett create to keep their works unified. In " 'For This Relief Much Thanks': Leopold Bloom and Beckett's Use of Allusion," David Cohen explores the differing functions of allusions in *Ulysses*. When he turns his attention to Beckett, he notes that the use of allusions is more closely allied to Bloom's than it is to the larger narrative voice of *Ulysses*. In "Beckett Re-Joycing: *Words and Music*," James Acheson finds himself similarly attracted to the allusions in Beckett's play and concludes that a full appreciation of Beckett's achievement in *Words and Music* can be attained only if the reader keeps in mind that the play constantly makes allusions to *Krapp's Last Tape* and the "Sirens" and "Cyclops" episodes of *Ulysses*. Acheson's essay, in part, suggests how subtly Beckett's "minimalism" expands.

Allusion, of course, is only one technique; we have paired the next two essays because they both concentrate on larger narrative structures and patterns. Alan Loxterman's essay " 'The More Joyce Knew the More He Could' and 'More than I Could': Theology and Fictional Technique in Joyce and Beckett" focuses on the repeated emphasis in both Joyce and Beckett of observers observing observers. Such scenes raise the question of who is observing—another character? the readers? the author? the author's Author, God? The metaphysical teasing of both readers and characters imparts to Joyce and Beckett a serio-comic philosophical perspective that, to a degree, toys with the problems of theology. Michael Patrick Gillespie in his "Textually Uninhibited: The Playfulness of Joyce and Beckett," on the other hand, foregrounds the impulse for gaming that Joyce and Beckett alike use as narrative strategies. With specific examples from *Ulysses*, Gillespie deals with the framing of games in Joyce's works, and then he extrapolates from this to consider how Beckett drew upon the tradition of game playing established in Joyce.

Two essays deal primarily with concepts of the artist. Phyllis Carey in "Stephen Dedalus, Belacqua Shuah, and Dante's *Pietà*," focuses on the differences between Joyce's and Beckett's appropriations of the Dantean portrayal of piety/pity in *The Divine Comedy*. Her argument is that while the young Joyce transforms Dante's spiritual and moral piety into an aesthetic worship of beauty, the young Beckett dichotomizes Dantean *pietà* into paradox to question the possibility of pity. Susan Brienza is also interested in aesthetics, but she strikingly inverts the usual paradigms by exploring the images of flow and elimination as central motifs of artistic creation.

The concluding essays of the volume pursue the problems of "authority" in writing, particularly in how Joyce and Beckett explore reference, self-reference and textual author-ity. In Steven Connor's "Authorship, Authority, and Self-Reference" and in Ed Jewinski's "James Joyce and Samuel Beckett: From Epiphany to Anti-Epiphany," the apparent dichotomy between modernist authority (in Joyce) and postmodernist surrender of authority (in Beckett) masks the point that both authors exercise a high degree of anxious, proprietal control over their texts. The "anxiety of influence," to borrow Harold Bloom's phrase, is a striking feature in the texts of both Joyce and Beckett. An analysis of that "anxiety" clarifies why "textual self-reference" is so dominant in both writers' works. An original one-act play and the first cumulative bibliography on the Joyce–Beckett relationship conclude the volume. Denis Regan's "Beckett et Joyce et Beckett-esque" lightheartedly looks back at Beckett's life, works, and relationship with James Joyce from the vantage point of Beckett's "afterlife mind." The concluding bibliography lists the major comparative studies of Joyce and Beckett, thereby providing an invaluable resource for present and future scholars of both Joyce and Beckett.

II

Our decision to end the essay-portion of the book with studies focusing on the "authority" of the writer was made, in part, because it brings many of the arguments concerning Joyce and Beckett full circle. Most of the early responses to Beckett abound with references to Joyce's "influence." Eric Bentley, for example, resorts to redundancy to make the point: "Mr. Beckett is excessively—if quite inevitably—over-influenced by Joyce" (21).

Given that the young Beckett met Joyce and was welcomed not only into the Joyce household but also into the group of early Joyce apologists, and given Beckett's leading essay in *Our Exagmination*, it is not surprising that readers have seen Beckett as under "the influence of those masters who have made *transition* their permanent resting place" (Thomas 454–55). While "influence"—most frequently in the form of imitation—was assumed for roughly half of Beckett's career, critics have increasingly focused on the contrasts between Beckett and Joyce, perhaps stimulated by the famous—and infamous—Israel Shenker "interview" that critics perhaps erroneously took for some time as Beckett's own assessment of the relationship when "evidently no direct interview ever took place" (Gontarski, " 'Illstarred Punster,' " 31; Bair 651 n. 22): " 'The kind of work I do is one in which I'm not master of my material. The more Joyce knew the more he could. He's tending toward omniscience and omnipotence as an artist. I'm working with impotence, ignorance. I don't think impotence has been exploited in the past' " (Shenker 3). Beckett's purported defining of himself in opposition to Joyce— an influence of a different kind—has been the focus of a number of studies, perhaps the most well known of which is Stanley Gontarski's *The Intent of Undoing*. As the frequently quoted passage from Shenker illustrates, however, critics can perhaps be misled into seeing the exact contours of what is at the least an extremely ambiguous relationship. Nevertheless, the contrast between Beckett's "impotence" and Joyce's "omnipotence" serves as a useful strategy to disclose other elements in their respective arts as two of the essays in this volume (see Loxterman; Jewinski) point out in different ways.

That the similarities and differences between Joyce and Beckett have taken on almost mythic proportions is only one problem in the study of these writers. Erroneous notions, too, have been perpetuated, even though critics have attempted on numerous occasions to stamp them out. The notion that Beckett was Joyce's amanuensis still survives although Bair (71) and Gluck (27) have pointed out that Beckett's willingness to assist Joyce does not support the view that Beckett acted as a secretary. The proliferation of such misunderstandings is hard to eradicate, and John P. Harrington's essay in this volume shows how such errors are multiplied and later re-defined (see Harrington).

A "misreading" of another kind is also frequent. Several Beckett critics have commented on a passage of *Finnegans Wake* as a direct reference to the young Beckett, when Joyce, in fact, had not even met Beckett prior to writing the passage originally:

> Sam knows miles bettern me how to work the miracle. And I see by his diarrhio he's dropping the stammer out of his silenced bladder since I bonded him off more as a friend and as a brother to try and grow a muff and canonise his dead feet down on the river airy by thinking himself into the fourth dimension and place the ocean between his and ours, the churchyard in the cloister of the depths, after he was capped out of beurlads scoel for the sin against the past participle and earned the factitation of codding chaplan and being as homely gauche as swift B.A.A. Who gets twickly fullgets twice as allemanden huskers. But the whacker his word the weaker our ears for auracles who parles parses orileys. Illstarred punster, lipstering cowknucks. 'Twas the quadra sent him and Trinity too. And he can cantab as chipper as any oxon ever I mood with, a tiptoe singer! He'll prisckly soon hand tune your Erin's ear for you . . . [FW 467].

Barbara Gluck saw in this passage a "reference to Beckett's alma mater and an apparent allusion to his first work of fiction, *More Pricks than Kicks*" (28). Stanley Gontarski used the quote as an epigraph for his essay "Samuel Beckett, James Joyce's Illstarred Punster" in *The Seventh of Joyce*. Deirdre Bair asserted that Joyce was disparaging Beckett in the quote (70), while Eoin O'Brien quoted the passage as a tribute by Joyce to the potential of the young Beckett (267). And, as recently as February 1989, according to *The New York Times* and *The "Beckett Circle,"* Barry McGovern introduced his performance of *Stirrings Still* by "reading a passage from *Finnegans Wake* in which James Joyce called Beckett 'a tiptoe singer' and said, apparently in reference to Beckett's book *More Pricks than Kicks*, "He'll prisckly soon hand tune you Erin's ear for you' " (Gussow 13).

If Joyce, like many of his readers, noted that the passage could, by mere chance and circumstance, refer to Beckett, then so be it. But as Phyllis Carey discovered while preparing a paper for the

Frankfurt Joyce Conference (1984), the famous passage was published in *transition* before Beckett met Joyce. Unless the written
records were in error, Beckett did not arrive in Paris until the fall
of 1928, after the printing of the now famous section in the
summer of 1928 (Number 13). Puzzled by the seeming applicabil-
ity of the passage to Beckett, Carey wrote to Beckett, asking him
to solve the mystery. He replied in his usual succinct fashion: "I
first met Joyce late 28. The passage cannot refer to me" (Letter to
Carey, 27 January 1984).

Continued research into the problem led Carey to several interesting discoveries. The fair copy of "Dave the Dancekerl" (Chapter 2, subsection B), generally dated April 1926, has the original
passage in kernel form (JJA: 57:200). The phrases "illstarred
punster" and "tiptoe singer," however, were added after the
publication of the version printed in *transition*, probably in the
early thirties (see JJA 61:230, 423, 650). The original passage, then,
was composed while Beckett was still, at least to Joyce, an
unknown student at Trinity. It seems, therefore, an inaccurate
reading of the passage whenever it is understood to be intentionally referring to Beckett, particularly the alleged allusion to *More
Pricks than Kicks* since the publication of the passage from the *Wake*
in *transition* predates the publication of Beckett's book by six
years. The moral seems to be—as Beckett put it when acting as
the first official critic of the *Wake*—that "The danger is in the
neatness of identifications" (*Disjecta* 19). Throughout this book,
the neatness of "identifications" will be questioned in a variety of
ways, and as a result, we believe, not only will Beckett and Joyce
be more fully understood, but their "influence" upon each other
expanded and clarified. In that endeavor, we offer this volume to
present and future scholars of Joyce and Beckett, who, we are
confident, will continue to explore in the Joyce–Beckett literary
relationship the facts, the unfacts, and that vast, rich region in
between.

PHYLLIS CAREY
Mount Mary College

ED JEWINSKI
Wilfrid Laurier University

WORKS CITED

Bair, Deirdre. *Samuel Beckett: A Biography*. New York: Harcourt Brace Jovanovich, 1978.

Beckett, Samuel. Letter to Phyllis Carey. 27 January 1984.

Bentley, Eric. "The Talent of Samuel Beckett." *The New Republic* 14 May 1956: 20–21.

Friedman, Melvin J. "Prefatory Note." *The Seventh of Joyce*. Ed. Bernard Benstock. Bloomington: Indiana University Press, 1982, 27–28.

Gluck, Barbara. *Beckett and Joyce: Friendship and Fiction*. Lewisburg, Pa.: Bucknell University Press, 1979.

Gontarski, S.E. *The Intent of Undoing in Samuel Beckett's Dramatic Texts*. Bloomington: Indiana University Press, 1985.

——. "Samuel Beckett, James Joyce's 'Illstarred Punster.' " *The Seventh of Joyce*. Ed. Bernard Benstock. Bloomington: Indiana University Press, 1982, 29–36.

Gussow, Mel. "New Book by Beckett in Dramatic Entrance." *The New York Times* 4 February 1989: sec. Y; 13.

The James Joyce Archive. Ed. Michael Groden et al. New York and London: Garland Publishing, 1978.

O'Brien, Eoin. *The Beckett Country: Samuel Beckett's Ireland*. Monkstown, Co. Dublin: Black Cat Press, 1986.

Shenker, Israel. "Moody Man of Letters." *The New York Times* 6 May 1956: sec 2; 1,3.

Thomas, Dylan. "Recent Novels." *New English Weekly* 12.23 (17 March 1938): 454–55.

RE: JOYCE'N BECKETT

Richard Ellmann's *James Joyce* and Deirdre Bair's *Samuel Beckett: A Biography*: The Triumphs and Trials of Literary Biography[1]

Melvin J. Friedman

THE LATE RICHARD ELLMANN was simply the nonpareil literary biographer of our era. Other biographies, when measured against Ellmann's *James Joyce*, seem always to be wanting, to come up short in some essential way. It is no accident that reviewers, despairing at other biographical offerings, often invoke Ellmann. Thus, for example, a dispirited Irving Howe, unhappy with Carlos Baker's *Ernest Hemingway: A Life Story*, makes this observation: "During the past few decades, when our professors have been composing a large number of Definitive Lives, often on the premise that truth is a by-blow of bulk, we have had only one major work in this genre, Richard Ellmann's *James Joyce*, a book endlessly pleasing for its ability to evoke the spiritual history of a great novelist without slipping into pedantry or cozy sentimentalism" (96).

Katherine Frank, in assessing the generic possibilities of literary biography, starts her discussion by coupling Ellmann's *James Joyce* with Leon Edel's *Henry James*, "two of the greatest modern biographies" (500). She proceeds to locate "the distinctive voice of Richard Ellmann" and finds that "the success of *James Joyce*, for all its thematic acuteness and historical breadth and soundness, derives from this voice" (502). Frank has here, I think, defined the one *essential* characteristic of Ellmann's labors as a biographer,

1. An earlier version of the first half of this essay appeared as "Ellmann on Joyce" in *Re-Viewing Classics of Joyce Criticism*, ed. Janet Egleson Dunleavy (Urbana: University of Illinois Press, 1991), 131–41. The second half of this essay is based in part on my "Beckett's Life Story," *Contemporary Literature* 20.3 (Summer 1979): 377–85.

that which distinguishes his efforts from so many pedestrian practitioners of the form.

The notion has occurred to me that *James Joyce* occupies the same position in the history of modern literary biography as Erich Auerbach's *Mimesis* occupies in the history of modern literary criticism and theory. Ellmann's "voice" as a biographer–critic and Auerbach's "voice" as an unerring reader of texts appear to have determined the contours of two types of literary discourse. The ambition of both enterprises seems absolutely stunning, Ellmann's perhaps in a less obvious way than Auerbach's. *Mimesis* closely examines texts from Homer and the Old Testament through Virginia Woolf while *James Joyce* treats a single literary life—but one that engaged and refashioned many of Auerbach's texts. Ellmann charts the circuitous course that the "myth-hopping" Joyce (words he later used in *Ulysses on the Liffey*) took as he wandered across the literary terrain from Greek antiquity to French Symbolist expression. To sound the litany of Joyce's sources and forebears, from Homer and Aristotle down to Dujardin and Mallarmé, passing by Dante, Vico, Goethe, Flaubert, Tolstoy, and Ibsen, is to engage in something quite as elaborate as Auerbach's schema.[2]

To conclude the counterpointing of Ellmann and Auerbach, one might suggest that neither limits himself to a single method, that neither falls victim to a single approach. Ellmann, for example, is quite aware of the seductions offered a biographer by Freud, but unlike Leon Edel "in his search for the figure under the carpet" (Frank 501), he seems to keep a respectful distance. Ellmann, in fact, concludes his "Freud and Literary Biography" somewhat equivocally:

> That Freud makes biography difficult does not mean that he should be put aside. Biographers need a depth psychology, and Freud, with his followers and deviationists, offers one. . . . Perhaps we should be gingerly in applying Freud's theories, for it is when they are most ostentatious that they awaken the most uneasiness. . . .

2. Ellmann, in a sense, starts the task in *James Joyce* and completes it in such elegant studies as *Ulysses on the Liffey*, *The Consciousness of Joyce*, a series of prefaces and introductions, and scattered essays. These critical writings serve almost as addenda to the Joyce biography.

For all this Freud remains a model, though no doubt a tricky one [478].

Auerbach, in *Mimesis*, also eschews any kind of narrowing critical persuasion. Thus he remarks in his epilogue:

> The method of textual interpretation gives the interpreter a certain leeway. He can choose and emphasize as he pleases. It must naturally be possible to find what he claims in the text. My interpretations are no doubt guided by a specific purpose. Yet this purpose assumed form only as I went along, playing as it were with my texts, and for long stretches of my way I have been guided only by the texts themselves [556].

Indeed "the texts themselves" seem to be what matter to both Ellmann and Auerbach, who manage to seduce their readers through the clarity and elegance of their language and devotion to literary study rather than through any kind of ostentatious, doctrinaire theorizing.

I

Katherine Frank rightly points out that *James Joyce* was published "before the recent flurry of biographical criticism" (501). It is a work conceived, as she indicates, before biography "lost its critical innocence" (499). Ellmann brought out *James Joyce* in 1959, a year after his edition of Stanislaus Joyce's *My Brother's Keeper* appeared (see Friedman, "Out of His Brother's Shadow" 18–20). This seemed to begin the second phase of his scholarly career, which brought him from Yeats to Joyce. Not only did the Joyce biography win the National Book Award, but it kept attracting the adjective "definitive"—which survived into Walter Goodman's Ellmann obituary in the May 14, 1987 *New York Times*: ". . . his 1959 biography that is considered the definitive work on the Irish novelist. . . ." (What was once "definitive biography" now is broadened to become "definitive work"![3])

3. A less than laudatory review of the second edition of *James Joyce* by Hugh Kenner carries the title "The Impertinence of Being Definitive." Phillip Herring, in discussing Kenner's review and other matters pertinent to my present labors, speaks of "the advertised definitiveness of *James Joyce*" (116). I am indebted to Herring for allowing me to see his "Richard Ellmann's *James Joyce*" in its manuscript form. It has been published in *The Biographer's Art* (see Herring). See also my "Joyce's Life," *The Progressive* 23.12 (December 1959): 49–50.

This time of "critical innocence" about the nature of biographical art was also one of relative scholarly innocence about Joyce's work. The early seminal criticism of Harry Levin, William York Tindall, Hugh Kenner, and Richard M. Kain was already in place, but the scholarly paraphernalia was still awaiting the editorial skills of Richard Ellmann, Robert Scholes, Richard Kain, David Hayman, Phillip Herring, Michael Groden, and Hans Walter Gabler, among others. *James Joyce* appeared at that restless moment in Joyce commentary when the early critical soundings were about to give way to more substantial and sophisticated scholarship. Many of the works that passed for scholarship before Ellmann's biography were "authorized" and orchestrated by Joyce himself, including *Our Exagmination Round His Factification·for Incamination of Work in Progress* (1929), Stuart Gilbert's *James Joyce's "Ulysses"* (1930), Frank Budgen's *James Joyce and the Making of "Ulysses"* (1934), and Herbert Gorman's *James Joyce* (1939). Stuart Gilbert's 1957 edition of the letters was the last of the works that seemed to carry Joyce's own signature of approval.

Ellmann's biography removed many of the cobwebs that were accumulating about the life and the work, especially those placed there by Gorman's *James Joyce*. The final sentences of Ellmann's introduction express with clarity and eloquence what Joyce is about:

> Implicit in his work there is a new notion of greatness, greatness not as an effulgence but as a burrowing that occasionally reaches the surface of speech or action. This kind of greatness can be perceived in his life, too, though camouflaged by frailties. To be narrow, peculiar, and irresponsible, and at the same time all-encompassing, relentless, and grand, is Joyce's style of greatness, a style as difficult, but ultimately as rewarding, as that of *Finnegans Wake*.[4]

4. Richard Ellmann, *James Joyce* (New York: Oxford University Press, 1959), 5. I will refer to the first edition of *James Joyce* throughout my essay. Reviewers of the 1982 second edition were generally agreed that the additions and alterations were not earthshaking. Philip Gaskell, for example, remarked: "This method of producing *JJ* II has not altered the tenor and conclusions of Ellmann's biography in important ways" (253). Denis Donoghue concurred: "Indeed, the revision is pretty light. Ellmann has retained the old structure, and has inserted the new stuff at appropriate points" (15). The one clear advantage of the second edition, as many reviewers have remarked, is Mary Reynolds' scrupulously detailed index. The three sentences quoted in my text, by the way, remain intact in the new edition.

Ellmann's is emphatically a "critical biography" in that it mixes life with letters in a most intriguing and original way. There is no formula for what he has done. Details of the life play off against commentary on the work in a kind of seamless fashion; one tends to reinforce the other at every turn. It is the "voice" of Ellmann, as Katherine Frank remarked, that gives a shape to his biographical–critical enterprise, rather than any theoretical predispositions.

Ellmann is faithful to chronology. On each left-hand page are the inclusive dates of the chapter; on each right-hand page, Joyce's age. The critic in Ellmann will occasionally take over for the biographer, with something of an entr'acte effect. Such a sustained critical interlude occurs when Ellmann abandons his narrative and offers twenty-five of the most incisive pages we have on *Ulysses* (see chap. 22, 367–90). In *Lives and Letters*, Richard D. Altick interestingly explains Ellmann's rhythm on this occasion:

> He described the origins of *Ulysses'* characters, places, and events in the order in which Joyce encountered them as a child and young man. Then, having reached the year 1914, Ellmann stopped the film and in a retrospective chapter reran the reels with a different filter, this time drawing out from the chaos of events a leading theme previously undiscussed: Joyce's artistic development, the emergence of peculiarities of technique which were destined to make *Ulysses* so revolutionary a work of fiction, and the slow formation of an over-all plan for the book. Once Joyce was seen to be prepared for the great work of his life, Ellmann resumed the narrative and watched the author putting his long-meditated plans into execution [381].

Ellmann, then, simply does not conform to what Leon Edel called in *Writing Lives: Principia Biographica* (while speaking of *James Joyce* and two other biographies) "the old-fashioned Victorian chronological manner." Ellmann's own critical urgencies break in on the narrative, unsettling, even undercutting, its forward movement. This surely is a kind of experimentalism, and would seem to give *James Joyce* an honored place among what Edel classifies as "the more experimental kinds of biography in our century" (185; see also Nadel, esp. 173–74).

A closer look at Ellmann's innovative Chapter 22 demonstrates that it is not what one usually expects from "old-fashioned

Victorian" biography. There are relatively few biographical details in this chapter, a great many critical insights. Ellmann discusses such matters of technique as Joyce's use of interior monologue (inspired by Dujardin, George Moore, Tolstoy, Stanislaus' journal), his flirtation with literary counterpoint, his positing of "undependable narrators," his blurring of the line separating fact and fiction. He also discusses characters, sources, themes, and events in convincing and vigorous new ways. The significance of Homer, Dante, and Shakespeare to Joyce's enterprise is given fresh emphasis. Ellmann moves back and forth through the oeuvre showing how *Ulysses* profits from earlier Joycean techniques and anticipates certain things in *Finnegans Wake*. Chapter 22, in breathtaking, telegraphic fashion, offers a showcase for the biographer's critical skills. It has firm ties to Ellmann's two later Joyce books, *Ulysses on the Liffey* (1972) and *The Consciousness of Joyce* (1977).

In these two studies he fleshes out matters that he could only suggest in *James Joyce*. The patterning of *Ulysses*, with its "triadic organization" (space/time/space–time), resulting in six sections of three chapters each, is the basis of Ellmann's schema in *Ulysses on the Liffey*. Homer is made to wrestle with Aristotle and David Hume for ascendancy as Ellmann rarely restricts his discussion to Odyssean parallels. Indeed he finds help from an enormous number of literary texts, both ancient and modern, insisting on the importance of *The Divine Comedy*, *Faust*, *Candide*, and the *Argonautica* of Apollonius of Rhodes, among many other works, in illuminating sections of *Ulysses*. *Ulysses on the Liffey*, a short book of barely two hundred pages, has something of the large lines and epic sweep of Auerbach's *Mimesis*. Ellmann proves, finally, how textually complex *Ulysses* is by mounting evidence of the staggering number of literary and mythical echoes sounded in its pages. (His contribution to *Ulysses* study here seems to me of the same order as David Hayman's justly applauded theory of the arranger in his *"Ulysses": The Mechanics of Meaning*.)

The Consciousness of Joyce is more directly concerned with sources and scrupulously lists in an appendix the contents of Joyce's Trieste library. While Ellmann's critical gifts were stunningly on display in *Ulysses on the Liffey*, his scholarship was a dominant presence in his 1977 study. When commenting on the labors involved in assembling the appendix, Michael Patrick Gil-

lespie remarked: "While often the task must have seemed daunt-
ing, scholars familiar with the list have already testified to the
merit of Ellmann's work. As researchers develop the information
on Joyce's intellectual background, the debt to Ellmann's industry
will continue to grow" (12). *The Consciousness of Joyce* also has the
usual Ellmann finesse; there are many passages that display his
accustomed pacing, his assurance about the critical act, such as:
"Joyce felt more than most writers how interconnected literature
is, how to press one button is to press them all. He exhibits none
of that anxiety of influence which Harold Bloom has recently
attributed to modern writers. Yeats said, 'Talk to me of originality
and I will turn upon you with rage.' If Joyce had any anxiety, it
was over not incorporating influences enough" (47–48). The tidy
juxtapositions, the elegance of phrasing make for vintage Ellmann. Goethe joins the triumvirate of Homer, Dante, and Shakespeare as being essential to Joyce's enterprise in *Ulysses*. While the
German writer was mentioned only in passing in the Joyce biography, he plays a crucial role in *The Consciousness of Joyce*. For
example, Ellmann points out that the likely source for Leopold
Bloom's taking on the name Henry Flower in his epistolary
exchanges with Martha Clifford is Faust's taking on the name
Heinrich in his relationship with Gretchen.

While the *Ulysses* criticism offered in *James Joyce* is especially
notable, Ellmann "reran the reels with a different filter" on two
earlier occasions (chapters 15 and 18) with discussions of "The
Dead" and *A Portrait of the Artist as a Young Man*. Aside from these
set pieces there are critical insights sprinkled throughout the
narrative—on virtually every page—so many as to overwhelm the
casual reader of biography. The biographer as critic, a role Ellmann is comfortable with, is in no sense a given. Even though
many biographers have also written criticism, there is no assurance
of the coupling of the two. Here, for example, is Carlos Baker
speaking to this point in the Foreword to his *Ernest Hemingway: A
Life Story*: "Again, although the present work offers a substantial
amount of information about the origin, development, and reception of his writings, it is not what is commonly called a 'critical
biography,' in which the biographer seeks to explore, analyze,
and evaluate the full range of his subject's literary output simultaneously with the record of his life" (5). Something of the opposed

tendency was expressed by Joseph Frank in the Preface to his *Dostoevsky*: "I sketch in the background of the events of Dostoevsky's private existence, but I deal at length only with those aspects of his quotidian experience which seem to me to have some critical relevance—only with those that help to cast some light on his books. . . . I do not go from the life to the work, but rather the other way round" (xii). (Ellmann is fondly acknowledged, by the way, in Frank's Preface.) Ellmann's position is somewhere between Baker's and Frank's although it tilts in Frank's direction. The difference between Ellmann and Joseph Frank is that the Joyce biography starts with the life (actually the pre-life, with a chapter entitled "The Family Before Joyce"), which is allowed free reign in determining the contours of the enterprise. The life and the work are securely tied together whenever possible, but the life story seems to pre-empt everything, even, to the despair of a number of reviewers, the details of his creative process.[5]

If the glimpses at Joyce's workshop are offered at oblique angles, one still comes away with a precise sense of how his talent matured. Ellmann is careful to show us how the "epiphanies" Joyce wrote between 1900 and 1903 offered the beginnings of a career conceived in the shadows of the French Symbolist prose poem. He observes the opening out and gradual thickening of the texture as the works gain in complexity and assume new experimental possibilities. But Ellmann never really makes the claim that the historian David Donald made in the Preface of his *Look Homeward: A Life of Thomas Wolfe*: "But chiefly this book is a study of the creative process, the story of Thomas Wolfe's evolution as a writer" (xvi–xvii). This is a surprising emphasis for an historian, but Donald does manage to discredit the widely circulating image of Wolfe as a "literary naif" and a "Bunyanesque epic singer" in favor of a more conscious writer aware of the problems of his craft. But he is not able, it seems to me, to offer new readings of Wolfe's fiction in the way that Ellmann does with Joyce.

5. Phillip Herring raised this point in his "Richard Ellmann's *James Joyce*" when discussing the second edition: "It does not seem too much to ask that a revised biography of one of the century's greatest writers reveal more about his creative process," especially in light of *The James Joyce Archive*'s appearing in sixty-three volumes several years before 1982 (124).

II

Most literary biographers manage to use the words "life" or "biography" in their subtitles. Witness, for example, Virginia Spencer Carr's *The Lonely Hunter: A Biography of Carson McCullers*, Joan Givner's *Katherine Anne Porter: A Life*, Matthew Bruccoli's *Some Sort of Epic Grandeur: The Life of F. Scott Fitzgerald*, Joseph Blotner's *Faulkner: A Biography*, Baker's *Ernest Hemingway: A Life Story*, and Donald's *Look Homeward: A Life of Thomas Wolfe*. Ellmann uses neither of these words nor does he offer a subtitle. None of the above books, not even Donald's, is in any real sense a critical biography. Analysis of the work is usually kept to a minimum. The life is, fittingly, of supreme importance in all these biographies. But so is it in *James Joyce*, despite the fact there is no subtitle to call attention to it.

A number of the above biographies have been criticized for being mainly inventories of their subjects' "laundry lists." George Steiner, for example, saw in Baker "an interminable record of Hemingway's 'life story' while leaving out all that matters" (147). Even Ellmann's least sympathetic reviewers shy away from that kind of condemnation. Throughout *James Joyce*, Ellmann's biographical "voice" never seems to permit the accumulation of monotonous detail. It is always hard at work introducing surprising juxtapositions, making incisive comparisons. The first meeting with Yeats, for example, is described in a paragraph that should be the envy of every literary biographer.

> Their meeting has a symbolic significance in modern literature, like the meeting of Heine and Goethe. The defected Protestant confronted the defected Catholic, the landless landlord met the shiftless tenant. Yeats, fresh from London, made one in a cluster of writers whom Joyce would never know, while Joyce knew the limbs and bowels of a city of which Yeats knew well only the head. The world of the petty bourgeois, which is the world of *Ulysses* and the world in which Joyce grew up, was for Yeats something to be abjured. Joyce had the same contempt for both the ignorant peasantry and the snobbish aristocracy that Yeats idealized. The two were divided by upbringing and predilection [104].

The details are more figural than literal. Another biographer might have busily accumulated more conventional information

but would probably have ended up with a far less suggestive
vignette.

Ellmann's method seems to thrive on juxtaposition. He often
manages his balancing technique in a single sentence: "Before
Ibsen's letter Joyce was an Irishman; after it he was a European"
(78). When Joyce arrives in Rome, an event recounted at the
beginning of chapter 14, another nod is made in the direction of
the Norwegian playwright: "Forty-two years before, Ibsen had
whiled away a period of exile in Rome thinking about Norway,
and Ibsen's example was still one to which Joyce attended. But
Ibsen, secure with his small pension, could afford to debate with
friends whether it was better to become an office clerk or to
swallow the latch key and die of starvation. Joyce, like T. S. Eliot
after him, chose to be a clerk" (232). Ellmann manages a number
of juxtapositions involving the brothers. One of the most persua-
sive occurs at the end of Part III: "It is easy to see that James was a
difficult older brother, yet Stanislaus was a difficult younger one.
If James was casual and capricious, Stanislaus was punctilious and
overbearing. James knew his laxity of behavior to be an appearance
he could, in sudden tautness, brush aside; Stanislaus knew his own
self-discipline to be largely a revolt against his brother's faults"
(496).

III

Among the most engaging of Ellmann's juxtaposed portraits is
one involving Samuel Beckett. A Flaubertian tableau is managed
when master and disciple are brought together: "Beckett was
addicted to silences, and so was Joyce; they engaged in conversa-
tions which consisted often of silences directed towards each
other, both suffused with sadness, Beckett mostly for the world,
Joyce mostly for himself. Joyce sat in his habitual posture, legs
crossed, toe of the upper leg under the instep of the lower; Beckett,
also tall and slender, fell into the same gesture" (661). The modern
and postmodern perform on stage together here.

There is nothing, alas, in Deirdre Bair's *Samuel Beckett: A
Biography* that approximates this passage. Ellmann himself was an
early reviewer of Bair's biography. Writing about it in the June 15,

1978 *New York Review of Books*, he found very little to his liking. He shook his head sadly at "that continuous slight distortion which Miss Bair performs on Beckett in the absence of interpretation. With so amorphous a conception of him, the biography often seems to be a collection of learned gossip." Hugh Kenner, who has rarely agreed with Ellmann during one of the few careers in literary criticism that rivals Ellmann's in versatility and distinction, on this occasion could only assent. In the August 1978 *Saturday Review* he observed, among other things, how "Bair has pieced together a mosaic of baffling glimpses." The chorus of detractors came finally to include such eminent critics as Ruby Cohn and Martin Esslin and such an important poet as John Montague. The Esslin review, "Scandalising Samuel Beckett: The Coarse Art of Biography," in the March 1979 *Encounter*, was especially scathing.

Yet despite the uncommonly harsh reception *Samuel Beckett: A Biography* received at the hands of reviewers, it seems to have held up rather well. Virtually every critical book on Beckett makes reference to it and offers it a privileged position in its bibliography. A dozen years after its publication, it seems to have found a relatively secure niche for itself.

Bair entered the arena with something of a handicap. Her name had never before been linked with that of Beckett. She had not tested the waters by writing criticism before turning to biography. Ellmann, by the time he published *James Joyce*, had already established himself as a distinguished Yeats scholar and had edited Stanislaus Joyce's memoir, *My Brother's Keeper*. Bair's brashness is a bit off-putting, especially in her Preface where she makes clear how little regard she has for the efforts of most Beckett critics:

> I wrote the biography of Beckett because I was dissatisfied with existing studies of his writings. . . . It seemed to me that many of the leading Beckett interpreters substituted their own brilliant intellectual gymnastics for what should have been solid, responsible scholarship; that they created studies that told more about the quality of the authors' minds than about Beckett's writings. This exasperating situation made me aware of the need for a factual foundation for all subsequent critical exegesis [xii].

In all fairness, the hostile tone of Bair's above remark gives way to more humility and affirmation in the remainder of the Preface and, indeed, in much of the biography proper.[6] But hers is still a curiously negative stance for a fledgling biographer and critic to take, especially when writing a book about a still-living writer whose response to the enterprise was no more positive than "that he would neither help nor hinder [her]" (Bair xi).

Bair's *Samuel Beckett: A Biography* might be thought of as a kind of work in progress, what the French would call a *biographie-en-train-de-se-faire*—a systematic gathering of interviews, letters, manuscripts, and other raw data that attaches a certain chronological coherence to a life and a work not yet finished. There is no distinctive voice apparent here comparable to "the distinctive voice of Richard Ellmann" which Katherine Frank found so essential to "the success of *James Joyce.*" There is a breathless quality to Bair's open-ended enterprise that goes against the grain of certain accepted views that the final judgment of any kind of literary–artistic success should be based on what is left out rather than what has been put in. Deirdre Bair seems not to admire ellipses and Mallarméan blank spaces; she clearly prefers the large-limbed, the oversized to the svelte and streamlined.

The great value of *Samuel Beckett: A Biography* lies in the astonishing amount of new information uncovered. Bair spent six years replacing myths with documents, undertaking a series of literary "digs" with the steadfastness of an archaeologist—almost as if she were trained as a scientist rather than a humanist. Nothing is held sacred, nothing is accepted without questioning, not even Beckett's birth date—declared to be May 13 despite Beckett's insistence that he was born on Good Friday, April 13, and that his life and his literature have been shaped accordingly. (Kenner saw here "in microcosm, the character of Bair's book.") With the myth of Beckett's birthday disposed of, Deirdre Bair proceeds to question the oft-quoted remark made to Alec Reid and others, "You might say I had a happy childhood." Her first chapter,

6. In a piece Bair later wrote for Jeffrey Meyers' edition *The Craft of Literary Biography* (199–215), she made clear the curious circumstances surrounding the composition of her biography in its passage from Columbia University Ph.D. dissertation to published book. Much of Bair's sympathetic essay is devoted to her perplexing encounters with Beckett who, in the end, is generously praised for allowing her to "write a fully independent book" (210). The Bair who emerges from this brief memoir is agreeably modest and self-effacing.

which bears this comment as epigraph, manages to mount impressive evidence to the contrary.

These strategies as a biographer, settled on in her opening pages, serve her well through the remainder of her long narrative. She never hesitates to go against the grain of accepted interpretation, opinion, or conjecture when her findings urge her to do so. Her final authority is often something like the following: "I use here the exact words of persons cited in interviews" (see, for example, 702 n. 51). Indeed the interview seems a crucial ingredient of her biographical excavations, second in importance only to the letters she has examined (especially that trove of "more than three hundred" Beckett wrote to Thomas McGreevy[7]). As she painstakingly chronicles Beckett's life, she documents every questionable statement, every suspect judgment. Her eighty-three pages of notes, discreetly placed at the back of the book where they do not interfere with the reading of her agreeably paced narrative, attest to her vast energy and her dedication to the task of uncovering the authentic Beckett stripped of all disguises.

The man who emerges surprises one a bit, but no more than the Joyce who survived Ellmann's biography and his edition of the letters. Ellmann removed the literary halo from Joyce that Herbert Gorman and Frank Budgen had placed there for an earlier generation. Now Deirdre Bair does something of the same with Beckett, although clearly with a difference. With the notable exception of Lawrence Harvey, who did some modest things with biography in the course of writing one of the best critical studies on the Irish-born writer (*Samuel Beckett, Poet and Critic*), most commentators have stated the known details of his life and avoided any serious biographical commitment. So Beckett's life was still very much virgin territory when Deirdre Bair turned to research her Columbia doctoral dissertation. The perils were painfully evident to her as she suggests on the final page of her text: "In all

7. In her contribution to Jeffrey Meyers' *The Craft of Literary Biography*, Bair commented tellingly: "Therefore, I knew that only the McGreevy letters contained the truth about Beckett's feelings and that only they should be trusted. They came to me fairly late in the writing of the biography, and I remember how many times I was grateful that I had instinctively distrusted the earlier collections and had continued to look for 'just one more source' to verify my hunches" (212).

of this century, it would be difficult to come upon another writer who has so lived through his art that it has become the substance of his life" (640). But she plowed ahead with grim determination, a quality that characterizes every page of her book, perhaps aware all the time that some reviewer would compare her efforts with those of the acknowledged master of the genre, Richard Ellmann.

With Ellmann, as I remarked earlier, groundbreaking critical insight and biographical detail reinforce each other at every turn; this is not the case with Bair, who often allows the work to limp along as an intermittent footnote to the life. She shies away from extended critical analyses; those she offers are intelligent, restrained, sober, but usually quite ancillary. While her notes are filled with references to interviews, letters, manuscripts, photographs, etc., there are remarkably few nods toward critics. The standard names do appear—John Fletcher, Ruby Cohn, Lawrence Harvey, Hugh Kenner, Vivian Mercier, often more for biographical than critical reasons—but there is no feeling that anyone has been of more than passing help in explaining the work to her. Does the statement from the Preface quoted above mean that she has painstakingly been through the criticism and rejected almost all of it? Has Estragon's expletive "Crritic!"—sounded so aggressively in *Waiting for Godot* (48[b])—taken its toll? In any case, one might suspect that one of the happier aspects of the biography for Beckett, if he ever read it, would have been the little criticism in evidence and the absence of the names of the vast majority of his interpreters.

Perhaps because Joyce mattered far more to Beckett than Beckett to Joyce, Deirdre Bair devotes many more pages to the relationship than Ellmann did, although I don't feel that I understand it much better than I did before. Bair, however, is quite good on the Beckett–Lucia Joyce relationship, which she amply documents in its every phase. Indeed she is very successful with the portraits of the women in Beckett's life, including his mother May, Peggy Sinclair, Betty Stockton, Peggy Guggenheim, and Suzanne Deschevaux-Dumesnil,[8] who eventually became his wife. We are told

8. One day a biographer may turn to the life of Suzanne Deschevaux-Dumesnil, just as Brenda Maddox recently produced a life of Nora Barnacle Joyce, *Nora: The Real Life of Molly Bloom*.

that the writer's relationships with all these women were determined by passivity, which explains much about the man, and, perhaps obliquely, something about the work.

The kinds of things we learn from Bair about the work are in the way of pinning down detail and enhancing the bibliographer's fare. Thus we discover that the line from *Krapp's Last Tape*, "Scalded the eyes out of me reading *Effie* again, a page a day, with tears again" (K 25), is a slightly misspelled reference to Theodor Fontane's novel, *Effi Briest*, which Beckett and Peggy Sinclair both read in the summer of 1929. The Elsner sisters, who turn up briefly in the second part of *Molloy* ("The Elsner sisters were not bad neighbours, as neighbours go" [MO 143]), were named after the elderly German women of the same name who ran a kindergarten that Beckett attended. An unfinished play is introduced, based on Samuel Johnson's "The Vanity of Human Wishes," that did not find its way into the "Known Unpublished Works" section of Fletcher's and Federman's *Samuel Beckett: His Works and His Critics, An Essay in Bibliography*. This abandoned work, *Human Wishes*, is important, Bair tells us, because of the crucial role Johnson played in the shaping of Beckett's career. This should give the influence-hunters—and there are many among the Beckettians—another tempting lead in the tracking down of Beckett's seemingly endless inspirations and sources.

Deirdre Bair does artfully bring the life and work together in her discussion of *Watt*. One of the high points of her biography, certainly, is chapter 14, which bears as epigraph the enigmatic final words of this work: "no symbols where none intended." Her discussion of this novel and its relevance to Beckett's sanity during an especially grim period of his life reveals her tact and finesse as biographer and critic. She achieves a fine balance of the two in several elegantly turned sentences: "For Beckett, sanity became analogous with secrecy and cunning. He had to work to stay sane; thus *Watt* became his daily therapy, the means with which he clung to the vestiges of his idea of sanity. . . . Beckett wrote *Watt* in a desperate attempt to stave off complete mental breakdown and filled the book with dialogues and scenes from his own life" (328). Earlier she had skillfully detailed the "more than two years" of therapy Beckett underwent with Dr. Wilfred Ruprecht Bion in the mid-1930s, a time when it was not uncommon for writers to submit to analysis.

She can on occasion press too much the relationship between the life and the work. She offers a long rehearsal of the autobiographical in her discussion of the trilogy:

Beckett's characters either have paralyzed legs or none at all. In his family, two uncles and a cousin each had one leg amputated due to what the Beckett family refers to jokingly as "the family circulatory problem." A third uncle, Dr. James Beckett, a well-known and beloved figure in Dublin, lost both legs through diabetic complications, had severely restricted use of both his arms because of a debilitating muscular disease and became blind. He ended his life in much the same manner as Beckett's *Unnamable*, telling amusing stories to cheer up visitors who usually were horrified and depressed when they arrived to visit the once vital champion swimmer reduced to immobility, but went away in high spirits and good humor because of his infectious, indomitable optimism [371].

Her apparent enthusiasm for these grim details makes one think a bit of those pages describing the Lynch family ("this fortunate family") in *Watt*. But such details do not help especially in understanding the work. Close examination of texts too often takes a back seat to statements like "It is not surprising . . . that *Malone meurt* is the most autobiographical of all Beckett's fiction" (376); "*Fin de partie* also incorporates snatches of his life, but they are far fewer and more impersonal than in *Godot*" (464); "It [*Krapp's Last Tape*] is one of the most openly autobiographical of his writings . . ." (490).

It is rather a shame that Bair did not more closely model the other twenty-five chapters of *Samuel Beckett: A Biography* on the *Watt* chapter—which manages the confrontation between life and work so gracefully and even effortlessly. But Deirdre Bair is no Richard Ellmann, and his subtle mingling of biography and criticism is not easy to come by. (Ellmann, by the way, was apparently one of the people approached who refused to cooperate in Bair's enterprise: "Richard Ellmann would not consent to be interviewed for this book" [699 n. 40].) If Bair does not supply us with new optics for reading the work, for resolving that "blooming buzzing confusion" (words which come to us in *Murphy* by way of William James), she offers an immense amount of valuable background material that does help to bring the writer and his art into something of a new focus.

IV

When Richard Ellmann died in May 1987, there was no doubt remaining that he was not only the foremost literary biographer of his time but one of the two or three most accomplished Joyceans. He had something of a triadic career, which seemed to touch down invariably on Irish soil, as he moved from Yeats to Joyce to Wilde.[9] Deirdre Bair, now in mid-career, seems to have moved from Beckett to Simone de Beauvoir.[10] (Her biography of Beauvoir did appear early in 1991.) Yet she has not entirely abandoned the subject of her first biography, as evidenced by occasional writing on Beckett in the past decade. Among the high points are contributions she made to two volumes of the ongoing series *Dictionary of Literary Biography*[11] and an essay *"Dream of Fair to Middling Women*: A Preface and Postscript" written for a special Beckett number of *The Review of Contemporary Fiction* (Summer 1987). But she has never established herself as a major interpreter of Beckett's work. Her staying power with Beckett indeed falls far short of Ellmann's with Joyce. While he devotedly tilled Joycean soil for the better part of three decades, she seems content with the role of biographer and occasional critic.[12]

9. See the fine appreciative piece by Steven Serafin, "Richard Ellmann," DLB Yearbook 1987, *Dictionary of Literary Biography* (Detroit: Gale, 1988), 226–30. See also the important volume that appeared after the completion of my essay: *Essays for Richard Ellmann: Omnium Gatherum*, ed. Susan Dick, Declan Kiberd, Dougald McMillan, and Joseph Ronsley (Kingston and Montreal: Mc-Gill-Queen's University Press, 1989).

10. She comments in her contribution to Jeffrey Meyers' *The Craft of Literary Biography:* ". . . as I reached the end of that book, and as I began to write a second biography of a living subject, Simone de Beauvoir this time . . ." (206).

11. She did the entries on Beckett for Volume 13, *British Dramatists Since World War II*, edited by Stanley Weintraub, 1982, and for Volume 15, *British Novelists, 1930–1959*, edited by Bernard Oldsey, 1983. These are both substantial essays.

12. James Knowlson is currently at work on what promises to be the definitive biography of Beckett. As Director of the Beckett International Foundation and the Samuel Beckett Archive, he has access to everything necessary to produce the final version of Beckett's life.

WORKS CITED

Altick, Richard D. *Lives and Letters: A History of Literary Biography in England and America*. New York: Knopf, 1965.

Auerbach, Erich. *Mimesis: The Representation of Reality in Western Literature*. Trans. Willard R. Trask. Princeton: Princeton University Press, 1953.

Bair, Deirdre. "*Dream of Fair to Middling Women*: A Preface and Postscript." *The Review of Contemporary Fiction* (Summer 1987): 21–27.

———. *Samuel Beckett: A Biography*. New York: Harcourt Brace Jovanovich, 1978.

———. "Samuel Beckett." *British Dramatists Since World War II*. Ed. Stanley Weintraub. *Dictionary of Literary Biography* 13. Detroit: Gale, 1982. 52–70.

———. "Samuel Beckett." *British Novelists, 1930–1959*. Ed. Bernard Oldsey. *Dictionary of Literary Biography* 15. Detroit: Gale, 1983. 13–32.

———. "Samuel Beckett." *The Craft of Literary Biography*. Ed. Jeffrey Meyers. London: Macmillan, 1985. 199–215.

Baker, Carlos. *Ernest Hemingway: A Life Story*. New York: Bantam, 1970.

Dick, Susan, Declan Kiberd, Dougald McMillan, and Joseph Ronsley, eds. *Essays for Richard Ellmann: Omnium Gatherum*. Kingston and Montreal: McGill-Queen's University Press, 1989.

Donald, David Herbert. *Look Homeward: A Life of Thomas Wolfe*. Boston: Little, Brown, 1987.

Donoghue, Denis. "Denis Donoghue Examines the New Edition of *Ulysses*." *London Review of Books* 20 September–3 October 1984: 14–15.

Edel, Leon. *Writing Lives: Principia Biographica*. New York: Norton, 1984.

Ellmann, Richard. *The Consciousness of Joyce*. Toronto: Oxford University Press, 1977.

———. "Freud and Literary Biography." *American Scholar* 53 (Autumn 1984): 465–78.

———. *James Joyce*. New York: Oxford University Press, 1959.

———. "The Life of Sim Botchit." *The New York Review of Books* 15 June 1978: 3–8.

———. "Literary Biography." *Golden Codgers: Biographical Speculations*. London: Oxford University Press, 1973. 1–16.

———. *Ulysses on the Liffey*. New York: Oxford University Press, 1972.

Esslin, Martin. "Scandalising Samuel Beckett: The Coarse Art of Biography." *Encounter* 52 (March 1979): 49–55.

Frank, Joseph. *Dostoevsky: The Seeds of Revolt, 1821–1849*. Princeton: Princeton University Press, 1976.

Frank, Katherine. "Writing Lives: Theory and Practice in Literary Biography." *Genre* 13 (Winter 1980): 499–516.

Friedman, Melvin J. "Beckett's Life Story." *Contemporary Literature* 20.3 (Summer 1979): 377–85.

———. "Ellmann on Joyce." *Re-Viewing Classics of Joyce Criticism*. Ed. Janet Egleson Dunleavy. Urbana: University of Illinois Press, 1991. 131–41.

———. "Joyce's Life." *The Progressive* 23.12 (December 1959): 49–50.

———. "Out of His Brother's Shadow." *The New Republic* 10 February 1958: 18–20.

Gaskell, Philip. "Joyce Again." *Essays in Criticism* 33 (July 1983): 252–55.

Gillespie, Michael Patrick. *James Joyce's Trieste Library: A Catalogue of Materials at the Harry Ransom Humanities Research Center at the University of Texas at Austin*. Austin: Harry Ransom Humanities Research Center, The University of Texas, 1986.

Goodman, Walter. "Richard Ellmann Dies at 69; Eminent James Joyce Scholar." *The New York Times* 14 May 1987: sec. D, 26.

Herring, Phillip. "Richard Ellmann's *James Joyce*." *The Biographer's Art*. Ed. Jeffrey Meyers. London: Macmillan, 1989. 106–27, 178–81.

Howe, Irving. "The Wounds of All Generations." *Harper's Magazine* (May 1969): 96–102.

Kenner Hugh. "A Callithumpian Life: *Samuel Beckett: A Biography* by Deirdre Bair." *Saturday Review* (August 1978): 46–49.

———. "The Impertinence of Being Definitive." *Times Literary Supplement* 17 December 1982: 1383–84.

Maddox, Brenda. *Nora: The Real Life of Molly Bloom*. Boston: Houghton Mifflin, 1988.

Nadel, Ira Bruce. *Biography: Fiction, Fact, and Form*. London: Macmillan, 1984.

Serafin, Steven. "Richard Ellmann." DLB Yearbook 1987, *Dictionary of Literary Biography*. Detroit: Gale, 1988. 226–30.

Steiner, George. "Across the River and into the Trees." *The New Yorker* 45 (13 September 1969): 147–56.

2

Joyce, Beckett, and the Short Story in Ireland

John Fletcher

IN FRESHMEN CLASSES, I tend to define the short story as a short prose narrative of concentrated effect, complete within its own terms, showing a firm story-line and often an abrupt ending, limited in its temporal and spatial location and in the number of characters deployed, and tending to work through understatement and humor rather than explicit comment.

Joyce's *Dubliners* is one of the greatest short-story collections ever published. Beckett's *More Pricks Than Kicks*, an early book—one he refused for many years to allow to be reissued—is far from being in the same league. Still, they are worth comparing in the light of the above definition for a number of reasons. The first, and most obvious, is that the young Beckett greatly admired his older compatriot and sought to imitate him. Secondly, they are both set in Dublin and feature Dublin people, as Joyce's title explicitly acknowledges. Thirdly, they both deploy a particular sense of humor—at once intellectual, sardonic, and self-consciously literary—which readers tend to associate with Irish writing in general.

I would like in this essay to look closely at their art of the short story with particular reference to "Ivy Day in the Committee Room" from *Dubliners* and to the second story, "Fingal," in *More Pricks Than Kicks*. I have deliberately chosen, as being more typical of their respective authors, stories that are less frequently discussed than, say, "The Dead" in Joyce's case or than "Dante and the Lobster" in Beckett's collection; because they are not perhaps the "best" story by either writer, they are, arguably, more representative of each collection taken as a whole.

"Ivy Day in the Committee Room" is set, as its full title implies, in an electoral ward committee room in Dublin as dusk falls on

October 6 (Ivy Day, the anniversary of the death of Parnell) in a year early in the present century. A motley group of canvassers and election workers enter the room to warm themselves by the fire, to drink stout, and to chat. Warmed by liquor and fellowship, the half-dozen men become a trifle sentimental about their great hero, Parnell, and one of them, Joe Hynes, is prevailed upon to recite a piece of mawkish doggerel verse that he has written, being, in the eyes of his companions, "a clever chap . . . with the pen" (D 125). In an interesting use of what we now call intertextuality, Joyce gives the poem in extenso, all eleven stanzas of it. Deeply touched, Mr. Hynes's listeners give him a spontaneous round of applause. So moved is the poet himself that he pays no heed to the popping of the cork in his bottle of stout, and another prominent character (prominent in that he is present in the room throughout), Mr. O'Connor, starts to roll himself a cigarette, "the better to hide his emotion" (135). Even Mr. Crofton, who represents the Conservative interest (for the men, although in temporary electoral alliance, do not belong to the same political party), agrees that Hynes's panegyric is "a very fine piece of writing" (135). Joyce's irony is all the sharper for not being spelled out: drink and national sentiment temporarily unite these men who, otherwise, have little in common and who indeed (as their sarcastic remarks behind each other's backs reveal all too plainly) do not even greatly care for one another. They have, in other words, about as much charity as they have literary taste: precious little.

In Beckett's story, "Fingal," the hero Belacqua takes his girlfriend Winnie on a walk in the countryside near Dublin. Because she is "hot" (MPTK 23) (a sexist epithet that the author did not permit himself in later years), they take advantage of the fine spring weather to make love a couple of times. When not embracing, they gaze upon the Irish landscape in general and upon the Portrane Lunatic Asylum in particular, where Belacqua declares his heart to reside, and Winnie, a doctor friend of hers; so they agree to make for there. But Belacqua, his immediate sexual needs having now been gratified, abandons Winnie to her friend Dr. Sholto. He infinitely prefers to her company—now that the baser lusts of the flesh have been satisfied—that of a bicycle, which he steals from a farmworker. Much to Winnie's annoyance, he gets

clean away on it, and the author leaves him drinking and laughing
in a roadside pub. This is the "memorable fit of laughing" (23)
referred to in the opening sentence of the story, a fit which, we
are told, incapacitated Belacqua from further gallantry for some
time.

The style throughout "Fingal"—indeed throughout the entire
collection—is marked by elaborate and calculated allusiveness
combined with extensively developed verbal irony. At its best this
can give rise to suggestively witty prose, as in the coy way the
sexual act is referred to: "They had not been very long on the top
[of the hill] before [Belacqua] began to feel a very sad animal
indeed" (23). This is an erudite allusion to a saying usually
attributed to Galen, the most famous physician of ancient Rome,
to the effect that every creature suffers depression after intercourse
("*omne animal post coitum triste est*"); and the bawdy innuendo here
is that the first act of love must have been intensely pleasurable for
Belacqua since it leaves him feeling particularly sad, whereas the
second embrace, on the top of another hill, makes him only plain
sad. (What Winnie experiences is not specified, unless we are
meant to understand something quite abstruse from the assertion
that, after the first occasion, she appears to Belacqua to be in high
spirits; following the same logic, the author may be implying that
she did not have an orgasm and so escaped Galen's depression.
But this may be carrying obscene interpretation further than even
this witty author intends.)

At less than its best, this kind of writing is pedantry pure and
simple, arrogantly disdaining simple formulations and cloaking a
banal idea in an esoteric manner. On the second page of the story,
for instance, there is elaborate and rather fatuous play on the name
of the French poet Alphonse de Lamartine, and on the third, some
toying with Latin and Roman history. This is neither funny nor
particularly clever, unlike the rather effective joke upon Galen's
aphorism.

All the stories in *More Pricks Than Kicks* are set in Dublin and
its environs and are, like *Dubliners*, permeated with the atmosphere of the Irish capital. In snatches of dialogue that anticipate
the elegant Irishisms of *Waiting for Godot*, we hear the authentic
brogue of the people, which Beckett sometimes helpfully trans-

lates ("Now would they[1] do him the favour to adjourn . . .? This meant drink" [31]), and their characteristic accent ("Dean Swift" pronounced "Dane Swift" [33], for instance). Nevertheless, Belacqua is something of an outsider as far as ordinary Irish people are concerned: he is idle, he is educated, and above all, he is a Protestant, a "dirty lowdown Low Church Protestant high-brow" (172). Inevitably, then, one does not find in *More Pricks Than Kicks* the same intimate familiarity with Dublin life—the sense of belonging to a society that is unique with its particular customs, humor, and myths—as one experiences in *Dubliners*. The country and its people are contemplated in Beckett's collection from a certain distance, which is perhaps not so surprising in the work of a Protestant Irishman, but, for all that, the feeling of alienation cannot be explained solely in terms of religion and ethnic origin. Belacqua is not only a member of the "Protestant Ascendancy," which ruled Ireland until independence; he is also the first in a line of Beckettian heroes whose condition of exile becomes gradually more painful. He is, in fact, the natural precursor of Molloy and of the Unnamable.

Physically, indeed, Belacqua appears a bit of a clown, an early version of the Chaplinesque figures in *Waiting for Godot*. It is easy, for instance, for Dr. Sholto to give a "brief satirical description" (MPTK 34) of his person, which would run on these lines: a pale fat man, nearly bald, bespectacled, shabbily dressed, and always looking ill and dejected (he is suffering from impetigo on his face in "Fingal," much to the disgust of Winnie, who has been kissed by him). His appearance is in fact grotesque enough to provoke comment and even laughter in all places except where he is well known. He is a total eccentric; we have already noted his habit of preferring bicycles to women. This oddity in his reactions (or, rather, his incapacity for registering the normal reactions expected of him) is coupled with a faculty for acting with insufficient motivation, which his creator maintains is serious enough to make a mental home the place for him (hence his avowal that his heart resides in the Portrane Lunatic Asylum). But, even more than a

1. The phrasing "Now they would do . . ." is a misprint in the original. The order as printed makes no sense in Anglo-Irish. Also the question mark indicates an interrogative order.

padded cell, what Belacqua really longs for is to return to the
womb, where he fantasizes about lying on his back in the dark
forever, free from "night sweats" (i.e., sex). In default of such a
refuge, Belacqua enjoys to the full a melancholy indulged in for
its own sake: landscapes, such as Fingal, are of interest to him
only insofar as they furnish him "with a pretext for a long face"
(30).

Beckett uses this oddity—a person not quite at one with his
fellow men, often more an onlooker than active participant in
what goes on in the stories—for satirical ends. Inspired caricature
fixes the less amiable aspects of a person in few words as is the
case in "Fingal" with Dr. Sholto, "a pale dark man with a brow"
(31) who feels "nothing but rancour" (32) toward Belacqua,
evidently because Winnie prefers him to Sholto (which may
indicate that what made Belacqua "sad" was pleasurable for her,
after all). This is all the more galling to the pompous, prissy
doctor in that Belacqua patently prefers his own company, laughing out loud alone in the pub, to getting "sad" with Winnie: his
"sadness" falls from him "like a shift" (32) as soon as he finds the
bicycle, we are told. Despite an unsightly rash on his face, we are
meant to understand that Belacqua is "sexier" than Sholto, even
assisted, as the latter is, by the aphrodisiac of a glass of whiskey.

Belacqua's compulsive urge to retreat from the body and its
"night sweats" into the wider freedom of the mind springs from
a dualistic conviction that he shares with his successor-heroes in
the Beckett canon. They, too, are lovers of bicycles; man and
machine together form what Hugh Kenner calls, in an arresting
phrase, a "Cartesian centaur" (Kenner 132), from Descartes,
whose thought deeply influenced the young Beckett who wrote
More Pricks Than Kicks. In all his writing, indeed, Beckett advances
his own version of Cartesianism, in which the mental part of his
heroes seeks continually to escape from the physical part. In this
early story, therefore, there is already discernible a theme—not
quite drowned by the academic wit and the tiresome allusiveness—
which becomes increasingly central in Beckett's fiction: the radical
split between body and mind, a disconnection that allows the
mind to retreat progressively into itself, into an isolated life of its
own. In the later works, the body is left to break down, like a
worn-out piece of machinery, while the mind, panic-stricken at

the prospect of cessation, chatters on, rehashing continually its never-changing futilities.

Thus the seeds of *For to End Yet Again* were sown forty years earlier in *More Pricks Than Kicks*, just as the long road to Finnegan's wake starts out from the committee rooms and parlors of the Dubliners whom Joyce portrays so deftly in "Ivy Day" and the other stories. Just as the bicycle that enables Belacqua to escape from Winnie is the twin of the one that leads Molloy into his disastrous encounter with *his* mistress, Lousse, so the Liffey, which the friends cross in a ferryboat in the second story of *Dubliners*, is the same "riverrun," the same Anna Livia's "hitherandthithering waters of" *Finnegans Wake*.

Both writers, then, are supremely consistent with themselves: just as both—the senior, a Catholic; the junior, a Protestant—are intensely, politically, Irish. The political dimension is less in evidence in "Fingal," but it is there, discreetly, in references to Swift and to the potato famine (the tower near which Belacqua and Winnie make love the second time was, they learn, "built for relief in the year of the Famine" [28]). The Fingal landscape stretching out before them is, Belacqua asserts in stoutly patriotic tones, a "magic land" comparable at least to Burgundy and far superior to Wicklow (24).

But Beckett does not—perhaps understandably, given his background—comment upon or even reflect contemporary Irish political concerns: there is no trace in his work of any reference to the Easter Rising or to the civil war; his criticisms are purely social and cultural in nature. Developments like literary censorship or the ban on contraceptives[2] he does satirize and debunk, but he eschews party politics and above all the bitter struggles surrounding the birth of the Irish Republic. Joyce, as a member of the majority community, feels no such inhibitions about expressing his feelings in *Dubliners*. There is telling satire in "The Dead" of the kind of nationalist virago who hurls the insult "West Briton!" at anyone who does not wear his shamrock heart on his sleeve,

---

2. See "Censorship in the Saorstat" (*Disjecta* 84–88), and *Watt* for an extended joke about the aphrodisiac Bando which, like the humble condom, "cannot enter our ports, nor cross our northern frontier, [but] is immediately seized, and confiscated, by some gross customs official half crazed with seminal intoxication . . ." (170).

and in "Ivy Day in the Committee Room," as we have seen, mawkish patriotism is ridiculed in Mr. Hynes's ghastly doggerel. At the same time, the men's emotion is genuine enough, even if its expression is inflated and pretentious. The figure of Parnell himself, it is important to note, is not ridiculed; if anything, it emerges enhanced by the extremes of devotion to which his admirers will go, composing and applauding bad verse in homage to their "dead King," felt so much more truly to be their sovereign lord than Edward VII, who is about to pay a visit to his "wild Irish" subjects (132) and who is derisively referred to as "Eddie" (124) for his pains. Insofar as the views of the implied author can be surmised, they are those of moderate nationalism, unemphatic patriotism, and temperate republicanism. This tolerant, non-extremist position stands in sharp contrast to the intolerance of the harpy in "The Dead" and to the naïve hero-worship of Mr. Hynes in "Ivy Day in the Committee Room."

Thus far, for the purposes of comparison, I have been treating "Fingal" and "Ivy Day in the Committee Room" as more or less of equal interest, but, as I made clear at the outset, the two stories are not of equal merit. Joyce's story, even though not the finest story in *Dubliners*, is markedly superior to "Fingal." For one thing, Beckett's story is slighter, shorter than Joyce's by about a third, and it deploys fewer and less interesting characters. Belacqua engages our sympathy, no doubt because the author tends to treat him indulgently, but Winnie is not very plausible, and Sholto is no more than sketched. Joyce, by contrast, introduces seven main characters and brings them on like a competent dramatist at different points in the narrative. Old Jack and Mr. O'Connor are present as the story opens and remain in the room throughout; Mr. Hynes the poet enters, leaves, and re-enters later to deliver his composition; Mr. Henchy enters about one-third of the way through; Father Keon puts in a brief, rather sinister appearance at about the half-way mark; and Mr. Crofton and Mr. Lyons walk in shortly afterward and remain to the end. This deployment of characters gives a much tauter feel to the story than Beckett's does. The effect (to return to my simple definition of the genre outlined at the beginning of this essay) is therefore more noticeably concentrated in "Ivy Day in the Committee Room," and the story line is appreciably firmer, the end coming precisely when it should, with the emotional responses to Hynes's elegy undercut by the implied author's discreet mockery of the enterprise when he gets Mr. Crofton (normally a political opponent) to concede that it is "a very fine piece of writing." The manner in which the end of "Fingal" refers back to the beginning (confirming the previously enigmatic allusion to Belacqua's fit of laughing) is competent enough but feels rather contrived in comparison with the ending of "Ivy Day in the Committee Room."

Both stories are sensibly limited in terms of temporal and spatial location, each covering a few hours in real time and a single setting, the committee room in Joyce's case and the vicinity of the Portrane asylum in Beckett's. The closed space of the committee room symbolizes the inward-looking nature of the men's political and social concerns—parochial and mundane—just as Beckett's outing to the country in fine weather is the objective correlative of Belacqua's escaping from convention and flouting of social niceties. And, last but not least, both writers work their effects by understatement and humor rather than explicit comment, although Beckett is, rather curiously, more old-fashioned than Joyce in his occasional, admittedly muted, use of the authorial aside to the reader, a device that the modernist Joyce eschews altogether. Not only that, but the Beckettian asides reveal the writer's unease: he is not really at home in the short-story form, and rhetorical questions like "Who shall silence them, at last?" (26) betray his discomfort. We are, after all, nearly half a century away from the great brief texts *Imagination Dead Imagine*, *Lessness*, *Still* and the others, texts that are Beckett's supreme, unique contribution to the short prose form. The classic short story, on the other hand, the kind that Chekhov, Henry James, D. H. Lawrence, and Joyce himself developed to such a high pitch of aesthetic perfection and emotional power, was never (to use an apt colloquialism) Beckett's "scene," any more than the play in several acts was: he wisely abandoned about the same time an attempt to write a stage work in four acts, one act devoted to each of the four years between the widowing and the remarriage of Mrs. Thrale, Dr. Johnson's friend. In the only section actually composed, Act One, Scene One, the tone is already at odds with the realistic, historical material that Beckett was trying manfully to shape into dramatic form. The pauses, repetitions, and formal patterns in the fragment that survives are precisely those which he was to hone later, in *Waiting for Godot*, into a style that, even as early as 1937, is characteristically Beckettian. But the form available to him in the '30s was not suitable to his purposes, and he abandoned the project (*Disjecta* 155–66). He did not abandon *More Pricks Than Kicks*, but he did, as we saw earlier, refuse for many years to have it reissued. In his eyes the book was juvenile stuff, and although that judgment was not fair, he was correct in accepting that, as examples of the short story form, his collection did not begin to match up to those of his great mentor Joyce.

The difference is highlighted by the humor. In both cases, as I said at the outset, this is intellectual, sardonic, self-consciously literary, and characteristically Irish in manner. But in Beckett's case the intellectualism is just too clever by half, the wryness veers disturbingly close to spite, and the literary self-consciousness borders on the arch. The difference between a master of the form and an apprentice who is trying hard to do well can be seen in sharp focus if two characteristic passages of humorous dialogue are compared in detail. In *Dubliners* Joyce wrote:

> The old man watched him attentively and then, taking up the piece of cardboard again, began to fan the fire slowly while his companion smoked.
>
> "Ah, yes," he said, continuing, "it's hard to know what way to bring up children. Now who'd think he'd turn out like that! I sent him to the Christian Brothers and I done what I could for him, and there he goes boozing about. I tried to make him somewhat decent."
>
> He replaced the cardboard wearily.
>
> "Only I'm an old man now I'd change his tune for him. I'd take the stick to his back and beat him while I could stand over him—as I done many a time before. The mother you know, she cocks him up with this and that. . . ."
>
> "That's what ruins children," said Mr. O'Connor.
>
> "To be sure it is," said the old man. "And little thanks you get for it, only impudence. He takes th'upper hand of me whenever he sees I've a sup taken. What's the world coming to when sons speaks that way to their fathers?"
>
> "What age is he?" said Mr. O'Connor.
>
> "Nineteen," said the old man.
>
> "Why don't you put him to something?"

"Sure, amn't I never done at the drunken bowsy ever since he left school? 'I won't keep you,' I says. 'You must get a job for yourself.' But, sure, it's worse whenever he gets a job; he drinks it all."

Mr. O'Connor shook his head in sympathy, and the old man 25 fell silent, gazing into the fire [119–20].

Beckett's humor is quite different, as the following passage from *More Pricks Than Kicks* reveals:

A stout block of an old man in shirt sleeves and slippers was leaning against the wall of the field. Winnie still sees, as vividly as when they met her anxious gaze for the first time, his great purple face and white moustaches. Had he seen a stranger about, a pale fat man in a black leather coat. 5

"No miss" he said.

"Well" said Winnie, settling herself on the wall, to Sholto, "I suppose he's about somewhere."

A land of sanctuary, he had said, where much had been suffered secretly. Yes, the last ditch. 10

"You stay here" said Sholto, madness and evil in his heart, "and I'll take a look in the church."

The old man had been showing signs of excitement.

"Is it an escape?" he enquired hopefully.

"No no" said Winnie, "just a friend." 15

But he was off, he was unsluiced.

"I was born on Lambay" he said, by way of opening to an endless story of a recapture in which he had distinguished himself, "and I've worked here man and boy."

"In that case" said Winnie "maybe you can tell me what the 20 ruins are."

"That's the church" he said, pointing to the near one, it had just absorbed Sholto, "and that" pointing to the far one, " 's the tower."

"Yes" said Winnie "but what tower, what was it?" 25

"The best I know" he said "is some Lady Something had it."

This was news indeed [32–33].

Both writers feature characters who speak in Dubin dialect, but Beckett catches it less accurately (lines 17–19, 22–24 and 26) than Joyce does: the syntax in Joyce is exact and plausible, fully characteristic of the Dublin working class (in standard English "only I'm" in line 10 would be "if I were not," and "while" in line 11 would be "until," with "I could no longer" replacing "I could"; and "amn't I never done at" in line 22 would be "do I ever stop remonstrating with"). At the lexical level, words like "cocks up" (12–13), "sup" for "drink" (17), and "bowsy" (22) are authentic Irish idioms, non-standard English, as "somewhat" (7) would be "into someone" in standard speech. Grammatically, "done" for "did" (6) and "says" for "say" (23) are examples of dialectal deviations.

What these contrasted examples really show, of course, is not so much that Beckett could not reproduce dialect authentically as that he was not greatly interested in doing so. He was not concerned with realism at all, in fact, as is revealed stylistically by his use of non-realist features like free indirect speech (4–5), self-quotation or self-intertextualization (9–10), and authorial asides (16, 27).

This crucial difference between Beckett's approach and Joyce's affects the nature of their humor. Joyce's is mimetic; Beckett's is self-reflexive. Joyce's is satirical, that is, extroverted, while Beckett's is self-conscious, that is, introverted. Joyce's suits admirably the short-story form; Beckett's does not. Both men are great writers, but Joyce is already working at the peak of his form in *Dubliners*, whereas for Beckett, the works of his maturity have still to be written when *More Pricks Than Kicks* is composed. Had Beckett died in the same year as Joyce did, he would now be remembered, if at all, as a mere promising disciple of a great Irish writer. The world is fortunate that he lived, in fact, much longer than Joyce (who died at the age of fifty-eight) and became a great Irish writer in his turn. We, their readers, able to re-Joyce 'n Beckett, are thus doubly blessed.

WORKS CITED

Kenner, Hugh. "The Cartesian Centaur." *Perspective* 11 (Autumn 1959): 132–41.

3

Beckett, Joyce, and Irish Writing: The example of Beckett's "Dubliners" Story

John P. Harrington

AFTER HIS WORK had taken on characteristic form and after he had acquired the public stature usual on winning the Nobel Prize, Samuel Beckett described his younger self of the 1930s as " 'a very young writer with nothing to say and the itch to make' " (Harvey 273). The itch to make without anything much to say is, of course, no specifically Irish phenomenon, but it was a particularly acute and a particularly dismal predicament in Ireland in the 1930s. The predicament was not lack of models, for there was a wide choice of exemplary figures as well as regular public debate over the quest for that fabulous Irish chimera, a unified national aesthetic. Rather, the predicament lay in the embarrassment of conveniently located riches. Writing on this in 1976 when, presumably, that predicament remained a current concern, Denis Donoghue concluded that "the price we pay for Yeats and Joyce is that each in his way gave Irish experience a memorable but narrow definition. . . . the minor writers of the Irish literary revival were not strong enough to counter Yeats's incantatory rhetoric: no writer in Ireland has been strong enough to modify Joyce's sense of Irish experience in fiction" (131). Donoghue's "no writer in Ireland" qualification here may be a deliberate exclusion of Beckett. But most often Beckett is excluded from discussions of Irish writing by unexamined convention. However, Beckett offers the way out of memorable but narrow definitions of Irish experience. He offers no incantatory rhetoric or distinctly negative sense of Irish experience. Rather, Beckett's work offers a view of Irish experience that is not narrow, exclusionist, or otherwise provincial. Yeats and Joyce, of course, are not predominantly provincial, but the subsequent example of Beckett does throw into interesting relief the provincial strain of their work and that of others associated with the Irish literary revival and its aftermath.

The young Beckett seems to have dealt expeditiously with the spell of Yeats's incantatory rhetoric. Nevertheless, Beckett's Irish past is one of the more untidy areas of record. Richard Ellmann's recent revelation in *Nayman of Noland* (26) that Yeats himself praised and quoted *Whoroscope* to Beckett in Killiney in 1932 hints at passing literary relations then between Ireland's Nobel past and Nobel future. A fairly recent reminder of that relation's likely complexity was the basis of Beckett's 1976 teleplay ". . . but the clouds . . . ," an allusion to Yeats's "The Tower."

Young Beckett's fancy for cosmopolitanism and newness meant that the cost of being Irish and literary was to be exacted first by Joyce. Though by now Beckett has in many ways matched the stature of Joyce as a figure on the literary landscape, Beckett's first reception often included an almost persecutorial sort of circumstantial association with Joyce. At one time part of that association was rumored identity as "Joyce's secretary"; later that was improved to the now familiar "*not* Joyce's secretary." The sense of Beckett as formed by Joyce persisted even after he got as unlike Joyce as possible, even after he chose French over English and drama over fiction, changes as radical as possible but liable to perception as overreaction. Among the early responses to Beckett's first produced plays, for example, was Lionel Abel's commentary in 1959 on *Godot* and *Endgame* in an essay called "Joyce the Father, Beckett the Son": "Joyce is present in Beckett's plays; he is confronted and he is vanquished, though Beckett, whether as Lucky or Clov, is never shown to be victorious" (27).

In early critical apprehension of Beckett as epigone of Joyce and often in critical consensus today, that confrontation and vanquishment were not of Joyce as overbearing personal example, or of Joyce as formulator of Irish experience in fiction, but of Joyce the author of *Finnegans Wake*. This notion was epitomized in the Shenker "interview" in 1956 when Beckett was characterized as saying " 'The kind of work I do is one in which I'm not master of my material. The more Joyce knew the more he could. He's tending toward omniscience and omnipotence as an artist. I'm working with impotence, ignorance' " (3). The emphasis on the amount Joyce "knew," presumably cumulative, and the omnipotence to which Joyce was "tending" imply preoccupation with Joyce's last work. Even Beckett's decision to write in French is phrased and depreciated by Ellmann in terms of Joyce and *Finnegans Wake*: Beckett's "boldness was almost without precedent. It freed him from literary forefathers. It was a decision only less radical than Joyce's in inventing his extravagant *Finnegans Wake*-ese" (16). The Shenker portrayal of Beckett's work as mired in a kind of inverse relationship to Joyce's, tending to ignorance while Joyce's tended to omniscience, encouraged perception of Beckett's early work in terms of Joyce, in terms of *Finnegans Wake* and in terms of *Finnegans Wake*-ese as a great mistake. Vivian Mercier, an acquaintance of Beckett's and an estimable commentator on Irish letters, reiterated this view in the late 1970s: Beckett's "greatest folly consisted in attempting to imitate James Joyce: not the earlier work, either, but *Work in Progress*, the drafts of *Finnegans Wake*" (36).

There is some reason to see Beckett in the 1930s as largely motivated by emulation of and slow progress away from what was then Joyce's *Work in Progress*. Chronologies of his work, of course, usually begin with publication in 1929 of "Dante . . . Bruno . Vico . . Joyce" both in *transition* and in a celebratory volume of essays in anticipation and encouragement of Joyce's work. Beckett's first publications in Dublin, in *T.C.D.: A College Miscellany*, were the fragmentary, anonymous dialogues called "Che Sciagura" (1929) and "The Possessed" (1930). These were seen in Dublin as quite obviously written under the spell of Joyce and the style of *Work in Progress*: " 'In the Joycean medley,' " *T.C.D.* later commented on the second of these early works, " 'its anonymous author performs some diverting verbal acrobatics, but in the manner of a number of *transition*'s offspring, is too allusive to be generally comprehensible' " (quoted in Bair 131). Indeed, Beckett cultivated this association with Joyce by appending to his poems for a 1931 anthology called *The European Caravan* a contributor's note that read in part: " 'Samuel Beckett is the most interesting of the younger Irish writers. . . . He has a great knowledge of Romance literature, is a friend of Rudmose-Brown and of Joyce, and has adapted the Joyce method to his poetry with original results' " (quoted in Bair 129–30). The Joyce method of greatest interest then was the method of *Works in Progress*, which began sporadic publication in *transition* in 1927 as vanguard of its self-proclaimed revolution of the word. In this example of rather Whitmanesque arrogance, Beckett points to Rudmose-Brown, his mentor at Trinity College, as his background and to the Joyce method as his means to originality. The influence of *Work in Progress* is also clear in the excerpts from *Dream of Fair to Middling Women* published in 1932 under the titles "Sedendo et Quiescendo" in *transition* (misprinted as "Quiesciendo") and "Text" in *The New Review*. In Dublin, such progress as Beckett had made in freeing himself from *Work in Progress* as he refashioned material from *Dream* for *More Pricks Than Kicks* was seen as only a slight inverse movement through Joyce's works. " 'Mr. Beckett is an extremely clever young man,' " concluded *The Dublin Magazine* in its review of *More Pricks* in 1934, " 'and he knows his *Ulysses* as a Scotch Presbyterian knows his *Bible*' " (quoted in Bair 179).

However, the tendency to view the young Beckett as devoted exclusively to Joyce's last works oversimplifies Beckett's critique of his predecessor. Though "Dante . . . Bruno . Vico . . Joyce" was of necessity devoted almost entirely to *Work in Progress*, Beckett's essay also refers familiarly to *The Day of the Rabblement*, which was Joyce's own 1901 declaration of independence from Irish literary predecessors. Furthermore, early in this essay Beckett discusses Stephen Dedalus' attitude in *A Portrait of the Artist as a Young Man*, and later in it he quotes part of Stephen's assertions to Lynch on the aesthetic image. David Hayman, in "A Meeting in the Park and a Meeting on the Bridge" (373), has pointed to echoes of *Portrait* and of *Exiles* in Beckett's first published short story, "Assumption," which appeared in *transition* in 1929 in the same issue as "Dante . . . Bruno . Vico . . Joyce." Even "Sedendo et Quiescendo," which is obviously derived in style from *Work in Progress*, alludes in "art thou pale with weariness" (13) and in "a pale and ardent generation" (14) to Stephen's poem in *Portrait* and derivation of it from Shelley's "To the Moon." In addition, *More Pricks Than Kicks*, however stridently it demonstrates its author's knowledge of *Ulysses*, also includes a story, "A Wet Night," that gives its attention to *Dubliners* and in particular to "The Dead." Beckett's story, like "The Dead," describes a Christmas season party in Dublin hosted and attended by Dubliners who anxiously exude continental sophistication while showing irritability with Gaelic aficionados. At the end of Joyce's *Dubliners* story, of course, Gabriel Conroy approaches new self-knowledge as he views the snow from the window of his room in the Gresham Hotel: "It was falling on every part of the dark central plain, on the treeless hills, falling softly upon the Bog of Allen and, farther westward, softly falling into the dark mutinous Shannon waves" (223). In Beckett's *More Pricks Than Kicks* story, it is rain, not snow, that falls, and the character, Belacqua, is oblivious to rather than intent on the rain that "fell upon the bay, the littoral, the mountains and the plains, and notably upon the Central Bog it fell with a rather desolate uniformity" (83). Nevertheless, Beckett's reference to Joyce's story is scarcely devoted imitation. That clear echo of Joyce is followed in Beckett's story by an obviously parodic approach to self-knowledge by Belacqua: "What was that? He shook off his glasses and stooped his head to see. That was his hands. Now who would have thought that!" (83).

More Pricks Than Kicks was published on May 24, 1934. In July it was reviewed in *The Bookman* by Francis Watson, who, having mentioned Beckett's monograph on Proust and his involvement in the translation into French of portions of *Works in Progress*, asserted that "The influence of Joyce is indeed patent in 'More Pricks Than Kicks' but Mr. Beckett is no fashionable imitator. Like Joyce he is a Dubliner and an exile, and Dublin has for him that peculiar compulsion which it exercises upon all Irishmen except Bernard Shaw" (219–20). Watson's laudatory review, which praised *More Pricks Than Kicks* as "one of those rare books to be read more than once" (220), may have provided Beckett with the opportunity to contribute to the "Irish Number" of *The Bookman* in August of 1934. That issue included single essays by Stephen Gwynn, Lennox Robinson, and Sean O'Faolain. Beckett contributed two pieces to the issue. One was a review essay, now well known and reprinted, called "Recent Irish Poetry." The other was a short story, not well known and not reprinted, called "A Case in a Thousand."

"Recent Irish Poetry" unambiguously categorizes Irish poets as the "antiquarians" or the "others." The antiquarians are those working poets who adhere to "accredited themes" derived from the Irish literary revival's formulation of a national literary identity and sustained by Yeats. The "others," notably Thomas McGreevy and Denis Devlin, friends of Beckett's and within the brood *T.C.D.* called "*transition*'s offspring," pursue instead "awareness of the new thing that has happened, or the old thing that has happened again, namely the breakdown of the object, whether current, historical, mythical or spook" (*Disjecta* 70). Beckett had already reviewed a collection of McGreevy's poems in the July 1934 issue of *The Dublin Magazine*, and he would articulate his admiration for Devlin in a review for *transition* in 1938 (both reviews have been reprinted in *Disjecta*). In "Recent Irish Poetry," McGreevy, Devlin, and Brian Coffey are decreed "the nucleus of a living poetic in Ireland" (76). The bulk of the review, though, is given over to evisceration of the "antiquarians," including less than admiring references to fellow contributors to this special issue of *The Bookman*. One fellow contributor was Frank O'Connor, the only one other than Beckett with two pieces in the issue. Though no associate of *transition*, O'Connor was as effective as Beckett in lampooning the forms of antiquarianism in Ireland in the 1930s; his essay describes how nativism and the state revival of Gaelic in combination with censorship of writers like O'Faolain and Liam O'Flaherty had the result of government sponsorship of Gaelic translations of Emily Brontë, Dickens, and Conrad. Like Beckett, O'Connor signed his two contributions differently. O'Connor's story, "The Man That Stopped," appeared under the pseudonym he would maintain, while his essay, "Two Languages," appeared under his own name, Michael O'Donovan. Beckett's essay, "Recent Irish Poetry," appeared under a pseudonym he would never use again, "Andrew Belis," while his story, "A Case in a Thousand," appeared under his own name. One imagines that the short story of Samuel Beckett should not be construed as wholly apart from the living poetic in Ireland proclaimed by Andrew Belis.

"A Case in a Thousand" is the most apparent adoption in Beckett's early fiction of the style of Joyce's own early work. It is written with a scrupulous meanness uncharacteristic of Beckett's other early fiction, including precise but understated attention to descriptive details of principal and minor characters. Forms of address, variations in Anglo-Irish dialect, and trivial mannerisms indicate social distinctions among characters. The Dublin setting at a nursing home beside The Grand Canal is established unobtrusively and without the sort of painful and scatological imagery common in Beckett's Dublin poems of this period, such as "Eneug I." The narrative, in the third person, proceeds without the allusiveness and obfuscation usual in Beckett's "*transition's* offspring" fiction.

The story concerns a Dr. Nye and his treatment of a tubercular boy who is worsening since surgery by another doctor. Dr. Nye's treatment of the case is complicated by his discovery that the boy's mother, who watches the hospital room window from the bank of the canal outside, is in fact his own former nanny, a Mrs. Bray. Soon Dr. Nye must make a decision on a second operation. He chooses surgery, the boy dies, and Dr. Nye feels compelled to confront Mrs. Bray with his memory of infantile eroticism. Mrs. Bray clarifies the memory for Nye, in a conversation denied the reader, and they part: "Mrs. Bray to go and pack up her things and the dead boy's things, Dr. Nye to carry out Wasserman's [*sic*] test on an old schoolfellow" (242).

As the title suggests, Beckett's story echoes in important instances Joyce's "A Painful Case" story from *Dubliners*. Beckett's story opens with great economy and asserts in the opening of the second paragraph that "Dr. Nye belonged to the sad men, but not to the extent of accepting, in the blank way the most of them do, this condition as natural and proper. He looked upon it as a disorder" (241). Joyce's story opens with a more elaborate exposition of setting and scene and asserts in the opening of the second paragraph that "Mr. Duffy abhorred anything which betokened physical or mental disorder. A medieval doctor would have called him saturnine" (108). Both characters are troubled by women characters, who threaten the males' assumed roles and assured selves. Mr. Duffy's relationship with Mrs. Sinico begins when "little by little he entangled his thoughts with hers" (110). Beckett's character resists his thoughts and entanglement with Mrs. Bray when "little by little Dr. Nye reintegrated his pathological outlook" (242). The entanglements in both stories are confessional. "With almost maternal solicitude," Mrs. Sinico encourages Mr. Duffy "to let his nature open to the full; she became his confessor" (110). Mrs. Bray offers to Dr. Nye the opportunity to "disclose the trauma at the root of this attachment" (242). In

Joyce's story, the relationship ends on a trivial indelicacy, and years later Mr. Duffy learns in reports about Mrs. Sinico's death that she had become one of "the hobbling wretches whom he had seen carrying cans and bottles to be filled by the barman" (115). In Beckett's story, the relationship ends in Dr. Nye's childhood, and years later he is "troubled to find that of the woman whom as baby and small boy he had adored, nothing remained but the strawberry mottle of the nose and the breath smelling heavily of clove and peppermint" (242). Near the end of "A Painful Case" Mr. Duffy is revolted by "the threadbare phrases, the inane expressions of sympathy, the cautious words of a reporter" (115) used in the newspaper report of Mrs. Sinico's death. At the end of "A Case in a Thousand" such words are elided: Mrs. Bray "related a matter connected with his earliest years, so trivial and intimate that it need not be enlarged on here, but from the elucidation of which Dr. Nye, that sad man, expected great things" (242).

Both stories pivot on moments when the male characters recoil from their women confessors; when, in Beckett's words and in both cases, "he really could not bear another moment of her presence" (242). The consequence of Mr. Duffy's withdrawal is the eventual realization that he has sentenced himself, that his own "life would be lonely too until he, too, died" (116), and so, finally, that "no one wanted him; he was outcast from life's feast" (117). In "A Case in a Thousand" Dr. Nye has a comparable revelation, but at the beginning of the story and without context: "Without warning a proposition sprang up in his mind: Myself I cannot save" (241). Beckett's story most resembles those in *Dubliners* in the occurrence of such an epiphany, such a sudden perception of limitation. In the Beckett story, however, that epiphany is preliminary, not conclusive, and it is not explicitly connected with the subsequent events in the story. "A Case in a Thousand" demands comparison with "A Painful Case" in title, narrative, and style, but it manipulates the poetics of the Joycean model in a fashion that disrupts representation of oppressive determinacy. Beckett's story is an ironic form of this "Joyce method," as indeed his earlier use of the "Joyce method" of *Work in Progress* is ironic, though perhaps insufficiently so if it seems to later commentators a great mistake.

"A Case in a Thousand" is of interest in several respects other than the parallel with "A Painful Case." Deirdre Bair, for example, finds it most significant because it "seems in many respects to be Beckett's way of using his analysis creatively" and because "the story contains the same equivocal erotic attitudes toward women first introduced with Belacqua in *Dream* and *More Pricks*" (185). Eoin O'Brien, in *The Beckett Country*, identifies the setting of the story as the Portobello Nursing Home. O'Brien discusses that nursing home along with the Merrion Nursing Home, which is only two bridges away on the canal (195–201). At the Merrion Nursing Home Beckett attended his mother's final illness in 1950, and *Krapp's Last Tape* evokes the experience of watching a hospital room window from outside, like Mrs. Bray's. The setting of "A Case in a Thousand" is an early, more easily identifiable appearance in Beckett's work of the canal on the south side of Dublin, which reappears in many later works—for example, in *That Time*. Also, in this story Dr. Nye weighs the charms of a meditative life that spares the feet and thinks in bed in the fashion of Malone. Mrs. Bray is introduced into the story with an emphasis on hat and bosom and umbrella suggestive of Winnie in *Happy Days*.

Biography, autobiography, and portents of later work aside, "A Case in a Thousand" remains of interest for its indication of the kind of influence on Beckett's work of Joyce's work and for its appearance in a special issue on Irish writing. In the same "Irish Number" of *The Bookman* Norreys Jephson O'Conor, writing on "The Trend of Anglo-Irish Literature," offered the opinion that "younger [Irish] writers, brought up in the atmosphere of what is euphuistically called the 'trouble,' in their search for realism turned towards Russian and other Continental authors—an attitude strengthened by the experimentation and growing reputation of James Joyce" (234). O'Conor was no doubt thinking of Irish writers, such as Frank O'Connor, who advertised their admiration of the Russian short story. But Norreys Jephson O'Conor's observation indicates that Joyce's example could then, in 1934, be one of experimentation, including forms of realism like *Dubliners* and not only the polyglot allusiveness of *Work in Progress*. Consideration of "A Case in a Thousand" beside "Sedendo et Quiescendo" indicates the extent to which Joyce's example was less than monolithic, less a limitation than a liberation, and less one of a single experiment than one of the enterprise of experimentation. It is entirely in keeping with such an example that Beckett's "A Case in a Thousand" is less imitation of "A Painful Case" than ironic manipulation of its method. The effect of such use of a well-known model is a story that is a critique—in this case a commentary on the poetics and representation of contingent entrapments central to Joyce's story. "A Case in a Thousand" certainly is not the only critique of a model in Beckett's early fiction, or even the only critique of Joyce's works. But Beckett, as the prescient Francis Watson recognized as early as 1934, was "no fashionable imitator." "A Case in a Thousand" is an early instance of the project central to Beckett's later work, the play with epistemology—the project that propels the narratives of Molloy, Malone, and the Unnamable and preoccupies the characters waiting on stage for Godot.

The example of Joyce for a writer like Beckett in the 1930s ("nothing to say and the itch to make") entailed the influence of Joyce's work both in itself and as exemplar of new Irish writing. In the 1930s, when most apparently conscious of Joyce's work, Beckett was also most conscious of being an Irish writer. Soon after writing these two pieces for the "Irish Number" of *The Bookman*, Beckett wrote "Censorship in the Saorstat," an essay on the absurdity of the Irish Censorship of Publications Act of 1929. Derision of that piece of legislation was then a favorite pastime of Irish writers both "antiquarian" and "other," as witness Frank O'Connor's essay for the "Irish Number." Furthermore, writing on that subject gave Beckett the opportunity to include himself and *More Pricks Than Kicks* in the group of Irish writers and works, including Joyce and *Ulysses*, for whom and for which being banned at home was a badge of honor. "Censorship in the Saorstat" was prepared for *The Bookman*, but the journal ceased publication before that essay could appear.

Joyce could sustain younger writers in many ways, but for Beckett in the 1930s an important part of that sustenance lay in Joyce's example for consciously Irish writers. Irish writers younger than Beckett testify to the liberating effect of the example of Joyce and the connection of that example to Beckett. Thomas Kinsella, casting the influences on Irish writers in the same Yeats/Joyce terms as Denis Donoghue, concludes that "Yeats stands for the Irish tradition as broken; Joyce for it as continuous, as healed—

or healing—from its mutilation" (65). The mutilation in question here is precisely the rigidity of conventions, or imitation, termed antiquarianism by Beckett in "Recent Irish Poetry." Aidan Higgins, in the course of asking "Who follows Beckett, himself following so closely on Joyce?" characterizes those works not following Joyce and Beckett as "linear, traditional, benign, and dull" (60). Just those qualities were circumvented in Beckett's "A Case in a Thousand" because the story followed from, and did not merely imitate, Joyce's "A Painful Case." In David Hanly's novel *In Guilt and in Glory* two characters discuss Joyce and then continue, with ambivalent sarcasm, to Beckett: " 'He's a Protestant of English blood,' " says one, " 'educated at Trinity, a cricket player who lived in Paris and writes in French. Of course he's Irish' " (99). These approach definitions of Irish experience that are not narrow.

These examples, like that of "A Case in a Thousand," point to the interesting dimension of Beckett's work in the context of Irish writing. He is a complicated and enriching addition to the local literary history. In turn, Yeats helped define Ireland as a positivistic literary subject, Joyce offered a scrupulous critique of Ireland, and Beckett adumbrated the luxury of aloofness to Ireland. This last is, too, a liberation. "A Case in a Thousand" is a significant example of the extent to which the young Beckett was most conscious of himself as an Irish writer and, like many others, one most conscious of Joyce's own early work. In extricating himself from inherited cultural and national contexts, Beckett began the critique that extended to literary form and language in his major works. Though close attention to Irish literary precedents is for the most part a feature of Beckett's early work, the examination of inherited premises in "A Case in a Thousand" and other early pieces is compatible with the analysis of *Godot* or *How It Is*. Just that continuity and relevance of early work to late is one sense of the words of the narrator of *Company*, written in English and published in 1980: "Having covered in your day some twenty-five thousand leagues or roughly thrice the girdle. And never once overstepped a radius of one from home. Home!" (60).

WORKS CITED

Abel, Lionel. "Joyce the Father, Beckett the Son." *The New Leader* 14 December 1959: 26–27.

Bair, Deirdre. *Samuel Beckett: A Biography*. New York: Harcourt Brace Jovanovich, 1978.

Beckett, Samuel. "A Case in a Thousand." *The Bookman* 86 (1934): 241–42.

——. "Sedendo et Quiesciendo" [sic]. *transition* 21 (1932): 13–20.

Donoghue, Denis. "Being Irish Together." *The Sewanee Review* 84.1 (1976): 129–33.

Ellmann, Richard. *Samuel Beckett: Nayman of Noland*. Washington, D.C.: Library of Congress, 1986.

Hanly, David. *In Guilt and in Glory*. New York: Morrow, 1979.

Harvey, Lawrence. *Samuel Beckett: Poet and Critic*. Princeton: Princeton University Press, 1970.

Hayman, David. "A Meeting in the Park and a Meeting on the Bridge: Joyce and Beckett." *James Joyce Quarterly* 8 (Summer 1971): 372–84.

Higgins, Aidan. "Tired Lines, or Tales My Mother Told Me." *A Bash in the Tunnel: James Joyce by the Irish*. Ed. John Ryan. Brighton: Clifton, 1970. 55–60.

Irish Number. Special Issue of *The Bookman* 86 (1934).

Kinsella, Thomas. "The Irish Writer." *Davis, Mangan, Ferguson? Tradition and the Irish Writer*. By W. B. Yeats and Thomas Kinsella. Dublin: Dolmen, 1970. 57–66.

Mercier, Vivian. *Beckett/Beckett*. Oxford: Oxford University Press, 1977.

O'Brien, Eoin. *The Beckett Country: Samuel Beckett's Ireland*. Monkstown, Co. Dublin: Black Cat Press, 1986.

Shenker, Israel. "Moody Man of Letter." *The New York Times* 6 May 1956: sec. 2; 1,3.

Watson, Francis. Review of *More Pricks Than Kicks*. *The Bookman* 86 (1934): 219–20.

4

"For This Relief Much Thanks":
Leopold Bloom and Beckett's Use of Allusion

David Cohen

AS A SELF-REFLEXIVE NOVEL, *Ulysses* explores the means by which life imitates art and art fails to imitate life. The former can be illustrated by a brief passage in the "Nausicaa" episode: when Bloom is named just before the narrative point of view shifts from Gerty to Bloom, the line reads "Leopold Bloom (for it is he) stands silent . . ." (U 13.744), which recalls the way Mr. Guppy's presence is occasionally revealed in Dickens' *Bleak House*. The parenthetical "(for it is he)" is hardly sufficient to be considered an allusion in the usual sense, but it operates as one here, setting up a parallel between the Bloom/Gerty relationship and that of Guppy and Esther Summerson, who is the object of Guppy's desires until she is disfigured by illness. As the characters of *Ulysses* perform the same actions and submit to the same experiences that have been the stuff of fiction since Homer's time, they cannot help but invoke the language of their literary antecedents. That art fails to imitate life is implied by the intentional stylistic "failures" of some of the later episodes, most noticeably in "Oxen of the Sun," where the styles of the greatest prose writers in the English language fail to report events coherently and objectively.

A few paragraphs into "Scylla and Charybdis," Stephen Dedalus, about to embark on his lecture on Shakespeare's *Hamlet*, thinks: "Folly. Persist" (U 9.42). This is, arguably, Joyce's operating principle, and it is closely allied to that of Samuel Beckett: to persist in the face of inevitable failure. In *Worstward Ho*, Beckett's narrator writes: "All of old. Nothing else ever. Ever tried. Ever failed. No matter. Try again. Fail again. Fail better" (7). The philosophical and aesthetic implications of Beckett's art of "ignorance" and "impotence" have become a commonplace in Beckett criticism.[1]

Rubin Rabinovitz and Raymond Federman in their books on Beckett's early fiction describe Beckett's attempts to move away from traditional forms of writing by using parody, abandoning representation, and merging form (or style) and content. Beckett's comments in "Dante . . . Bruno . Vico . . Joyce," his defense of Joyce's *Work in Progress*, are also particularly illuminating when applied to his own writing. Beckett scolds the reader.

> You are not satisfied unless form is so strictly divorced from content that you can comprehend the one almost without bothering to read the other. This rapid skimming and absorption of the scant cream of sense is made possible by what I may call a continuous process of copious intellectual salivation. The form that is an arbitrary and independent phenomenon can fulfill no higher function than that of stimulus for a tertiary or quartary conditioned reflex of dribbling comprehension [*Disjecta* 26].

Of *Work in Progress*, Beckett writes: "Here form *is* content, content *is* form" (*Disjecta* 27).

Many of the stylistic devices Beckett uses in his early fiction have been traced to Joyce, whose writings are frequently parodied in Beckett's work, but Beckett did not accept Joyce's methods wholeheartedly and write "in his shadow" as some critics have suggested.[2] From the beginning, Beckett had his own agenda, and many of the staples of Joyce's art, primarily the omniscient narrator, did not figure in Beckett's plan for successful failure. The position of the storyteller in relation both to the author and to the story told is one fraught with complexities with which Beckett has grappled from the aborted novel *Dream of Fair to Middling Women* to *Worstward Ho*. Of interest here is the authority of the narrator, and particularly in his use of allusion.

Joyce's works are built on complicated systems of allusion. In

1. The Israel Shenker "interview" may be the source of this commonplace: " 'I am working with *impotence, ignorance*. I don't think impotence has been exploited in the past. . . . My little exploration is that whole zone of being that has always been set aside by artists as something unuseable—as something by definition incompatible with art' " (quoted in Federman 6; emphasis added).

2. In *Beckett and Joyce*, Barbara Gluck titled her chapter on *Murphy*, *Watt*, and *Mercier et Camier* "The Joycean Shadow."

Ulysses, where these systems begin to dominate the narrative, we can isolate three fairly distinct ways in which allusion is transmitted: that used by Stephen, that used by Bloom, and that applied to Stephen, Bloom, and the other characters by the narrator.

Leopold Bloom's interior monologue is peppered with references to scientific, musical, commercial, and literary texts; by finding analogies for Bloom's situation in the texts referred to, the reader is able to find possible meanings for their presence in *Ulysses*. For Bloom himself, however, unaware that he is a character in Joyce's fiction, the allusions do not have such a multifarious purpose. They are bits of language in Bloom's mind, many of which come to the surface because of their ironic relevance to his current situation. For example, Bloom's interior monologue in "Nausicaa" contains the following passage: "Did me good all the same. Off colour after Kiernan's, Dignam's. For this relief much thanks. In *Hamlet*, that is" (U 13.939–40). References to *Hamlet* litter Bloom's and Stephen's interior monologues as well as the narrator's own words, and readers may in consequence draw parallels between *Hamlet* and *Ulysses*. For Bloom, however, who is endowed with an unconscious version of the type of wit he recognizes and admires in people like Simon Dedalus,[3] the phrase "for this relief much thanks" leaps from his mind without dragging along a rattling chain of associations. It is simply appropriate and comic, the "relief" in the present case being that of Bloom's sexual tension. It is only after he uses the phrase that he remembers its source in *Hamlet*, and he does not pause to consider whether he is a character in a symbolic modern rendition of the play.

In contrast to Bloom and his idle use of allusion, we have Stephen Dedalus, who usually knows to what he is alluding and why. Stephen and Buck Mulligan toss off quotations and parodied quotations and communicate in literary riddles, such as the telegram Stephen sends Mulligan that paraphrases Meredith's *The Ordeal of Richard Feverel* (U 9.550–51). Stephen understands the signature of all things he is there to read, and has absorbed

3. I am thinking here primarily of Bloom's recollection in "Lestrygonians" of Simon's lightning-fast responses to the story about Reuben J. Dodd and his son in "Hades" (U 6.250–93): "One and eightpence too much. Hhhhm. It's the droll way he comes out with the things. Knows how to tell a story too" (U 8.53–55).

literature in an attempt to surpass it and establish himself as an artist. His interior monologue brims with his comprehension of the implications and applications of the texts to which he refers. Even Stephen's thought, "Folly. Persist," derives from one of the "Proverbs of Hell" in Blake's *Marriage of Heaven and Hell*: "If the fool would persist in his folly he would become wise."

Finally, we have the narrator, setting scenes in the early episodes and wearing masks later on, and, throughout, planting allusions which serve to remind the discerning reader of scenes from literary history that provide meaning for the scene at hand. Although I call the narrator's use of allusion a single distinct device, in fact the narrator tends to use the device differently in his treatment of Bloom and Stephen. In the example above, in which the narrator invokes Dickens' *Bleak House* to identify Bloom, Bloom is unaware that he is acting out a scene from literature and does not yet even know of Gerty's limp. The narrator recognizes an analogical framework that Bloom does not and uses the allusion to make an implied commentary on the similar relationships.

With Stephen, the narrator frequently provides allusion in a way that Stephen would probably approve of, referring to textual structures that Stephen can recognize.[4] In "Telemachus," an episode wherein Stephen imagines Mulligan is the usurper of his kingdom, several narrative allusions serve to reinforce Stephen's view. Of Mulligan, the narrator writes: "He turned asbruptly his grey searching eyes from the sea to Stephen's face" (U 1.86–87). Mulligan has throughout the episode been associated with light and the sun, as he will be again in "Scylla and Charybdis." Coupled with this, the narrator's reference to Mulligan's "searching eyes" recalls a line from Shakespeare's *Richard II* where King Richard explains to the Duke of Aumerle how Bolingbroke has usurped his throne:

> Discomfortable cousin! Know'st thou not
> That when the searching eye of heaven is hid
> Behind the globe, and lights the lower world,
> Then thieves and robbers range abroad unseen,
> In murders and in outrage bloody here . . . [III.ii.35–40].

4. This is not to imply that Stephen is or is not the narrator of *Ulysses*, but merely to point out that both Stephen and the narrator share a vast knowledge of literature and literary history.

Though the allusion is not Stephen's, it is likely that Stephen would have thought of making the analogy of Richard II and Bolingbroke to himself and Mulligan, which may behoove us to see it as a function of what Hugh Kenner, in *Joyce's Voices*, calls "The Uncle Charles Principle" (18). This is not to say that Stephen is in any way aware of these allusions; he, like Bloom and the other characters, is bound within the text. Stephen is certainly unaware that he is playing Telemachus to Bloom's Ulysses.

The highly visible narrators of Beckett's early novels, from "We," as the narrator of *Dream of Fair to Middling Women* refers to himself, to the storytellers of the French writings, use literary allusion very sparingly. We may be tempted at first to pounce on what we find and look for deeper significance, but it soon turns into the type of logical trap that Watt is prone to: "foisting a meaning . . . where no meaning appeared" (77). But when Beckett's narrators do allude, it is not with the confident erudition of Stephen Dedalus or the *Ulysses* narrator, but rather with the improvisatory wit of Leopold Bloom.

For example, the occasional references to Shakespeare's *Romeo and Juliet* in *Murphy* provide ironic commentary on the status of Murphy and Celia as "star-crossed lovers" without imposing a strong interpretive burden. The references to *Romeo and Juliet* continue into Beckett's next novel, *Watt*, where the very notion of love, "star-crossed" or otherwise, is absurd. The mechanical sexual congress between Watt and the fishwoman Mrs. Gorman takes its place as just one in a series of mechanical activities. What is perhaps most significant about the allusions in Beckett's early novels, then, is their very poverty of signification. When Sam, the narrator of *Watt*, writes ". . . if it was really day again already, in some low distant quarter of the sky, it was not yet day again already in the kitchen" (64), the phrasing recalls Act III, Scene V of *Romeo and Juliet*, the lovers' farewell before Romeo departs for Mantua, but beyond the phrasing there is no apparent application, except, perhaps, for a rather grim irony. Like Leopold Bloom, the narrator of *Watt* incorporates a phrase from Shakespeare into his monologue, apparently without premeditation or intent, almost by word association. In *Watt*, crafted by Beckett through several drafts to resemble an abandoned first-draft of a novel, this improvisatory alluding lends to the hurried, disorderly tone of the writing.

In an interview Beckett said that he was interested in "the shape of ideas," meaning that the form of the sentence, the very expression of the idea, was more compelling to him than the mere content. I suggest that this principle informs his use of allusions not so much as keys to interpretation as evocations of the shape of language. If the words are form and their meanings content, then Beckett's allusions are commonly made for the sake of form. Familiar shapes, both of allusion and cliché, frequently become containers that Beckett may fill with parodic substances, as in the following examples from *Murphy*:

> "Who ever met," said Miss Counihan, ". . . that met not at first sight [221]?"

> Turf is compulsory in the Saorstat, but one need not bring a private supply to Newcastle [197].

The humor in these passages depends upon the recognizable shape of the source quotations: for the former, "who ever lov'd that lov'd not at first sight?" from Marlowe's *Hero and Leander*, also found in Shakespeare's *As You Like It* (III.iv); for the latter, the cliché about carrying coals to Newcastle. Beckett also creates new patterns in his works, which are then repeated over and over with or without variation, and, again, they depend upon the reader's recognizing the unique syntax. From *Murphy*:

> It was at this moment that they all saw simultaneously for the first time, and with common good breeding refrained from remarking, the slender meanders of water on the floor [213].

> It was at this moment that they all caught simultaneously for the first time, and with common good breeding refrained from remarking, a waft of Miss Carridge's peculiarity [227].

In a 1937 letter to Axel Kaun, published in *Disjecta* and translated from Beckett's German by Martin Esslin, Beckett asked:

> is literature alone to remain behind in the old lazy ways that have been so long ago abandoned by music and painting? . . . Is there any reason why that terrible materiality of the word surface should not be capable of being dissolved, like for example the sound

surface, torn by enormous pauses, of Beethoven's seventh Symphony, so that through whole pages we can perceive nothing but a path of sounds suspended in giddy heights, linking unfathomable abysses of silence [172]?

Beckett wanted to free words from the tyranny of representation, to banish meaning and make the reader comprehend and appreciate the words themselves. He set out to manipulate words in the same way as a painter manipulates color or a composer manipulates sound. By quoting other texts and having the quotations stand for themselves as groups of words as recognizable as the group of notes that begin Beethoven's Fifth Symphony, Beckett has achieved this. Increasingly in later works, such as *Play* and *The Lost Ones*, he exploits the everyday language of cliché in a similar way, while references to literary texts disappear almost entirely. In his plays, many of which bear a heavier load of allusion than his fictions, there is no narrative presence, but his characters are not, like Stephen and his associates, learned men and women batting difficult concepts back and forth: they are like Bloom, letting the play of language run free, like Krapp taking pleasure in "spool."

Beckett is searching for the situation that has not previously attained literary utterance, instead of flaunting the fact that all have, as Joyce had done. By using the Bloomean form of Joycean allusion and placing this within his own narrative voices, Beckett at once distances himself from his narrators and allows "the shape of ideas" to take precedence over the ideas themselves. If *Ulysses* is about how life imitates art and art fails to imitate life, Beckett is concerned with an art that does not seek to represent anything but itself and is content to fail, but, if possible, to fail better.

WORKS CITED

Federman, Raymond. *Journey to Chaos: Samuel Beckett's Early Fiction.* Berkeley and London: University of California Press, 1965.

Gluck, Barbara Reich. *Beckett and Joyce: Friendship and Fiction.* Lewisburg, Pa.: Bucknell University Press, 1979.

Kenner, Hugh. *Joyce's Voices.* Berkeley and London: University of California Press, 1978.

Rabinovitz, Rubin. *The Development of Samuel Beckett's Fiction.* Urbana and Chicago: University of Illinois Press, 1984.

5

Beckett Re-Joycing: *Words and Music*

James Acheson

WORDS AND MUSIC WAS FIRST BROADCAST by the BBC on November 13, 1962. An audience research report conducted shortly afterward revealed that the play was not well received: it scored an appreciation index of 43, the lowest figure recorded for a Beckett production on the Third Programme (Zilliacus 115). It is not surprising that even the sophisticated radio audience that tuned in to *Words and Music* found it perplexing, for the play is densely packed with allusions; it embodies an unusual combination of the expressionistic and the medieval; and it requires that the listener be aware of Beckett's lifelong preoccupation with the unfathomability of the human mind, a preoccupation that surfaces near the end of the play in a less than immediately obvious form. Like the three other radio plays Beckett wrote at about the same time— *Rough for Radio I, Rough for Radio II,* and *Cascando*[1]—*Words and Music* needs not only to be heard in performance but to be studied as a literary text if the significance of its complexities is to be appreciated fully.

As Clas Zilliacus has observed, Beckett offers various hints that the play is set in a castle, with one of the characters, Croak, acting as feudal overlord, and the two others, Words and Music, as entertainers permanently attached to Croak's household:

> The mode of their attachment is unambiguous: they are, in Words' phrase, "cooped up here in the dark." At more or less regular intervals Croak visits them in their confinement, for such solace and entertainment as their art may provide. His artists address him [as] My Lord; the term of Beckett's French version is Milord, and that of a French MS. was Seigneur. Croak for his part calls them

---

1. For manuscript dates, see Admussen, 26, 47, 80, and 94.

his comforts, balms, or dogs, as his temper prompts him. The master-and-servant motif familiar from other Beckett works here appears in recognizably feudal costume [Zilliacus 106].

Zilliacus adds, however, that on closer examination, the setting of the play turns out to be not a castle but the interior of a mind (105). The play's medieval element emphasizes the nature of the relationship between Croak, on the one hand, and Words and Music, on the other. As Martin Esslin has suggested, Croak is the superior figure, the Self; Words is the mind's verbal component; and Music, the non-verbal (100). Each serves Croak in a different way.

Rather than being a young and virile warrior-hero, Croak is (as his name and faltering voice imply) an old man approaching death.[2] He is a partly pathetic, partly comic figure, who, despite his feudal aspect, derives not from Beckett's interest in medieval literature, as Zilliacus has claimed (105), but from his longstanding interest in Joyce's *Ulysses,* two of whose chapters, "Sirens" and "Cyclops," form a major source for the play. Words (in the form of conversation) are central to "Cyclops," and Music (in the form of song) to "Sirens." It is from these two chapters of a novel Beckett knows well that *Words and Music* derives.[3]

Beckett draws on "Cyclops" to set the tone of his play. In this chapter, a nameless first-person narrator reports the conversation of a rather shabby group of Dubliners who have gathered together in a public bar; Joyce intersperses the narrator's comments not only with dialogue but also with third-person passages phrased in high-flown, quasi-medieval language. The effect is mock-heroic, as the following excerpt illustrates:

—Ah, well, says Joe, handing round the boose. Thanks be to God they had the start of us. Drink that, citizen.

—I will, says he, honourable person.

2. Zilliacus points out that in the first draft of *Words and Music* Croak was initially called " 'Old man's whisper,' then 'Whisper,' then 'Senile Croak,' and finally 'Croak' " (100).

3. Cf. N. H., "Caviare to the General," a review of Beckett's *More Pricks Than Kicks* (London: Chatto & Windus, 1934), where the comment is made that "Mr. Beckett . . . knows his *Ulysses* as a Scotch Presbyterian knows his *Bible*" (85).

—Health, Joe, says I. And all down the form.

Ah! Ow! Don't be talking! I was blue mouldy for the want of that pint. Declare to God I could hear it hit the pit of my stomach with a click.

And lo, as they quaffed their cup of joy, a godlike messenger came swiftly in, radiant as the eye of heaven, a comely youth and behind him there passed an elder of noble gait and countenance, bearing the sacred scrolls of law and with him his lady wife a dame of peerless lineage, fairest of her race.

Little Alf Bergan popped in round the door and hid behind Barney's snug, squeezed up with the laughing. And who was sitting up there in the corner that I hadn't seen snoring drunk blind to the world only Bob Doran [U 12.238–51].

Though the medieval element in *Words and Music* is fully integrated into the dialogue, rather than being separately interjected into it, as in "Cyclops," it serves a similar, mock-heroic purpose. Croak, the governing faculty of an aging, failing mind, summons his servants Words and Music not to perform an act of heroism but to assist him in the humbler task of writing poetry and setting it to music. That the poetry and music will be less than great art is conveyed by the fact that Croak is a lord in decline and that Words and Music, castle poet and minstrel, respectively, are named "Joe" and "Bob," after two of the lowlife characters in the "Cyclops" episode, Joe Hynes and Bob Doran. It is appropriate that Words, the mind's verbal component, should bear Joe Hynes's name, for Hynes is distinguished from his companions by virtue of being "eloquent" (U 12.908). Similarly, just as Bob Doran is highly emotional, so Music represents, in Martin Esslin's words, "the non-verbal, non-articulated component of [the mind portrayed in *Words and Music*], the flow of the emotions themselves . . ." (100).[4]

4. See U 12.310ff., 388ff., 780ff. for instances of Bob Doran's emotional behavior. I am grateful to Professors Mary Gerhardstein and Ellen Shields of the University of Waterloo (Canada) for reminding me that Joe Hynes also appears in "Ivy Day in the Committee Room," where he recites a poem he has composed in honor of Parnell; and that a Mr. Doran (his first name is not given) figures in "The Boarding House." Doran has had an affair with the landlady's daughter and wavers between two emotions: love for the young woman and the desire to remain unmarried.

Croak's name, the title of the play, and much else derive from the "Sirens" episode of *Ulysses.* Here Leopold Bloom listens as Simon Dedalus sings "Come Back, Martha! Ah Return Love"[5] to the assembled drinkers in a bar. "Through the hush of air," comments Joyce, "[his] voice sang to them, . . . touching their still ears with words, still hearts of their each his remembered lives" (U 11.674–77). Like the others, Bloom is moved by the song and asks himself why: "Words? Music? No: it's what's behind" (U 11.703). Bloom realizes that it is neither the words nor the music that has touched him—neither the description of the lover's pain as he yearns for the return of Martha nor the melancholy tune to which it is set. Rather, it is the power the song has to evoke thoughts and feelings about his own situation—which includes his involvement in a furtive correspondence with a woman named Martha Clifford, in compensation for the fact that his wife Molly is being unfaithful to him.

Thoughts of infidelity lead in Bloom's mind to events that have taken place earlier in the day. Paddy Dignam has been buried; he (Bloom) has reflected that a certain Father Coffey has "a belly on him like a poisoned pup" (U 6.598–99); and he has several times recalled that his own father died by poisoning himself. "Cruel it seems. Let people get fond of each other; lure them on. Then tear asunder. Death. . . . Dignam. . . . Corncrake croaker: belly like a poisoned pup" (U 11.803–806). For Joyce, this passage serves to reveal Bloom's thoughts about the cruel inevitability of lovers being separated by death. For Beckett, however, "Words? Music? No: it's what's behind" (U 11.703) is the source of the title of *Words and Music,* and "Corncrake croaker"—a phrase associated in Bloom's mind with Simon Dedalus, a man with a good singing voice ruined by overindulgence in drink—the provenance of the name "Croak."[6]

Beckett uses these and other allusions to *Ulysses* in the same way as he uses major allusions to various literary and non-literary works in earlier plays—as points of departure for the creation of

5. For the words to this song see Bowen 178–79.
6. For reasons that will become apparent, this passage in *Ulysses* is a more probable source for the title *Words and Music* than Yeats's collection of late poems, *Words for Music Perhaps,* first suggested as a source by John Pilling (101).

an original work. Though Croak is neither Simon Dedalus nor
Leopold Bloom, he is allied to both. He resembles Dedalus in that
he has known better days; he is not, however, a naturalistic
character in a novel, but the governing faculty of a mind presented
to us in an expressionistic radio play. His resemblance to Leopold
Bloom consists in the fact that he finds the right combination of
words and music highly moving; but unlike Bloom, who hears
Simon Dedalus' song because he happens to be in the same pub
when Dedalus is asked to sing, Croak deliberately summons
Words and Music to entertain him. Beckett establishes these
differences for the sake of exploring the implications of Bloom's
reflection that "it's what's behind" the words and music of a song
that is important.

Croak is thwarted in his desire for entertainment because Words
is constantly in conflict with Music. Words would ideally like to
speak on the topics set him by Croak without having his statements colored by the emotion Music insists on providing, and for
that reason he repeatedly tries to silence him. Music, by contrast,
finds Words a useful complement to his compositions and often
invites him to provide lyrics to the melodies he has created. On
the few occasions when he drowns Words out, it is almost always
because he has been ordered to do so by Croak. Croak's interest,
however, is not in helping Music to triumph over Words but in
encouraging the two to come together as friends. What he wants
is to bring the verbal and non-verbal components of his mind into
a relationship productive of song. The particular song he yearns
to hear is one whose marriage of words and music will give rise
to pleasure on three topics that have hitherto given him pain: love,
age, and—mysteriously, for its significance is not immediately
apparent—"the face."

Croak's pain when thinking of the first topic, love, is intensi-
fied, however, by Words's dispassionate approach to it. Asked to
speak on this topic, Words formulates a trite, quasi-Scholastic
definition:

> WORDS (*orotund*): Love is of all the passions the most powerful
> passion and indeed no passion is more powerful than the passion
> of love. (*Clears throat.*) This is the mode in which the mind is
> most strongly affected and indeed in no mode is the mind more
> strongly affected than in this.

Pause.

CROAK: *Rending sigh. Thump of club.*

WORDS (*as before*): By passion we are to understand a movement of the mind pursuing or fleeing real or imagined pleasure or pain. (*Clears throat.*) Of all—

CROAK (*anguished*): Oh! [*Cas* 24].

To assuage the anguish Words's detachment has caused him, Croak calls on Music to furnish emotion. Music responds with "*Soft music worthy of foregoing, great expression, with audible groans and protestations—'No!' 'Please!' etc.—from* WORDS" (25). At Croak's insistence, Music drowns these protestations out; when Croak bids Words to resume, however, the latter persists in being cool and detached and at Croak's command is silenced by Music again.

When Croak next calls upon Words, it is to demand that he speak on the subject of age. Words begins falteringly, but more emotionally than before, and as he composes a short poem on the topic, joins with Music, and sings. The poem is a bleak description of old age and growing decrepitude which, though initially generalized, moves to the particular when it pictures an old man remembering a woman he once loved:

> Age is when to a man
> Huddled o'er the ingle
> Shivering for the hag
> To put the pan in the bed
> And bring the toddy
> She comes in the ashes
> Who loved could not be won
> Or won not loved
> Or some other trouble
> Comes in the ashes
> Like in that old light
> The face in the ashes
> That old starlight
> On the earth again [28].

Croak is interested less in Words's description of the old man and the music than in what lies behind them. He has earlier spoken of having seen or imagined a face "[o]n the stairs" (24), and it is in order to explore the poem's relationship to this experience fully that he asks Words to describe the face in detail.

> WORDS (*disregarding, cold.*): Seen from above at such close quarters in that radiance so cold and faint with eyes so dimmed by . . . what had passed, its quite . . . piercing beauty is a little . . . blunted. Some moments later however, such are the powers of recuperation at this age, . . . the eyes widen to a stare and begin to feast again. (*Pause.*) . . . Now and then the rye, swayed by a light wind, casts and withdraws its shadow.
>
> . . . .
>
> CROAK (*anguished.*) Lily! [29–30].

Clas Zilliacus has argued that this is a "postcoital" scene, the aftermath of Croak's lovemaking years before with a woman named Lily (109). Words's reference, however, to Lily's "powers of recuperation," and his comment that "a little colour comes back into [her] cheeks" (30) as she recovers herself, suggest instead that she has had a great shock, perhaps the shock of learning that Croak wants to bring their relationship to an end.[7]

It is significant in this connection that Words echoes a song from the "Sirens" episode of *Ulysses*, "When the Bloom Is on the Rye":

> My pretty Jane, my pretty Jane!
> Ah! never, never look so shy,
> But meet me, meet me in the ev'ning,
> When the bloom is on the rye.
>
> . . . .
>
> But name the day, the wedding day,
> And I will buy the ring,
> The lads and maids in favors white,
> And village bells shall ring.[8]

Although the ballad describes fulfillment in marriage, the allusion to it in *Words and Music* suggests that Croak suffered a great loss in

---

7. It is convenient to use the name "Croak" to refer to the person whose mind is portrayed in the play, since that person's name is not given. However, it must be remembered that, in the first instance, the name refers to the governing component of that mind.

8. Bowen quotes this song and identifies Joyce's allusions to it in the "Sirens" episode (163). See Bowen (372) for a list of Joyce's allusions to the song elsewhere.

breaking with Lily and is now troubled by a profound sense of regret.

Another song important in this context is "The Lily of Killarney," which perhaps contributed the name "Lily" to the play. Joyce alludes to this song in *Ulysses* and quotes part of it in *A Portrait of the Artist as a Young Man*:

> 'Tis youth and folly
> Makes young men marry,
> So here, my love, I'll
>   No longer stay.
> What can't be cured, sure,
> Must be injured, sure,
>   So I'll go to
>   Amerikay.
>
> My love she's handsome,
> My love she's bonny:
> She's like good whisky
>   When it is new;
> But when 'tis old
> And growing cold
> It fades and dies like
>   The mountain dew.[9]

Unlike "When the Bloom Is on the Rye," which takes a celebratory view of marriage, "The Lily of Killarney" is negative and spurning. If, as it seems, Croak did decide to break with Lily as a young man, it may have been because he believed that young love was not a proper basis for marriage, since it "fades and dies like / The mountain dew." Another, quite different possibility is suggested, however, by the resemblance between Words's description of the recuperating Lily and Krapp's account of the girl in the punt in *Krapp's Last Tape*. In picturing Lily to Croak, Words draws attention to the

—flare of the black disordered hair as though spread wide on water, the brows knitted in a groove suggesting pain but simply

---

9. Quoted in Bowen (37–38). See Bowen (369) for a list of the places in *Ulysses* and *Portrait* where Joyce either alludes to or quotes from this song. Beckett echoes the first of the two lines, "What can't be cured, sure / Must be injured, sure" in *Happy Days* (10).

concentration more likely all things considered on some consummate inner process, the eyes of course closed in keeping with this. . . . the whole so blanched and still that were it not for the great white rise and fall of the breasts. . . . Some moments later however, . . . the brows uncloud, . . . a little colour comes back into the cheeks and the eyes . . . (*reverently*) . . . open [30].

In its use of black and white imagery and its concentration on the girl's eyes, this passage echoes the scene in *Krapp's Last Tape* in which Krapp breaks off with a nameless girl:

TAPE: I said again I thought it was hopeless and no good going on, and she agreed, without opening her eyes. (*Pause.*) I asked her to look at me and after a few moments—(*pause*)—after a few moments she did, but the eyes just slits, because of the glare. I bent over her to get them in the shadow and they opened. (*Pause. Low.*) Let me in [27]. [10]

What these similarities suggest is that in writing *Words and Music* Beckett drew not only on two chapters of *Ulysses* but also on *Krapp's Last Tape*. The contrast of black and white allows him to achieve a striking visual effect in an otherwise exclusively aural medium, and in Krapp he has a useful model for Croak. In *Words and Music*, the fact that Croak is haunted by the face of a woman he once loved suggests that, like Krapp, Croak chose as a young man to deny himself love in order to dedicate himself to art. Moreover, Becket hints that Croak's decision to break with Lily had an intellectual as well as an emotional side to it by ensuring that, as in *Krapp's Last Tape*, black and white, light and dark are associated with the intellect and the emotions. That on an intellectual level (the intellect being represented both here and in *Krapp's Last Tape* by white and light) [11] he is convinced that he was right to break with Lily is evident from his apparent unwillingness to halt Words's "cold" description of her face. Croak prefers to dwell on the dispassionate side of his decision and says nothing to encourage Music to drown out Words's description. On the other hand, it is also evident that, like Krapp, Croak is profoundly

10. Zilliacus (110) relates this passage from *Krapp's Last Tape* to the poem Words composes at the end of the play.

11. James Knowlson discusses the significance of the black/white, light/dark imagery (see Knowlson).

lonely, and on an emotional level (the emotions being represented by black and darkness) is all too aware of having made a mistake.

In old age he finds he is still obsessed with Lily and experiences pain rather than pleasure when Words sets a poem to music on the subject of her reaction to the ending of their relationship:

> WORDS:—the brows uncloud, the lips part and the eyes
> . . .(*reverently*.) . . . open. (*Pause.*)
> . . . .
> (*trying to sing, softly.*)
>   Then down a little way
>
> . . . .
>   Towards where . . .
>   All dark no begging
>   No giving no words
> . . . .
>   To whence one glimpse
>   Of that wellhead.
> (*Pause. Shocked.*) My Lord! (*Sound of club let fall. As before.*) My Lord! (*Shuffling slippers, with halts. They die away* . . . [30–32].

Croak seems, like Krapp, to have explored the eyes—traditionally the windows of the soul—of the woman he loved in order to gauge her reaction to the news that their love affair was to end. Evidently he managed to get only a glimpse of the "wellhead" of thought and feeling from which that reaction issued. That he did get only a glimpse is to be expected, for as Beckett emphasizes in various of his novels and plays, the workings of another person's mind are ultimately unknowable.

Croak, however, not only is barred from knowing what Lily thought and felt, but bars himself from even speculating on it, finding the whole matter too distressing to contemplate. Where the dispassionate Words is shocked at his sudden departure, the reader or radio listener alive to Beckett's allusions to Joyce and to *Krapp's Last Tape* finds it entirely consistent with what has gone before. Croak has been presented mock-heroically throughout the play, like the characters in the "Cyclops" episode of *Ulysses*; we expect him to avoid unpleasantness whenever he can. Moreover, we have come to understand that he is quite possibly a failed artist whose sacrifice of love to ambition as a young man has, like

Krapp's, been in vain. His departure at the end is an expression of profound regret over lost opportunities and his inability to compose, with the help of Words and Music, a song that will ameliorate his sorrow. That inability may derive from a lack of talent or, more generally, from the mind's ultimate lack of control over the emotions it generates. It is appropriate that Beckett, who has said that the key word in his plays is "perhaps" (Driver 23), should end this play by suggesting that it is impossible to be altogether certain "what's behind" the thoughts and feelings that the words and music of his title represent.[12]

WORKS CITED

Admussen, Richard. *The Samuel Beckett Manuscripts: A Study*. Boston: Hall, 1979.

Bowen, Zack. *Musical Allusions in the Works of James Joyce*. Albany: State University of New York Press, 1974.

Driver, Tom F. "Beckett by the Madeleine." *Columbia University Forum* 14 (Summer 1961): 21–25.

Esslin, Martin. "Beckett's *Rough for Radio*." *Journal of Modern Literature* 6 (February 1977): 95–103.

H., N. "Caviare to the General." *Dublin Magazine* 9 (July–September 1934): 84–86.

Knowlson, James. "*Krapp's Last Tape*: The Evolution of a Play, 1958–1975." *Journal of Beckett Studies* 1 (Winter 1976): 50–65.

Pilling, John. *Samuel Beckett*. London: Routledge & Kegan Paul, 1976.

Yeats, W. B. *Words for Music Perhaps*. In *The Winding Stair and Other Poems, 1933*. Rpt. in *The Collected Poems of W. B. Yeats*. London: Macmillan, 1963.

Zilliacus, Clas. *Beckett and Broadcasting*. Abo: Abo Akademi, 1976.

12. I should like to thank Professor Eugene Benson of the University of Guelph (Canada) and Professor Colin Duckworth of the University of Melbourne for their thoughtful readings of a draft of this essay.

6

"The More Joyce Knew the More He Could" and "More Than I Could": Theology and Fictional Technique in Joyce and Beckett

Alan S. Loxterman

THROUGH THEIR FICTIONAL TECHNIQUE both James Joyce and Samuel Beckett articulate theological uncertainty, the uneasiness of twentieth-century readers about whether reality can be grounded in ultimate authority. In fiction such authority is represented by the godlike narrator who oversees characters and plot and who provides the controlling intelligence from which a normative set of values can be derived, no matter how eccentrically a work's characters might behave or how experimentally they might be presented in terms of narrative technique. The status of this traditionally godlike narrative authority is reinterpreted by Joyce, then challenged by Beckett.

Both Joyce and Beckett question the authority of the traditional omniscient narrator, but do so in ways expressed through opposite stylistic assumptions and techniques. Two examples from *Ulysses* illustrate how the questionable authority of interior monologue is replaced by a secular version of the controlling narrator, the author himself as manipulator of language. Such a narrator is too apt to call our attention to himself and his handiwork to be considered godlike. But, if not omniscient, he is at least omnipresent in terms of style. Two prayer scenes from *Waiting for Godot* and *Happy Days* demonstrate how Beckett seemingly reacts against Joyce's retention of narrative authority, with all its theological implications. Through incomplete or confused dialogue and monologue Beckett dramatizes the difficulty, if not the impossibility, of either the author or his central characters being able to com-

municate the sort of universal truths that we have come to expect
from omniscient narration.

Historically considered, Joyce and Beckett have become two of
the most influential writers of our century through their inclusion
of problematic interpretation as part of the aesthetic experience, a
degree of complexity that requires readers to acknowledge their
own complicity in making meaning out of what they perceive.
Joyce pioneers the inclusion of indeterminacy in his narrative, first
in the opening of *Portrait* and next in those later chapters of *Ulysses*
where his method of narration takes precedence over who and
what are being narrated. *Finnegans Wake* represents the culmination of a language and style which pre-empts that narrative
guidance through a story line which has traditionally been central
to the reading experience. Here readers must puzzle over each
syllable of the language from beginning to end, being perhaps
more consistently aware of their own attempts to interpret what
is being said than of anything else.[1]

It is tempting to speculate that Joyce had considerable influence
on Beckett since the broad outlines of Beckett's own development
appear so similar. First, for both came poetry and an analytical
essay on a major literary predecessor, Beckett on Proust and Joyce
on Ibsen. Then *More Pricks Than Kicks,* a series of stories set in
Dublin and united by a common character instead of a common
theme, as in *Dubliners.* Next apprentice work, *Murphy,* which is
indebted to Joyce as Joyce's play *Exiles* was to Ibsen. But the more
appropriate (and chronologically parallel) comparison for *Murphy*
is Joyce's *Portrait* since both seem experimental in terms of their
predecessors yet conventionally realistic in comparison to the
fiction that follows.[2] Since Beckett wrote many more separate

1. Some would deny this account by concentrating on the organization of
Finnegans Wake rather than on the chaos that is being organized. But the reader's
concrete experience of interpreting the language itself, word by word, is far
removed from the critic's delineation of whatever overall abstract schemes the
symbolic plot comprises. In *Finnegans Wake* the totality of the reading experience
is that there can *be* no totality, only a multiplicity of proliferating alternatives.

2. For example, one critic characterizes *Murphy* as a transitional work which
belies its own apparent "assumptions . . . that viable relationships exist among
the artist, his art, and the surrounding world, and that complete and absolute
structures can be fashioned and communicated." "As traditional as *Murphy*'s
form might appear initially, its language, characters, settings, and viewpoints
are in fact products of and consistent with the Beckettian themes presented [of
fluidity, uncertainty, and intentional ambiguity]" (Dearlove 15, 26).

works than Joyce, at this point I shall simplify the comparison by moving directly to some of Beckett's better-known fiction and drama. Like the second half of Joyce's *Ulysses*, Beckett's *Molloy*, *Malone Dies*, *The Unnamable*, and *Waiting for Godot* all represent a departure from the author's previous depiction of reality perceived in terms of plot, character, and setting. Finally, like Joyce's *Finnegans Wake*, Beckett's subsequent plays and later fiction increasingly concentrate on the interior processing of language itself, the interaction between author/narrator(s) and reader which produces fictional alternatives to an indeterminable exterior reality.

In parallel fashion, then, Joyce and Beckett have developed from realistic writers depicting characters in terms of situations into tragi-comedians exposing the provisional nature of what the reader perceives to be their enterprise, truth-telling through fiction. In both we can see the end implicit in their beginning. Even where they retain some conventions of fictional realism, their decentralization of the narrative, through substitution of first-person or interior monologue for omniscient direction, prepares the way for their subsequent shift to an emphasis on meaning as autonomous illusion. Their fiction becomes increasingly self-referential, no longer an interpretation of external reality so much as a construct of language open to multiple interpretations by different readers.

Two examples from the earlier and later types of narrative in *Ulysses* illustrate how the influence of the original Author, as the source of theological omniscience in one's view of reality, has been replaced by interior monologue and by the human author's exercise of his own omniscience through built-in reminders to his readers that he is always in control of his fictional world. When Stephen Dedalus shuts his eyes while walking on the beach, he can still hear the sound of crunching stones and shells, and thus concludes that he cannot ignore the existence of external reality: "There all the time without you: and ever shall be, world without end" (U 3.27–28). The double meaning of "without" establishes that reality must be independent of the perceiver as well as external to him, properties constituting possible evidence of an everlasting Creator, as his echo of the conclusion of the "Gloria" in the Book of Common Prayer acknowledges.

Yet Stephen refuses personal assent to that creed by not pro-
nouncing his "Amen." To begin with, there is considerable doubt
about how well Stephen is able to read "[s]ignatures of all things"
(U 3.2). With respect to his own art, at least, the signature is not
Stephen's own, but that of Douglas Hyde on the poem Stephen is
composing in this chapter (Gifford 44). That night, in Circe's
brothel when he is trying to pick out a tune on the piano and is
asked by a prostitute to sing (accompanied by the inevitable *double
entendre* of having intercourse), Stephen admits that, creatively and
procreatively, he is "a most finished artist" (U 15.2508).

In aspiring to be an artist, Stephen seeks a kind of immortality.
As he would read "signatures of all things" himself, so he wishes
to be read rightly, in his essence, by others: "I throw this ended
shadow from me, manshape ineluctable, call it back. Endless,
would it be mine, form of my form? Who watches me here? Who
ever anywhere will read these written words?" (U 3.412–15).
Considering the literary and traditional associations of one's
shadow with the soul, Stephen seems to be wondering here if he
has an eternal essence that will continue to be him, "endless" after
the death of his human form. If so, can that be expressed in words
as a "signature" to be fully understood through all space and time
to come ("ever anywhere") by others? The answer to Stephen's
question is both someone and no one. Later Leopold Bloom does
pick up the scrap of paper on which Stephen has jotted his
fragment of a poem. But it has become too blurred for Bloom to
read (U 13.1244–48).[3]

Stephen's desire to be understood is religious, as well as personal and artistic. At the chapter's end, his original desire to be
noticed expands beyond the artist's need for recognition. Wist-
fully he touches on the Cartesian solution of an omniscient entity
bridging the dualistic gap between concept and percept: "Behind.
Perhaps there is someone" (U 3.502). The name of this chapter is
"Proteus," the god identified with the shifting flux of phenomena.

3. Perhaps Bloom has sensed Stephen's inner need to communicate and be
understood, though, for Bloom next attempts a composition of his own,
scratching on the sand a message intended for Gerty MacDowell to find later.
Yet he too gets no further than "I. AM. A.," with the curious excuse (considering
that he is writing on a vast expanse of beach) that he has "no room" left to
continue (U 13.1246–65).

So is Stephen looking for the existence of a Cartesian God "behind" that flux capable of unifying internal ideas and the external reality to which they refer? What Stephen sees behind him when he does turn around holds theological promise: "Moving through the air high spars of a threemaster, her sails brailed up on the crosstrees, homing, upstream, silently moving, a silent ship" (U 3.503–505). The "threemaster" (three crosses, or Christ as the "master" part of the Trinity?) and the echo between "brailed up" and "nailed up" (especially in conjunction with "crosstrees") both provide a possible answer to Stephen's question in an image of Christian afterlife, a funeral ship of crucifixion "homing" toward resurrection.

Yet, as we might expect in a chapter on appearance and reality, this ending remains decidedly ambiguous. For the actuality of the situation undercuts any theological interpretation of what Stephen may see in the ship. He has just placed a piece of snot on a rock, observing "For the rest let look who will" (U 3.501). Coming after such a melodramatic gesture, his query about someone behind him may simply indicate Stephen's desire to be caught in the act by some passerby. Or is it guilt over desecrating the rock of Peter's church? In an intrusion rare in the early chapters of *Ulysses*, the narrator inserts "rere regardant," the stiff, even precious, language of striking an heraldic pose, to describe Stephen's turning to look behind him (U 3.503). Even the image of the sailing ship may be another example of Stephen's second-hand creativity since it is described in the manner of Tennyson.[4] As a

4. Before he sees the ship Stephen has already sneered at the Victorian respectability of "Lawn Tennyson" (i.e., a pun on "son of lawn tennis") (U 3.490–92; Gifford 47). Since "mother" appears together with "new year" when Stephen thinks about Tennyson, the text he is recollecting must be the opening of "The May Queen": "call me early mother dear; / Tomorrow'll be the happiest time of the glad New-year" (lines 1–2), probably in its setting as a popular song (Gifford 47).

So, with Tennyson recently on his mind, when Stephen sees the ship after having been thinking about a drowned man, he is prepared to recall Tennyson's better-known reference to the new year as the hopeful turning point in *In Memoriam* (stanza 106). Early in that poem Tennyson expressed his grief in an image that merged the movement of the ship with Hallam's body, as if the sea were now doing the breathing for the corpse it contained: "dead calm in that noble breast / Which heaves but with the heaving deep" (stanza 11, lines 19–20). The metaphorical implication that Hallam's mortal energy has been absorbed

final indignity, this otherworldly, silent vessel's actual cargo is later revealed to be decidedly earthy, politically charged ballast: bricks from England (U 10.1098–99; Gifford 47).

When Haines presses Stephen to describe his religious belief, Stephen responds "You behold in me . . . a horrible example of free thought"; and the narrator notes that he says this not jokingly, as Buck Mulligan would, but "with grim displeasure" (U 1.625–26). "Proteus" shows that Stephen's misery derives not so much from atheism itself as from Stephen's inability to be a freethinker, to believe in it wholeheartedly as a substitute for the unswerving commitment that he had previously reserved for Catholicism. What begins as comparatively pure internal monologue, a philosophical reflection that reaffirms Cartesian dualism, ends in a yearning for theological reconciliation. Yet such a hope (as Stephen bitterly appreciates better than anyone) contradicts his role of freethinking atheist, which he first revealed publicly when he refused to kneel and pray for his dying mother at her request (U 1.207–208). Against the personal melodrama of inner conflict between Stephen's doubt and would-be (or has-been?) faith Joyce overbalances an array of ironic complications. The possible self-mockery of Stephen's viewing the sailing ship in terms of Tennyson's Christian consolation is augmented by the incongruous insertion of the language of heraldry. Perhaps the narrator is insinuating that the reader ought to view Stephen's dramatic "turnaround" toward the heavenly promise of the ship with the

---

into the endless rhythms of nature foreshadows the source of consolation announced in terms of the new year. Tennyson is able to reconcile himself to Hallam's death by the end of the poem, seeing it as part of an ultimate convergence between nature's evolutionary process and God's plan, "one far-off divine event, / To which the whole creation moves" (Epilogue, lines 143–44). As poet laureate, this "gentleman poet" has supplied a transcendental view of history which, in the popular mind, can be used to justify British imperialism. As Mr. Deasy had observed to Stephen in the previous chapter, "All human history moves towards one great goal, the manifestation of God" (U 2.380–81): and this is the Tennysonian "nightmare from which [Stephen is] trying to awake" (U 2.377).

Considering such a subconscious network of religious and political associations, Stephen could be describing the ship in his own mind as Tennyson might, ridiculing his own former credulity with this parody of Tennyson's complacent assurance ("homing, upstream, silently moving" also evokes the mood and imagery of "Crossing the Bar").

same skepticism accorded to his absurd posturing with the snot. At the end of "Proteus" it is impossible to distinguish between the reader's response to the otherworldly appearance of the ship— which, in his earlier works, Joyce might have regarded as an epiphany—and the narrator's own mockery of the notion that any such object could constitute an epiphany.[5]

For the most part, "Proteus" is notable for the difficulties it poses as an example of pure interior monologue uncontaminated (and therefore unshaped) by narrative control.[6] Yet one narrative intrusion, "*rere* regardant," is enough to put the reader in the position of being as uncertain about Stephen's attitude toward God as Stephen himself is. Thus when the narrator subsequently

5. Earlier in "Proteus" we see an older Stephen mocking the religious aesthetic that he once took so seriously in *Portrait*: "Remember your epiphanies written on green oval leaves, deeply deep, copies to be sent if you died to all the great libraries of the world, including Alexandria?" (U 3.141–43). Whether we regard the description of the ship which concludes "Proteus" to come from Stephen himself or from the narrator, it is too unlike both of them in the rest of *Ulysses* to be anything but ironic. The description of the ship must therefore be a satire of Stephen's and Joyce's own former emphasis on *quidditas* as leading to epiphany, Stephen's former belief that the artist can express what is already inherent in the object, its soul or essential reality (Hendry 451–52). For it is the very idea of essence residing in being that Stephen questions in this chapter through his inconclusive Cartesian experiment on the beach. Alternatively, we would be agreeing with Marilyn French how remarkable it is that "Stephen, who responds to everything else, makes nothing of [the sailing ship]: he simply sees it" (55).

6. Marilyn French observes that such pure inner monologue causes so much difficulty for the reader because of the removal of "the summarizing phrase, such as 'she thought,' " the removal of the omniscient narrator as a source of truth and value, "the removal of censorship" in terms of subject matter, and "the relaxation of grammatical form" (58–64). But the last page of "Proteus" is replete with phrases like "he said," and I do not believe that the other criteria adequately account for the difficulty here. For "Proteus" I find it more helpful to draw an analogy with reading *The Waste Land*. In both, the consciousness belongs to someone adept at introspection on abstruse subjects and abstract concepts, someone so widely read that he habitually thinks in terms of fragmentary allusions and subtle associations of other thinkers in many disciplines with personal experience. So with both narrators we are being required to decode the shorthand musings of an intellectual who would test our mental agility even in actual conversation when he would be conscious of adapting his interior discourse to the needs of communicating with an audience. The narrators of Beckett's fiction present many of the same difficulties because they tend to be as intellectually allusive as Stephen. In this respect they differ even from Beckett's own central characters in his plays who, while somewhat philosophical, nevertheless draw on a more commonplace frame of reference (Webb 131–32).

takes complete control, as in "Sirens," the realistic psychological rendering of character through interior monologue becomes problematic.

Leopold Bloom's interior monologue designates him as the main character, among those listening to sentimental songs in the Ormond Bar. Yet Bloom's own sentimental (and voyeuristic) anticipation of his wife's adulterous appointment with Blazes Boylan is overwhelmed by the narrator's larger view of organizing the whole chapter as if its language were subject to the same patterns of sound as the music that is being performed. Consider the chapter's opening: "Bronze by gold heard the hoofirons, steelyringing. Imperthnthn thnthnthn" (U 11.1–2). By the second line the narrator begins treating words abstractly, solely according to their value in creating patterns of sound. Since his epic parallel with the sirens and the situation in the hotel requires that the sound be singing, Joyce adopts the organizational technique of an operatic composer. As a musician might represent his operatic arias abstractly, through instrumental fragments of melody in the overture, so Joyce begins with an abstract sound pattern, the "melody" only, to which the words will be added later. Each of the lines in this excerpt represents some incident that will later be more fully developed as an "aria" set within a narrative sequence. "Bronze by gold" in Joyce's overture later turns out to be a pair of red- and yellow-haired barmaids, the sirens of this chapter who regard a waiter's casual attitude toward them as "impertinent insolence" (U 11.99). In the excerpt above, however, we see not their admonishment of the waiter but a typographical representation of the waiter's own sonic parody of their attitude toward him. Closing his nostrils with one hand as he speaks, the waiter snorts out a derisive distortion of "impertinent insolence," an echo (note the number and division of the syllables) "imperthnthn thnthnthn" of the sound included at the opening of this chapter (Blamires 109). Initially Joyce violates our expectations about linear narrative so that we will be more attuned to these fragmentary phrases in the overture when we encounter them again later, as aural motifs repeated within the dramatic context of the narrative.

Of course, the use of words as abstract sounds works against their usual connotations and denotations. The very fact that Joyce's analogy between words and music in "Sirens" repeatedly breaks down is what makes the narrator's arrangement call attention to itself. During the rest of the narrative that follows his verbal overture Joyce introduces rhythmic patterns and words distorted for time and sound values to remind us continually of his narrative concept of comparing words with music, even as we also try to follow the story.[7]

In most of the other chapters after chapter 6 of *Ulysses* ("Hades"), Joyce's narrators arrange chapters according to other abstract concepts. Character and plot are diminished as we become aware, before anything else, of Joyce exposing his artistic manipulations of reality so that readers may see his narrators laboring mightily to create the illusion of significance. Joyce delights in making more out of his subject than it inherently deserves; and he lets us in on his joke. He calls his novel *Ulysses,* the Latin name of Odysseus, to alert the reader that he will be drawing parallels between his own characters and the classical characters of Homer's epic. Such problematic interpretation is also a source of comedy, as we detect these elaborate parodies of well-known works like *The Odyssey* and *Hamlet* and watch for underlying organizational concepts like the one of music just described in "Sirens." Both the parodies and the narrative manipulations operate to distance readers from characters and plot, even as they keep them conscious of the comic presentation, of how hard the narrator must work to invest one rather ordinary Dublin day with epic scope and significance.

Thus far we have seen how in *Ulysses* character and plot are first de-emphasized by concentration on interior monologue in "Proteus," then superseded altogether by a conceptually organized narrative in "Sirens." For the reader who surveys the flux of narrative phenomena throughout *Ulysses,* the answer to Stephen's speculation in "Proteus" of who or what lies behind the shifting appearance must be Joyce's narrators and their various organiza-

---

7. Stuart Gilbert argues against Professor Curtius' contention that Joyce's analogy breaks down in the relationships between the *leitmotifs* in Joyce's verbal overture and the narrative itself (225–26). But debate over theory does not alter the fact that all Joyce's technical devices reinforcing the analogy between words and music deflect even the most experienced readers' attention from characters and plot toward the narrator's organizational ingenuity.

tional strategies. They are perhaps too numerous and various to
represent omniscience; yet they do strive to approximate omnipotence by imposing on plot and character a total conceptual order
within their individual chapters. Once we view *Ulysses* in terms
of this shift from the microcosm of interior monologue to the
macrocosm of exterior narrative control, then *Finnegans Wake*
represents a culmination of Joyce's narrative development, a merging of the microcosm with the macrocosm. Through the creation
of his own time and space Joyce here invents a language that more
closely approximates music than that of "Sirens" because it has
become more abstract and self-referential. In *Finnegans Wake* the
autonomous narrators of *Ulysses* become one, representing a
universal consciousness that is both interior monologue and exterior narration. Godlike, Joyce begins his creation with the *logos* so
that his narrator may finally exercise both omniscience and omnipotence, the development of the fiction being the reader's witnessing of a new world being created syllable by syllable.

Like Joyce's Stephen on the beach, some of Samuel Beckett's
characters speculate inconclusively about who or what lies "behind" external reality. But Beckett takes the conclusion of Stephen's experiment in introspection, that an external world is
"there all the time without you" (U 3.27), and shows how this
disproves Descartes' *cogito*. Stephen's external world is there
"without" him, independent of his being aware of it. Reality is
also "without" Stephen in the sense of being outside, external to
his perception of it in a spatio-temporal presence that enables him
to read its "signatures" (U 3.2) as evidence for God's being the
prototype of artist as creator. But Beckett's fictions minimize such
distinctions between internal and external reality. Consciousness
expressed in language through character and narration exists prior
to (and so perhaps independent of) physical identity, as a voice
without determinate location in time or space. Beckett repeatedly
questions the logic of Descartes' "I think; therefore I am" by
demonstrating the way introspection discloses no contingent "I"
but only the self-questioning consciousness itself (Hesla in Morot-
Sir 18–19). In Beckett's fiction, as in Joyce's, loose associative
links within the consciousness of narrators replace the more
traditional cause-and-effect sequencing of character and plot
(Wicker 173). Joyce's novels compensate for loss of such causal

coherence through rhetorical strategies that reinstate purposeful control of the narrative. But Beckett's lack coherence; their associative links are minimal because their narrators establish no clear purpose or identity. Whereas Joyce reinstates a full narrative agent, the omnipotent narrator, Beckett progressively moves toward narrative vacuity to demonstrate that there can be no such entity to control the telling; there is only "the weak old voice that tried in vain to make me" (STFN 137), the thought process failing to manifest itself convincingly in language.

Throughout a series of novels from *Molloy* to *Malone meurt* (1951) to *L'Innommable* (1953) Beckett successfully undermines both the omniscience of impersonal narrators and the personal identity of narrators as characters. Sometimes first-person narrators within the same novel even have multiple names, confirming their indeterminacy. *The Unnamable* culminates Beckett's series of minimally narrated novels with an unidentified witness, a protean narrative voice which can be anything from a finite consciousness to an omnipresent metaphysical abstraction. Not only does Beckett's fiction lack the central consciousness of a narrator who knows more than particular characters; it lacks the presence of those characters themselves as multiple consciousnesses who remain sufficiently coherent to reveal discrete points of view on a common subject. For Beckett all conventional narration, from omniscient to first-person, becomes problematic.

In Beckett's first published novel the narrator confidently asserts that "All the puppets in this book whinge sooner or later, except Murphy, who is not a puppet" (MU 122). But since it takes a narrator to make such a distinction between puppets and free agents, is not Murphy that narrator's puppet? In fact, who is this narrator who remains bodiless, just a voice that does not (like Joyce's later narrators in *Ulysses*) draw attention to itself *as* narrator? Does this lack of presence imply that there is another narrator narrating this narrator?

The theological implications of such an infinite narrative regression are most clearly stated in one of the *Stories and Texts for Nothing*. In this work the writer reformulates the prime mover into a prime observer, in terms of Beckett's Cartesian consciousness: "at the end of the billions [of all the peoples of the earth,] you'd need a god, unwitnessed witness of witnesses" (STFN 135).

But, of course, the work that most extensively dramatizes the impertinence of fallible witnesses trying to imagine an "unwitnessed witness of witnesses" is *Waiting for Godot*. Early in the play, while they wait, Vladimir and Estragon decide to kill time by killing themselves. But they realize this might be impractical because the branch of a nearby tree might not be strong enough to hang both of them, and then one would be left alone—presumably a fate worse than death (12–12[b]). So to pass the time, instead of committing suicide, they begin to reflect on the efficacy of prayer:

VLADIMIR: Well? What do we do?

ESTRAGON: Don't let's do anything. It's safer.

VLADIMIR: Let's wait and see what he says.

ESTRAGON: Who?

VLADIMIR: Godot.

ESTRAGON: Good idea.

VLADIMIR: Let's wait until we know exactly how we stand.

ESTRAGON: On the other hand it might be better to strike the iron before it freezes.

VLADIMIR: I'm curious to hear what he has to offer. Then we'll take it or leave it.

ESTRAGON: What exactly did we ask him for?

VLADIMIR: Were you not there?

ESTRAGON: I can't have been listening.

VLADIMIR: Oh . . . Nothing very definite.

ESTRAGON: A kind of prayer.

VLADIMIR: Precisely.

ESTRAGON: A vague supplication.

VLADIMIR: Exactly.

ESTRAGON: And what did he reply?

VLADIMIR: That he'd see.

ESTRAGON: That he couldn't promise anything.

VLADIMIR: That he'd have to think it over.

ESTRAGON: In the quiet of his home.

VLADIMIR: Consult his family.

ESTRAGON: His friends.

VLADIMIR: His agents.

ESTRAGON: His correspondents.

VLADIMIR: His books.

ESTRAGON: His bank account.

VLADIMIR: Before taking a decision.
ESTRAGON: It's the normal thing.
VLADIMIR: Is it not?
ESTRAGON: I think it is.
VLADIMIR: I think so too [12[b]–13].

The composite image of God that emerges here is so concrete because both Vladimir and Estragon share a concept of what is for them "the normal thing," prayer as a potential material transaction. Godot puts off an immediate answer to their prayer so that he can consult family, friends, and business associates. The progression of consultants grows increasingly impersonal and business-oriented until it results in a personal decision reached impersonally, one based on the proverbial bottom line: "his [account] books" and "his bank account."

But before we blame Godot, their version of God, for being calculating, we should note that Beckett takes pains to remind us that this is *only* their version. At first they are inclined to do nothing because they fear what Godot might do: "it's safer." The scene that shows the tramps getting their first glimpse of other people suggests why they fear Godot. Pozzo appears with a whip, driving Lucky who is tied to him by a rope, a concrete image of the way they have just been discussing themselves as being "tied to Godot" (14–14[b]). So it is not surprising that they should mistake Pozzo as being Godot (13[b]–15[b]). When Vladimir and Estragon try to put off Pozzo by not calling him by his own name, Pozzo reminds them that they are "of the same species as Pozzo! Made in God's image!" (15[b]); and later Pozzo admits that he is "perhaps not particularly human," when they reprove him for his cruelty to Lucky (19[b]). So perhaps cruelty is that common denominator that entitles man to claim a resemblance to God. To Vladimir and Estragon God is an authority figure responsible for the "muck" of living (14[b]) and therefore to be regarded with suspicion rather than the awe accorded God in a more traditional role as parental authority.

When Vladimir and Estragon summon their courage to make the first move in prayer, it is with the object of finding out "what [Godot] has to offer." Their responses to the way they have formulated their prayer, "precisely" and "exactly," are ironically inappropriate since the prayer itself is "nothing definite." They deliberately keep it a "vague supplication" since they are feeling out someone they know only by reputation and therefore mistrust, hoping to "hear what he has to offer" without committing themselves prematurely to their end of a business deal.

Vladimir and Estragon are not surprised by Godot's noncommittal response, then, because they get what they ask for. Godot's lawyer and agents seem entirely "normal" because this "vague supplication" is tentative bargaining toward a potential contract, not the implicit communication of traditional prayer which George Herbert summed up as "something understood" (Prayer [I], line 14).

Of course, Beckett is suggesting not that Vladimir and Estragon misunderstand the nature of prayer but that they understand the nature of a God who will never answer. If we follow the logic of Descartes' *cogito,* as he himself did not, thinking must be prior to being (Hesla in Morot-Sir 18–19). So there can be no God as "unwitnessed witness of witnesses." Stephen's imperfectly entertained notion of God as creator "behind" the external world may have satisfied Descartes, but it is no longer enough for Beckett. There is only Godot, for only in theory are we made "in God's image," as Pozzo would have it. In practice, as the prayer of Vladimir and Estragon demonstrates, God must be made in man's image, his own language and metaphors based on his own experience.

When Estragon asks Vladimir. "Do you think God sees me?" (49[b]), Vladimir's answer, predictably tentative, comes in an unusually rhetorical passage replete with poetic imagery and allusion:

> Was I sleeping, while the others suffered? Am I sleeping now? To-morrow, when I wake, or think I do, what shall I say of today? . . . Astride of a grave and a difficult birth. Down in the hole, lingeringly, the grave-digger puts on the forceps. We have time to grow old. The air is full of our cries ([*Vladimir*] *listens.*) But habit is a great deadener. ([*Vladimir*] *looks . . . at Estragon* [*dozing*].) At me too someone is looking, of me too someone is saying, He is sleeping, he knows nothing, let him sleep on. (*Pause.*) I can't go on! (*Pause.*) What have I said [58–58[b]]?

If it were not for its new context, this striking image of a gravedigger superimposed over an obstetrician might be as suspect as the Christian ship in "Proteus." For Vladimir has borrowed it from the self-conscious orator Pozzo (57[b]), who (complete with atomizer) strikes poses and speaks primarily to hear the sound of his own voice (20[b]). But here the complex emotional resonance of this birth/death soliloquy contrasts movingly with the asperity of the more customary single-line dialogue exchanged between Vladimir and Estragon. Overall, this passage alludes to God's two punishments by which Christians measure their mortality after the Fall: from the "difficult" beginning of birth to the inevitable sentence of death. However painful they may be, our lives seem so short that death appears superimposed upon us from the very moment of our birth. As if to establish that this heritage of suffering after Adam and Eve remains all-encompassing, Vladimir listens for the cries that must constantly be in the air everywhere; and when he hears none, he concludes not that they are not there, but that he has been tuning them out for too long: "habit is a great deadener." At least he can see one other person, Estragon, who is perhaps suffering less than usual because he is dozing.

Vladimir's response to Estragon's query about whether God sees him has been so evocative and compassionate that Vladimir himself finds it inexplicable: "What have I said?" The prospect that Vladimir too may be asleep raises one of Descartes' fundamental doubts about our senses. Since consciousness precedes everything else, how can we know for sure whether, at any given moment, we are dreaming or not? The issue has already been raised:

ESTRAGON: I had a dream.
VLADIMIR: Don't tell me!
ESTRAGON: I dreamt that—
VLADIMIR: DON'T TELL ME!
ESTRAGON: (*Gesture towards the universe.*) This one is enough for you? (*Silence.*) [11].

Vladimir seeks to get outside his own consciousness by supposing a "someone" watching him sleep, just as he now watches Estragon. But this raises the prospect of that infinitely regressive series of narrators, God as "unwitnessed witness of witnesses" (STFN 135). Estragon's original question about whether God sees him (49[b]) is unanswerable because witnessing is all there is. Vladimir can only posit a "someone" beyond himself in a replication of his own experience.

In *Happy Days* Winnie steadfastly avoids wondering what lies beyond her set of circumstances, perhaps because they are so inexplicable. Being buried alive under the constant glare of the sun, Winnie insists that she is satisfied merely to have Willie be her witness. But the way she states it implies that, like Vladimir and Estragon, she would prefer to be a witness herself, in "the old style" of praying to a God who watches over all.

At the beginning of Act II Winnie's invocation leads us to expect that the "someone" looking on is the One speculated about by Stephen, Vladimir, and Estragon, the One whose presence continues to be evoked by our experience of His absence. But Winnie must also "confess" that "I used to pray" and acknowledges that she has "changed from what [she] was" (50–51). Her peremptory invocation, borrowed from Milton, distinguishes the opening of Act II from that of Act I where Winnie prayed personally in silence and then (unlike Stephen) completed the Anglican "Gloria" with her own "Amen." But now the only eyes watching her are secular, borrowed from an "unforgettable" popular song, which of course she has forgotten. So, while Stephen still longs for a transcendent witness, Winnie has settled for Willie. Like Vladimir and Estragon, Winnie fears loneliness most. The prospect of an unwitnessed monologue is her "wilderness" (50), perhaps madness; and she keeps her revolver closer to hand in Act II, just in case.

In one respect, though, Willie is to Winnie as Godot is to Vladimir and Estragon. Most of the time he can only be posited as a witness, and that makes him a source of great distress. Winnie continues to *feel* like her old self, even though from Willie's point of view she will have changed because the mound has advanced to hide her arms and breasts. She is most likely correct in fearing that Willie will lose interest. For sex, including a "disgusting" photo, was most of what captured his attention in Act I. Now she cannot see him and repeats his name ever more loudly in a parallel series of phrases beginning with "what" ("What arms?" "What breasts?" "What Willie?") (51), which suggests that she fears Willie may be her next appendage to disappear.

But concentration on all these changes makes the play seem more dynamic, in the traditional manner of character and plot development, than it actually is. As in the other prayer scene from *Waiting for Godot* where God's lack of response was "normal," here too a countermotion works to neutralize change so that the overall impression an audience receives continues to be stasis, or at least circularity. No wonder Winnie inquires doubtfully, "May one still speak of time?" The constant glare of light, punctuated only by the bells, suggests that the "old style" cycle of night and day has been superseded. Yet Winnie concludes that "one does" continue to speak of time since that is all one knows; the very term "old style" requires a conceptual distinction between past and present to be intelligible. Amidst so much suffering and uncertainty, what seems to be a fundamental change in time could be illusory too. So why not retain the more comfortable older illusion rather than multiply the unknown by accepting a different order of reality? Winnie herself best sums up the effect of her temporal paradox: "Then . . . now . . . what difficulties here, for the mind. (*Pause.*) To have been always what I am—and so changed from what I was" (50–51).

As with people, so it is with events: the more they change, the more they remain the same. Everything—the necessity of talking, Winnie's fear of talking to herself, her need to be overheard by Willie, even the "hail holy light" of her prayer—has already been mentioned in the first act. The repetitive nature of the material, the frequency of pauses designated between Winnie's phrases and sentences, and some remarks in Act I, such as "To sing too soon is a great mistake" and "Do not overdo the bag" (32), all indicate that Winnie's primary objective is time management (to speak in the old style). She must conserve her limited amount of material and pace herself in such a way as to get through each interval between the bells for waking and sleeping. Her smile—flashing on, then off—is as consciously controlled as the bells themselves; and the directions she gives herself to begin and end Act I, "Begin your day, Winnie" (8) and "Pray your old prayer, Winnie" (48) suggest the effort of will that she must exercise to maintain the endless repetition of this circular routine. She calls it doing "all one can." Tersely Winnie also sums up both the problem and the effort required: "There is so little one can say, one says it all" (51).

Even what seems most spontaneous, Winnie's specious reformulation of the *cogito* (I speak; "ergo" you exist to overhear) is less a rationalization than a verbal equivalent of the comic capers of Vladimir and Estragon, intended mainly to keep up morale while passing the time. Winnie's next statement shows that she well knows Willie's presence is unrelated to the sound of her voice (50). He could leave any time, if he has not already. For, despite all her strenuous efforts to continue singing "Happy days are here again" (the song from which the play's title derives), the audience's overall assessment must be that Winnie is singing in the dark. Even Winnie herself concludes that there is "no truth in it anywhere" (51).

Bleak as it first sounds, however, even this statement harbors a saving contradiction. In itself it sounds like a truth, belying its own meaning. Thus, even after saying it, Winnie can continue to be thankful, this time for the "great mercy, all I ask" of incertitude: "not to know, not to know for sure" (51). Winnie's relentless determination to be cheerful, no matter what the circumstances, is her equivalent of Vladimir's determination, against all the evidence, to wait for Godot.

In their different ways both Joyce and Beckett offer us philosophical comedy that challenges our traditional assumptions about the nature of external reality. Joyce's Stephen is ambivalent about rejecting the God of Descartes; the price he pays for such uncertainty about his unbelief is being haunted by his mother's ghost. Beckett's narrators, on the other hand, are haunted by the provisional nature of their own existence. His philosophical comedies demonstrate our desperate attempts to clothe the nudity of nothingness with the illusion of everyday reality, from the tramps waiting for Godot to Winnie's "another happy day" (HD 64). Joyce moves in the opposite direction, celebrating his own ability as an artist to exceed reality. Rather than wryly reminding his audience how much his characters lack, as Beckett does, Joyce achieves his own comic effects by encouraging readers to see his narrator trying to make both his characters and what happens to them mean more than they inherently deserve.

Even though they approach the problem differently, both Joyce and Beckett have accepted Descartes' challenge: to explore the paradox of a consciousness having as its object an external world that, experience proves, is both independent of and resistant to such exploration. Critics have often pointed out that Beckett's approach to Descartes (thinking must be prior to being) also makes Beckett a literary exponent of existentialism and of phenomenology.[8] But there is evidence to the contrary: "Once Beckett was asked if his system was the absence of system. He replied, 'I'm not interested in any system. I can't see any trace of any system anywhere' " (Shenker 3).

Here I have placed less emphasis on formal philosophy and more on Beckett's intuitive response to the theological implications of Joyce's fictional technique, elaborating on a contrast suggested in what Shenker has represented as an interview with Beckett (Bair 651 n. 22).

> "In the last book [before this interview]—'L'Innommable'—there's complete disintegration. No 'I,' no 'have,' no 'being,' no nominative, no accusative, no verb. There's no way to go on. . . .
>
> "With Joyce the difference is that Joyce was a superb manipulator of material—perhaps the greatest. He was making words do the absolute maximum of work. There isn't a syllable that's superfluous. The kind of work I do is one in which I'm not master of my material. The more Joyce knew the more he could. He's tending toward omniscience and omnipotence as an artist" [Shenker 1, 3].[9]

Beckett's *The Unnamable* must remain unnamable because it "is that impersonal consciousness which simply 'goes on' thinking and speaking, and which, as such, is always an instant ahead of the namable self which is constituted by its being conscious" (Hesla in Morot-Sir 19). Perhaps this is why, despite the comedy, Beckett's explorations of his characters seem so tortuous. They

---

8. Existential parallels between Beckett and Heidegger and Beckett and Sartre are explored in length in Butler. They are also mentioned more briefly in Hesla, *Shape of Chaos,* which provides the fullest discussion of Beckett and phenomenology, particularly in terms of Husserl and Hegel.

9. Actually the words quoted here are not precisely Beckett's. Shenker both gives and takes away authority in his article: "if [Beckett] would relax his rule on [not granting] interviews, this is what he would say (he has said it all, in precisely this phrasing)." What can "precisely" mean here? When did Beckett "[say] it all"? In a letter to Deirdre Bair (which is not directly quoted either), Bair states "Shenker said that he had been careful not to say anywhere in the article that he had actually interviewed Beckett, but had used an obvious literary device in order to write it as one long quotation" (Bair 651 n. 22). So did Beckett grant Shenker an interview, then allow him permission to print it on the condition that Shenker not admit it *was* an interview? Whatever Beckett did or did not do, this is a narrative tangle that might have pleased him—if he had read footnotes.

turn out to be infinite spirals around a self whose existence cannot be adequately explained because it can never be prior to the thought being expressed in the language that articulates it. So Beckett views Joyce's technique as being radically opposed to his own. He excludes and Joyce includes; he underexpresses and Joyce overexpresses. As Beckett moves from creation toward destruction, the artist's failure of silence, Joyce moves "toward omniscience and omnipotence," a return, through narrative "manipulation," to the artist as godlike creator. In contrast, Beckett sums up his own composition of *Endgame* as " 'all I can manage, more than I could' " (letter to Alan Schneider, quoted in Bair 470). Yet Beckett's self-proclaimed failure succeeds in affording us critical insight into the nature of Joyce's success. Compared to Beckett, groveling in the muck, Joyce has scaled the Tower of Babel, taking us from the babble at the opening of *Portrait* through the embryonic development of the English language in "Oxen of the Sun," beyond Berlitz to a multinational language suitable for proclaiming his own cosmic myth in *Finnegans Wake*. The Joycean narrator has become a god for whom Christianity is but sacred metaphors, a series of epiphanies suitable for the revelation of his own artistic development.

In his first published story Beckett proposes an artist-hero who comes close to achieving Stephen's dream of being "made not begotten" (U 3.45), yet without attaining Stephen's concomitant goal of escaping from history (U 2.377). So instead of seeming like an apotheosis, the deification of Beckett's first artist remains static and timebound in its infinite circularity: " 'Thus each night he died and was God, each night he revived and was torn, torn and battered with increasing grievousness, so that he hungered to be irretrievably engulfed in the light of eternity' " (quoted in Bair 271). The Joycean analogy between man as artist and God as creator breaks down in Beckett. His fictional narrators (often writers themselves) inevitably fail because their aims are contradictory. The I/eye of their art is fixed and finite in its narrative perspective, whereas their art's object, life itself, is that dynamic process of becoming which remains so unattainable that we have ascribed it to deity. As finite beings we can never capture conceptually (much less in language) the fluidity, dynamism, and comprehensiveness of infinite Being. Joyce's narratives strive to bridge the gap between infinite aspiration and finite performance with a series of rhetorical strategies that become increasingly extroverted, from absence in *Dubliners* to overwhelming presence in *Finnegans Wake,* where the comic texture of the language controls the narrative by calling attention to its own supremacy at every moment. But Beckett's narrative remains introverted, as he makes more out of less through negation. His later short fiction surpasses his former subversion of narrative perspective by undermining language's very location of concepts in time and space. In works like *Imagination Dead Imagine, Ping, Lessness, The Lost Ones,* and *Not I,* "the two-dimensional structure of language itself is all but obliterated in a kaleidoscope of word-fragments endlessly juggled together. There can be . . . no progress of meaning from one statement to the next, no story, no narrator, no fictional world" (Wicker 180). Beckett's increasing cosmological asperity seems an inversion of Joyce's final gesture of plenitude, an unprecedented constriction of meaning in response to the expanding ambiguity of word and world in *Finnegans Wake.*

Yet, for all their different aims and techniques, Joyce and Beckett share a hopefully negative theology. As philosophical tragic-comedians haunted by the loss of ultimacy, they both, like Stephen in "Proteus," turn around to look behind every thing. Yet, even as they turn, the very movement reveals another of Joyce's manipulative narrative strategies, another of Beckett's futile comic "turns." Stephen's parody of Tennyson, the tramps' composite image from popular culture of God as a prudent businessman, and Winnie's dimly recollected snatches of her classics foreshadow no metaphysical future. They remain vacant gestures measuring only the loss of our corporate past. Joyce's and Beckett's profound absurdities seem poignantly appropriate for an age intermittently aware that traditional philosophy has reached its end. Their wit simultaneously diverts us from, and reminds us of, the fact that we can no longer, like Descartes, rely on metaphysics to resolve our ontological dilemmas. The Teller of all Tales has become a fiction. We ought to be forewarned by the excesses of both rhetorical stances, both Joyce's strenuous affirmation of narrative omnipotence and Beckett's desperate denial of it. Even before we turn around, we should suspect what we will find: nothing behind these fictions but ourselves, the readers of our own tale.

WORKS CITED

Bair, Deirdre. *Samuel Beckett, A Biography*. New York: Harcourt Brace Jovanovich, 1978.

Blamires, Harry. *The Bloomsday Book*. London: Methuen, 1966.

Butler, Lance St. John. *Samuel Beckett and the Meaning of Being: A Study in Ontological Parable*. New York: St. Martin's, 1984.

Dearlove, J. E. *Accommodating the Chaos: Samuel Beckett's Nonrelational Art*. Durham: Duke University Press, 1982.

French, Marilyn. *The Book as World: James Joyce's 'Ulysses.'* Cambridge: Harvard University Press, 1976.

Gifford, Don, and Robert J. Seidman. *Notes for Joyce: An Annotation of James Joyce's 'Ulysses.'* New York: Dutton, 1974.

Gilbert, Stuart. *James Joyce's 'Ulysses.'* New York: Knopf, 1930.

Gluck, Barbara Reich. *Beckett and Joyce: Friendship and Fiction*. Lewisburg, Pa.: Bucknell University Press, 1979.

Hendry, Irene. "Joyce's Epiphanies." *The Sewanee Review* 54 (Summer 1946): 449–67.

Herbert, George. *Works*. Rev. ed. F. E. Hutchinson. London: Oxford University Press, 1945.

Hesla, David H. *The Shape of Chaos: An Interpretation of the Art of Samuel Beckett*. Minneapolis: University of Minnesota Press, 1971.

———. "Being, Thinking, Telling, and Loving: The Couple in Beckett's Fiction," *Samuel Beckett: The Art of Rhetoric*. Ed. Edouard Morot-Sir, et al. Chapel Hill: University of North Carolina Press, 1974.

Shenker, Israel. "Moody Man of Letters." *The New York Times* 6 May 1956: sec. 2; 1, 3.

Tennyson, Alfred. *Poems and Plays*. London: Oxford University Press, 1965.

Webb, Eugene. *The Plays of Samuel Beckett*. Seattle: University of Washington Press, 1974.

Wicker, Brian. "Beckett and the Death of the God-Narrator," *The Story-Shaped World: Fiction and Metaphysics, Some Variations on a Theme*. Notre Dame: University of Notre Dame Press, 1975. 169–83.

7

Textually Uninhibited:
The Playfulness of Joyce and Beckett

Michael Patrick Gillespie

AMBIVALENCE, PERHAPS MORE THAN ANY OTHER TRAIT, stands as the distinguishing feature of English literature in the twentieth century. Readers encounter a persistent deferral of closure and a recurrent shift of perspective resonating from precursors of modernism like Ford Madox Ford's *The Good Soldier,* through modernist novels like those of Virginia Woolf, to the postmodern work of writers like John Fowles and John Berger. As a natural consequence, the fragmentation of traditional protocols of expression and the exploration of the erosion of epistemological certitude have made the search for alienation the critical centerpiece of many contemporary interpretive strategies. Often such an approach seems eminently justifiable, and it allows the individual critic to articulate sensitive responses to a specific work under consideration. Nonetheless, the temptation to make isolation and despair the bywords of current critical methodologies can foreclose examination of particular aesthetic features central to many works: "No, assuredly, they are not justified, those gloompourers who grouse that letters have never been quite their old selves again since that weird weekday in bleak Janiveer (yet how palmy date in a waste's oasis!) when to the shock of both, Biddy Doran looked at literature" (FW 112).

One can find in the works of both James Joyce and Samuel Beckett ample reflections of the terrors of our age. Their fictions constantly reiterate the plight of individuals (both writers and readers) caught up in intellectual and emotional environments that defy the comfortable assumptions of Cartesian thinking. Nonetheless, neither Joyce nor Beckett succumbs to an embittering nostalgia for predictability. Rather, throughout their works, they persistently invite readers to embrace the freedom of uncertainty and to indulge in imaginative connections made possible by the disruption of causal relationships.

> You is feeling like you was lost in the bush, boy? You says: It is a puling sample jungle of woods. You most shouts out: Bethicket me for a stump of a beech if I have the poultriest notions what the farest he all means. Gee up, girly! The quad gospellers may own the targum but any of the Zingari shoolerim may pick a peck of kindlings yet from the sack of auld hensyne [FW 112].

The invitation to "any of the Zingari shoolerim" (gypsy scholars) to participate actively in the completion of meaning by developing elements of their narratives ("the sack of auld hensyne") lies at the core of the work of both Beckett and Joyce. In this essay I would like to foreground one shared aspect of their writing that encourages reader extrapolation by examining selected instances of depictions of the impulse for game playing. Gaming itself, of course, does not fully encompass the imaginative ambiance of either of the two authors; nor does either writer invite the reader to engage in games in exactly the same manner as the other. In fact, both Joyce and Beckett carefully maintain the idea of games as a specific rather than as a generic concept. Nonetheless, gaming can provide a useful objective correlative for many of the aesthetic assumptions operating in their fictions.

By this introduction, however, I do not mean to foreclose interpretation with epistemological prescriptiveness, for although one might reasonably expect the introduction of games to enforce a degree of order and of predictability on a narrative discourse, in the works of Joyce and of Beckett it functions outside the usual parameters laid down in formal contests. The games themselves generally remain unidentified as such, with the distinctions between random play and organized sport intentionally blurred. As such, they often unfold without any clear demarcation of their beginnings or their conclusions, operating according to rules and guidelines left to the reader to determine.[1] These conditions impel

---

1. Jorij Lotman has offered a fairly formal model of the game as an aspect of narrative discourse in *The Structure of the Artistic Text* (see especially chapter 4, "Text and System," 57–77). See also Peter Hutchinson, *Games Authors Play*. My own concept is a bit looser and probably closer to the approach followed by Roland Barthes in *S/Z*.

anyone seeking to comprehend the dynamics of the narrative first into a delineation of the game itself and then into active participation. This engagement in turn allows one to develop a broader sense of the alternatives for response inherent throughout the work. A clear instance of such possibilities occurs midway through Joyce's *Ulysses*.

For many readers, the performance of Stephen Dedalus in the "Scylla and Charybdis" chapter may bring to mind analogous scenes of youthful efforts to play the prodigy before a group of baffled elders. By now the memory of the successes enjoyed or of the failures endured has faded, yet one can still recall a sense that a formal, if unarticulated, protocol shaped the roles that one assumed and governed the demeanor that one affected. Consequently, when we consider a similar situation unfolding in the National Library, impressions of the games and of the gaming that we ourselves have experienced (directly or indirectly) subtly impinge upon our views of the individual elements constituting the episode and upon our conception of the chapter as a whole.

Several men—representatives of the Dublin literati—have gathered in an office adjacent to the main reading room. Stephen Dedalus presents a disquisition on the conditions—emotional, intellectual, and artistic—informing Shakespeare's process of composition. The narrative bifurcates their discussion into the dialogue of the characters and the interior monologue of Stephen that forms a silent, running commentary on their remarks. At the same time, the most significant elements of the interchange, the motivations informing the responses of the characters, often remain unarticulated, but the attention drawn to aspects of the narrative through the interplay of Stephen and the others gives one ample opportunity for speculation.

In essence, the reader engages in the shifting debate in the library while retaining a sense of detachment not shared by the other participants. This privileged perspective subsequently conditions our response on several levels. Publicly, in the dialogue between Stephen and the others, it leads one to note unmistakable signs of a contest. All the participants are aiming at the same specific goal, self-affirmation, and each in varying degrees is shaping his behavior in accordance with the same specific, though unspoken, rules: the tenets of conversation that trace the limits of verbal aggressiveness tolerated by polite society. On the personal level, Stephen's persistent refusal to confer more than a provisional seriousness on any of his logical efforts also signals a commitment to an agenda conditioned by gaming. Thus, as diverse aspects of Stephen's consciousness vie for interpretive control of his actions, he bifurcates his interior monologue, replicating the decorum governing the debate going on in the library. As a consequence, in our view of the various levels of gaming in the episode we see the fluidity and unpredictability of play unfolding beside the orchestration and inevitability of games. The chapter leaves open the question of emphasis, for it invites us to discard the presumption of the primacy of a particular perspective and to turn instead to the creation and manipulation of provisional texts, guided but not prescribed by elements inherent in the episode.

Approaching Scylla and Charybdis from the perspective that incorporates play and games into a broad concept of gaming (or game playing) provides the reader with a clear-cut strategy for entering into the discourse as a means of interpreting a rich and divergent narrative. Unfortunately, this method, initially at least, presents as many problems as it promises to solve. By the very ambiguity of the dialogical interchanges, we sense the discourse refusing to provide explicit guidelines for clarifying the nature of our participation. Instead, the episode persistently challenges us to delineate our own rules for engaging whatever games we perceive as being under way. At the same time, the mutability inherent in the process of reading the chapter forces us to revise continually the very rules we rely upon for stability. Such a condition constantly undermines certitude by its deferral of closure and challenges us to reorder our own assumptions toward games and play.

The debate over perceptions of Shakespeare stands as the most overt level of discourse in the chapter and the one calling for our most immediate participation. By observing Stephen Dedalus' witty evocation of the scholarly ethos, the reader becomes not so much a critic of literary theory as an evaluator of rhetorical gamesmanship. Stephen's playfulness, however, should not be seen as mere clowning, for a complex agenda governs his every gesture. Throughout the episode we see him struggling to expound his theories on Shakespeare's creative impulse against varying degrees of opposition from others in the room. This approach leads him to assume a tone that may call to mind the carnivalesque form that Bakhtin has found in the discourse of Rabelais (see Bakhtin). At the same time, unlike that of Bakhtin's Rabelais, Stephen's behavior indicates a less than full commitment to a posture of anarchy, for his repeated equivocations and diplomatic deflections suggest, at least to his readers, that he does not wish to overturn the concept of authority. Consequently, we judge his success in his version of the game not simply according to the gains that he makes in his arguments but also by the facility with which he avoids allowing rancor to mar the contest.

Stephen, in fact, plays a multilevel game of literary criticism with the men in the room. He fights to assert the validity of his own epistemology, working to establish his readings, at least provisionally, as legitimate alternatives to those advocated by the others in the library. At the same time he intentionally blunts the force of his views to diminish their threat to the complacent attitudes of his listeners. They, on the other hand, respond single-mindedly, attempting to discredit his assertions by remarks aimed at maintaining their own authority and dignity.

> —All these questions are purely academic, Russell oracled out of his shadow. I mean, whether Hamlet is Shakespeare or James I or Essex. Clergymen's discussions of the historicity of Jesus. Art has to reveal to us ideas, formless spiritual essences. The supreme question about a work of art is out of how deep a life does it spring. The painting of Gustave Moreau is the painting of ideas. The deepest poetry of Shelley, the words of Hamlet bring our minds into contact with the eternal wisdom, Plato's world of ideas. All the rest is the speculation of schoolboys for schoolboys.
>
> A. E. has been telling some yankee interviewer. Wall, tarnation strike me!
>
> —The schoolmen were schoolboys first, Stephen said super-politely. Aristotle was once Plato's schoolboy.
>
> —And has remained so, one should hope, John Eglinton sedately said. One can see him, a model schoolboy with his diploma under his arm [U 9.46–59].

The game is complicated for Stephen, who wishes both to avoid a clear-cut victory and to avert an obvious defeat. He endeavors instead to maintain a delicate balance between personal and public power: a both/and condition that allows him to establish intellectual independence without provoking ostracism. Some would say that his exclusion from the literary soirée that George Moore has organized for later that evening makes the ostracism a foregone conclusion. In terms of the discussion in the library, however, that assumption goes too far. The efforts of the others to rebut Stephen underscore the effectiveness of his arguments, and their continuing presence during his talk legitimizes, to a degree at least, his own views. (A.E.'s abrupt departure in the middle of Stephen's talk requires another defensive digression. While his leaving signals the forceful impact of Stephen's argument on at least one of his interlocutors, Stephen's game is not dependent upon a single individual. Eglinton and the others remain, and the incident gives Stephen benefits from seeing just how far he can push his views before losing one of the players.)

Despite these complexities, this perspective of game playing gives us, as readers, an advantage in judging the effect of this interchange, especially if we operate along rhetorical or even dramatic lines rather than along semantic ones. As we follow the exchanges, we are drawn to respond to the suppleness, the malleability of Stephen's argument even if we cannot always construe a satisfactory meaning out of statements such as his metaphysical genealogy:

> When Rutlandbaconsouthamptonshakespeare or another poet of the same name in the comedy of errors wrote *Hamlet* he was not the father of his own son merely but, being no more a son, he was and felt himself the father of all his race, the father of his own grandfather, the father of his unborn grandson who, by the same token, never was born, for nature, as Mr Magee understands her, abhors perfection [U 9.865–71].

This is the playfulness that will come to dominate the narrative of *Finnegans Wake*, and its appearance in *Ulysses* invites the same type of (dis)engagement. As in responses to *Finnegans Wake*, if one reads only linearly, in search of a Cartesian certitude, then much of the pleasure inherent in the episode will be lost. Near the end of the chapter, for example, when John Eglinton asks Stephen if he believes his own theory, Stephen ostensibly concedes defeat by answering no. Yet if we see that statement as a reversal in the contest—a disclaimer of all that he has said or, more properly, done—we are in danger of missing the very playfulness that he has worked into all of his discussion. By assuming, as Eglinton does, that such a gesture signals closure, we foreclose encounters with the broader, unarticulated issues of the interaction, for throughout the chapter, Stephen has based his theory on relative concepts rather than on absolutes. His assertions function as synecdoches, hinting at much broader connections. Those who presume that the goal of all debate is to arrive at certitude fall into the same trap that snares the disgruntled A. E., and they avoid one of the central issues that Stephen raises in his discussion: the mutability of perception.

I do not, however, mean to label all Stephen's gaming as superficial self-aggrandizement. He clearly places a great value on the reception of his performance, and he plays seriously at social dominance. Although his efforts are restrained when dealing on this level with A. E. or with John Eglinton, he holds nothing back when he struggles with Buck Mulligan to establish his own credentials as an entertainer. In many ways Mulligan complements Stephen perfectly, for Buck's bawdy humor goads Stephen to enhance the dimensions and the force of his argument, countering slapstick humor with wit and erudition. As they vie for the attention of the others, style takes on a more important function than content, and emotionally evocative assertions supercede the significance of intellectually grounded arguments. Their struggle underscores their awareness—cynical on Mulligan's part, idealistic on Stephen's—of the inherent subjectivity of criticism, and their interchanges undercut any effort that one might wish to make to rely upon absolute logical criteria for evaluating the impact of a particular intellectual position.

Nonetheless, their repartee does more than serve as satirical illustration of ludicrous critical pretensions. It reflects, to readers attuned to the episode's sense of play, the narrative's impulse to go beyond simple parody. When viewed in the context of gaming and with the freedom to interpret suggested by Roland Barthes and others, these interchanges reflect the inherent aim of criticism.[2] They introduce others to the pleasure to be derived by

2. Besides Barthes' *S/Z* two works of critical theory have been most useful

accepting the provisionality of any particular perspective for seeing a critical work.

The games, of course, do not stop at this stage. Through his interior monologue, Stephen continues the play, moving it to an ontological level. He applies his own aesthetic and artistic beliefs to a critique of the very posturings that seemed so important to him in his contest with the Dublin intellectuals, and he quite often undercuts his putative views with great effectiveness. In the following example he reviews and then rejects his rationalization for not repaying a loan made to him by George Russell:

> Steady on. He's from beyant Boyne water. The northeast corner. You owe it.
>
> Wait. Five months. Molecules all change. I am other I now. Other I got pound.
>
> Buzz. Buzz.
>
> But I, entelechy, form of forms, am I by memory because under everchanging forms.
>
> I that sinned and prayed and fasted.
>
> A child Conmee saved from pandies.
>
> I, I, and I. I.
>
> A.E.I.O.U. [U 9.203–13].

In such dialogues with himself, Stephen mixes humor and concern to question the validity both of his way of knowing the world around him and also of his perception of his self. As Stephen critiques his own performance, he gives explicit evidence of the elements of it that he values, and he chastises himself for the hypocrisy and the timidity that he has intermingled with them.

> His glance touched their faces lightly as he smiled, a blond ephebe. Tame essence of Wilde.
>
> You're darned witty. Three drams of usquebaugh you drank with Dan Deasy's ducats.

to me in this study: Wolfgang Iser's *The Act of Reading* and Hans Robert Jauss's *Aesthetic Experience and Literary Hermeneutics.*

How much did I spend? O, a few shillings.

For a plump of pressmen. Humour wet and dry.

Wit. You would give your five wits for youth's proud livery he pranks in. Lineaments of gratified desire [U 9.531–38].

Stephen's concern for recognition foregrounds his double bind. While he endeavors to maintain a logical consistency within his statements, he cannot deny at some level the significance of the responses of the others as a form of validation for his own views. In each reading of the episode, we must confront these conflicting attitudes and Stephen's response to them, and we must, in assessing Stephen, determine the weight we wish to give to the various roles he assumes and then rejects or amalgamates.

Whatever significance we assign to the diverse narrative elements, however, certain broad features of the discourse maintain a mutual dependence that renders artificial any single effort at evaluating play. None of the games operates independently. Each takes its cues from the others, and each alternately extends the range of the others. Nonetheless, the development of a sense of play remains skewed. Only Stephen and the reader are aware of the full operations of all three games, and only the reader enjoys a position of sufficient distance to render an inclusive, if provisional, judgment of the success of each effort.

Ultimately, all Stephen's games must end in foolsmates. They ostensibly aim at impressing three recognizable groups—his listeners, himself, and the reader—yet, given the constraints of the episode, none can ever reach a satisfactory or definitive conclusion. Although Stephen himself may not be fully aware of these goals, we cannot engage the narrative without evaluating to some degree, varying with each reading, the impact of each effort. In this respect the ultimate goal of these games becomes the engagement of the reader in the act of play.

In postmodern writing, this inclination for play extends well beyond the discursive limits of *Ulysses* or *Finnegans Wake*. Consequently, once a reader has entered the game by rescripting Joyce's polyphonic narratives, it becomes almost inevitable for the reader to search for similar opportunities in the fiction of his contemporaries. The writing of Samuel Beckett insistently offers a form most responsive to such an approach. The friendship of these two writers and Beckett's deep admiration for the achievements of Joyce had a pronounced and direct effect upon his own writing, and, like Joyce, Beckett repeatedly demonstrates a playfulness that challenges one's ability to respond while encouraging the impulse to extrapolate. This does not mean that Beckett's fiction merely mimics the styles of his predecessor. It has a less overt yet more sustained strategy for gaming. Nonetheless, it depends to some degree, at least, on the predispositions toward gaming cultivated in readers by their previous encounters with Joyce's work.

In the "Scylla and Charybdis" chapter of *Ulysses*, Stephen's gaming implies at least a tacit acceptance of the modernist reverence for the position of the artist as arbiter of conventions and of meaning. The insistent metadiscursive impulse maintained throughout *Finnegans Wake* goes a step further. Its decentered narrative prevents any figure from assuming such a privileged role and gives the reader the opportunity to play out a range of games more diverse but equally as valid as those that take place in the "Scylla and Charybdis" chapter. Beckett takes up this inclination for metadiscursive play on a less expansive level in his own work, consciously limiting the immediate elements making up the game while inviting uninhibited elaboration of their potential.

Consequently, although Beckett's writing evolves along roughly the same lines as Joyce's, several prominent features immediately distinguish it. Grounded in an insistent solipsism, Beckett's minimalist fiction eschews the implicit optimism of *Ulysses* and *Finnegans Wake*. His characters find themselves in appropriately postmodern ambiances where all boundaries to the discourse, whether imposed by author or by readers, remain provisional. Nonetheless, many individuals, especially those figures appearing in the early works, have a nostalgia for Cartesian thinking that removes them from direct participation in Beckett's gaming strategy. Instead, the reader takes on an increasingly significant role as player, bringing to each work the unfettered imagination necessary to complete the creative process that Beckett has initiated.

As the importance of the reader's role as game player grows in Beckett's canon, characterization diminishes exponentially. In its place gaming becomes an increasingly complex function of the discourse. As part of this development, the changing dimensions of play rather than the development of individuals or even of action emerge as the central aspects of Beckett's creative strategy. Characters like Belacqua, Murphy, Watt, Vladimir, Estragon, Molloy repeatedly enmesh themselves in games. As often as not, however, while the putative rules and the presumed goals may seem clear to the individuals directly involved, the ultimate purpose of the gaming often remains ambiguous to them. Unlike Stephen, they lack the dialogic detachment necessary to form more than a rudimentary assessment of their own actions. Instead, the function of the reader takes on increasing significance as the figure upon whom the responsibility for the reconciliation of contradictions falls. In the remaining portion of my essay, I would like to present selected examples illustrating this process and to comment upon the protocols for interpretation encouraged by Beckett's writing.

During his debate in the National Library, Stephen Dedalus fluidly shifts his attention back and forth between discrete levels of discourse. While aware of the mutability of the signifiers that accompany him on these moves, he feels a degree of confidence in his ability to recognize semantic variance. In fact, he derives his gaming strategy from that assumption, initiating play on several levels based on the changes in meaning that accrue. The reader, privy to Stephen's thoughts, can play along, inferring rules for the games as they unfold. Within Beckett's narratives, however, a sharp dichotomy dominates. Characters adhere to a strict, even inflexible, regime founded on a near unshakable faith in cause-and-effect logic. For the reader, however, even the limited certitude afforded by the presumption of a structural integrity in the relationship between signifiers and signified cannot be sustained. As a result, the reader does not simply engage in a repeated reordering of the rules of each game being played but time and again redefines the nature of a continually changing series of games.[3]

In Beckett's earliest published fiction, the short stories of *More*

---

3. Because of Stephen's deferral of closure, it would be reductive to see his attitude as analogous to that of structuralist critics and those of Beckett's characters as analogous to post-structuralists. Nonetheless, similarities do appear.

Pricks Than Kicks, the strategy of gaming appears in a relatively basic form, but it bears the hallmarks of patterns of play that will be replicated time and again in subsequent writing. The first story of the collection, "Dante and the Lobster," exemplifies this approach. It begins with an elaborate description of the ritual that the central character, Belacqua Shuah, follows in the preparation of his noon meal: "Lunch, to come off at all, was a very nice affair. If his lunch was to be enjoyable, and it could be very enjoyable indeed, he must be left in absolute tranquillity to prepare it" (10).

The narrative goes on to describe in meticulous detail the care taken to prepare a sandwich: the effort to prevent interruption, the steps followed to toast the bread precisely, and the skill required to apply the condiments. For Belacqua the immediate goal seems rather self-contained, for he labors to please himself and regards everything else as a potential impediment to achieving his end. Consequently, throughout the routine he struggles to assert his authority not simply over a specific individual but over all the forces, animate and inanimate, of the world that he encounters. Like Stephen, Belacqua bases his actions on a deep faith in his sense of signifiers, but his behavior assumes that words maintain a linear integrity that Stephen disdains: "He laid his cheek against the soft of the bread, it was spongy and warm, alive. But he would very soon take that plush feel off it, by God but he would very quickly take that fat white look off its face" (11). The description continues on for a half-dozen more pages. It follows Belacqua, intent upon avoiding any distraction, through his neighborhood to "a little family grocery" (13) in search of "a good green stenching rotten lump of Gorgonzola cheese" (14). His efforts apparently end in shambles when a nasty scene ensues because the cheese that the grocer has set aside for him does not appear to have reached an acceptable level of corruption. Only later, at lunch in a nondescript pub, does Belacqua discover "that he had been abusing himself all these years in relating the strength of cheese directly to its greenness" (17), for the cheese in his sandwich proves as offensive as any he could have hoped for. Belacqua's putative defeat becomes a triumph because of this difference between what he initially perceives and what he eventually comes to understand, and without a second thought he realigns his sense of cheese.

The incident, however, has no effect upon Belacqua's epistemological assumptions. His faith in the relationship between signified and signifier remains unshaken, for he retains a commitment to cause-and-effect logic. On the other hand, by this point in the story the reader, attentive to the flow of the discourse, no longer shares this assurance. From its opening, the narrative has been playing with our sense of the meaning of words. "It was morning and Belacqua was stuck in the first of the canti in the moon. He was so bogged that he could move neither backward nor forward." Only in the ensuing lines does the narrative make it explicit that Belacqua's dilemma is not physical but metaphysical:

> Blissful Beatrice was there, Dante also, and she explained the spots on the moon to him. She shewed him in the first place where he was at fault, then she put up her own explanation. She had it from God, therefore he could rely on its being accurate in every particular. All he had to do was to follow her step by step [9].

Belacqua's struggles to translate a passage from Dante's *Divine Comedy* testify to his belief in the integrity of meaning, his devotion to the concept of the recoverability of signification. (Here, struggle stands as the key concept. If Belacqua were able to respond freely to any word he encountered, he would be playing a game similar to that in which the reader is invited to participate. Instead, he labors to recuperate an ideal/idealized version.) Although the narrative opens with a sentence introducing a sense of displacement and mutability into the discourse, only the reader is attuned to the play of language within the story. Even after his experience with the Gorgonzola, Belacqua still allows a rigid and simplistic literalism to shape his discourse. Speaking of a punning passage in Dante, Belacqua says to his Italian tutor: "I wonder how you could translate that?" "Do you think" she murmured "it is absolutely necessary to translate it" [19]? A few moments later, still persisting in his pursuit of certitude, Belacqua tries to resume the translation and asks "Where were we?" But Neapolitan patience has its limits. "Where are we ever?" cried the Ottolenghi, "where we were, as we were" (20).

For the reader, the entire discourse has become a game, conditioned by repeated displacement and vigorous resistance to any simple recuperation of meaning. Part of the significance of this game comes from the exclusion of Belacqua through his repeated refusal to embrace its elements of play. At the end of the story, when he learns to his horror that his conception of how one cooks a lobster is incorrect and that the creature is actually boiled alive, he still steadfastly adheres to a monocular mode of perception that the counterpoint within the discourse has taught readers to reject.

> She lifted the lobster clear of the table. It had about thirty seconds to live.
>
> Well, thought Belacqua, it's a quick death, God help us all.
>
> It is not [22].

"Dante and the Lobster" contains many of the features that have come to characterize Beckett's gaming, and its structure outlines the process of play in which the reader is invited to participate. The narrative introduces a game (generally taken quite seriously by the individual or individuals involved) putatively governed by established rules often fully articulated within the discourse. The central character adheres to them with a determination bordering on fanaticism, and although the results of these efforts are patently obvious, their significance remains ambiguous. In essence, from the start of each discourse, the reader has been taught to view language as unreliable, while the central character remains committed to a belief in the integrity of meaning conveyed by each word. As the central character becomes involved in the overt contest dictated by the narrative, the reader engages in an alternative one.

To break free of the linguistic trap that ensnares the central character, the reader must play with the same elements but change the game. As the narrative proceeds, we come to see the inevitable imprecision of attempts to evaluate the outcome of a particular incident in terms of success or failure. Rather, it stands as part of a larger game in which the central character, hampered by a misplaced confidence in his sense of perception, struggles to assert his own sense of order upon the world around him. The character always endures frustration because of an unwavering devotion to a flawed system. The reader, on the other hand, can acknowledge the mutability of words, enabling him or her to move freely between systems to derive new interpretations and experience new aesthetic sensations.

As with Stephen's efforts in the National Library, the conclusion of each contest has very little impact on the reader's overview of the narrative. Rather, the game itself stands as much more significant, for it reveals the combined dependence on and alienation from perceptions of the environment that the character experiences. This pattern repeats throughout Beckett's fiction, and it places the strategy of gaming in a complementary relationship to that pursued by Joyce. Unlike Stephen's disquisition, however, the contests of Beckett's characters do not admit our direct engagement. Rather, they serve as prolegomena for the act of reading Beckett's fiction.

This condition does not invite Beckett's readers to participate in the games along with the characters, amplifying their efforts at play. Instead, the narrative encourages us to construct countergames derived from those of the individuals in the fiction but operating independently. The narrative always retains a directive power over the reader's considerations, for it has introduced the basic elements of play. At the same time, since the discourse has encouraged the reader to reject the operative assumptions of the characters in the work (something that does not occur in "Scylla and Charybdis"), the dimensions of play can unfold free of the narrative's influence. This both/and condition does not constitute the derivation of meaning in the conventional sense—at the discursive level. The game functions not by explaining but by identifying alternative courses open to interpretation and available at the metadiscursive level. Specifically, the reader apprehends the action occurring within the narrative and then forms a game or text from it by re-creating the action in the form of a metadiscourse derived from the play of language. Beckett's work always invites extrapolation, with the reader playing by continuing the act of creation. The re-creation does not in itself constitute an act of interpretation, but rather serves to highlight some of the varied aesthetic responses that one might pursue. From these responses, one may derive a range of provisional meanings.

By the time he composed *Waiting for Godot*, Beckett had a fully developed rhetorical strategy of play integrated into his fiction. The open-ended word games obsessively engaged in by Vladimir and Estragon, for example, function as both proclamations and denials of the efficacy of discourse based upon the presumption that a monologic system governs their language. Responses logically follow from the statements that precede them. They do not, however, present structurally limited and linguistically naïve interchanges based on the presumption of the inviolate integrity of meaning. Instead, the dialogues follow patterns that seek to emphasize the suggestive rather than the denotative function of language.

Direct communication between the two characters dominates the drama, but the ability to maintain any sort of consistent topical agreement has disappeared from the ambiance in which they exist. As the play begins, Vladimir and Estragon converse apparently at cross purposes. After a relatively short time, however, the remarkable cohesion of the dialogue becomes apparent:

> VLADIMIR: When I think of it . . . all these years . . . but for me . . . where would you be . . . (*Decisively*.) You'd be nothing more than a little heap of bones at the present minute, no doubt about it.
> ESTRAGON: And what of it?
> VLADIMIR: (*gloomily*). It's too much for one man. (*Pause. Cheerfully*.) On the other hand what's the good of losing heart now, that's what I say. We should have thought of it a million years ago, in the nineties.
> ESTRAGON: Ah stop blathering and help me off with this bloody thing.
> VLADIMIR: Hand in hand from the top of the Eiffel Tower, among the first. We were respectable in those days. Now it's too late. They wouldn't even let us up. (*Estragon tears at his boot*.) What are you doing?
> ESTRAGON: Taking off my boot. Did that never happen to you?
> VLADIMIR: Boots must be taken off every day. I'm tired telling you that. Why don't you listen to me?
> ESTRAGON: (*feebly*). Help me!
> VLADIMIR: It hurts?
> ESTRAGON: (*angrily*). Hurts! He wants to know if it hurts!
> VLADIMIR: (*angrily*). No one ever suffers but you. I don't count. I'd like to hear what you'd say if you had what I have.

ESTRAGON: It hurts?
VLADIMIR: (angrily). Hurts! He wants to know if it hurts!
ESTRAGON: (pointing). You might button it all the same [7[b]].

As they continue speaking, the audience sees that each man has become adept at maintaining a cadence of continuity based not on strict contextual consistency but on an ability to make and sustain flexible connections. Superficially the dialogue seems a cohesive whole, but on close examination it becomes evident that the discourse does not develop linearly but rather shifts direction with each utterance.

In such an approach, clichés, non sequiturs, and malapropisms inevitably insinuate themselves into the dialogue. These forms do not, however, produce in Vladimir and Estragon admissions of the exhaustion of language. The central characters, in fact, take no notice of any infelicities. Rather they continue to assert their faith in cause-and-effect logic, (mis)using dialogue as a way of explaining and justifying the world in which they exist:

ESTRAGON: And what did he reply?
VLADIMIR: That he'd see.
ESTRAGON: That he couldn't promise anything.
VLADIMIR: That he'd have to think it over.
ESTRAGON: In the quiet of his home.
VLADIMIR: Consult his family.
ESTRAGON: His friends.
VLADIMIR: His agents.
ESTRAGON: His correspondents.
VLADIMIR: His books.
ESTRAGON: His bank account.
VLADIMIR: Before taking a decision.
ESTRAGON: It's the normal thing.
VLADIMIR: Is it not?
ESTRAGON: I think it is.
VLADIMIR: I think so too.
    Silence.
ESTRAGON: (anxious). And we?
VLADIMIR: I beg your pardon?
ESTRAGON: I said, And we?
VLADIMIR: I don't understand.
ESTRAGON: Where do we come in?
VLADIMIR: Come in?
ESTRAGON: Take your time [13[a]–13[b]].

Ultimately, of course, very little is said, but that becomes precisely the point. Dialogue, in fact, barely exists. Instead Beckett's drama offers the audience a series of overlapping monologues that occasionally connect with one another producing momentary consolation but no real comprehension. Vladimir and Estragon remain satisfied with the gaming at this level because it leads to that which they most desire: self-validation. The reader, with a wider range of motivation and desire, feels the invitation to return to these interchanges to explore their potential for multiplicity.

This division between the views of readers and those of the drama's characters blurs momentarily in the closing moments of the second act when Vladimir seems to break free of the tyranny of linear thinking to face incertitude squarely:

> Was I sleeping, while the others suffered? Am I sleeping now? To-morrow, when I wake, or think I do, what shall I say of to-day? That with Estragon my friend, at this place, until the fall of night, I waited for Godot? That Pozzo passed, with his carrier, and that he spoke to us? Probably. But in all that what truth will there be? (*Estragon, having struggled with his boots in vain, is dozing off again. Vladimir looks at him.*) He'll know nothing. He'll tell me about the blows he received and I'll give him a carrot. (*Pause.*) Astride of a grave and a difficult birth. Down in the hole, lingeringly, the grave-digger puts on the forceps. We have time to grow old. The air is full of our cries. (*He listens.*) But habit is a great deadener. (*He looks again at Estragon.*) At me too someone is looking, of me too someone is saying, He is sleeping, he knows nothing, let him sleep on. (*Pause.*) I can't go on! (*Pause.*) What have I said? (58[a]–58[b]).

This epiphanic moment, however, is short-lived. When Godot's messenger arrives announcing yet another postponement, Vladimir inverts the implications of what he has been told. He embraces the news not as an affirmation of ambiguity but as a projection of certitude: Godot is definitely not coming today, but I may expect him tomorrow. Once again a character irresolutely submits to the tyranny of linear perception and to the blindness of cause-and-effect logic: "Tell him . . . (*He hesitates*) . . . tell him you saw me and that . . . (*he hesitates*) . . . that you saw me" (59[a]). At the end of the drama, Vladimir and Estragon remain static, impotent figures.

VLADIMIR: Well? Shall we go?
ESTRAGON: Yes, let's go.
>   *They do not move.*
>   *Curtain.* (60[b]).

These endeavors with language, however, have provided readers with the opportunity to embrace a far greater range of perceptions than either Vladimir or Estragon have been able to comprehend. Beckett's gaming, in terms of its development over the canon, evolves in a paradoxical fashion. The goals of play emerge as increasingly ambiguous while at the same time the rules of each successive game, at least the games strictly situated within the narrative, become more rigid. (One can find analogues to this pattern throughout *Finnegans Wake* with perhaps the most obvious examples appearing in the children's games of II.1.) In the fiction written by Beckett over the last two decades the narratives tend to describe, with a high degree of specificity and with little room for deviation, the routine governing the actions of one or more nondescript central characters. At the same time, the actions of each figure seem almost devoid of motivation, offering little basis for immediate reader response yet inviting our elaboration and extrapolation to complete the sense of the work.

In *The Lost Ones*, for example, the narrative gives readers quite specific physical details, presenting a very precise picture of the dimensions and of the climate of the setting that bounds the action of the work:

> Inside a cylinder fifty metres round and eighteen high for the sake of harmony or a total surface of roughly twelve hundred square metres of which eight hundred mural. Not counting the niches and tunnels. Omnipresence of a dim yellow light shaken by a vertiginous tremolo between contiguous extremes. Temperature agitated by a like oscillation but thirty or forty times slower in virtue of which it falls rapidly from a maximum of twenty-five degrees approximately to a minimum of approximately five whence a regular variation of five degrees per second [16].

The narrative also gives a rough description of the people there: "One body per square metre or two hundred bodies in all round numbers. Whether relatives near and far or friends in varying degrees many in theory are acquainted. The gloom and press make recognition difficult" (13). They are divided into four groups differentiated by degree of movement and each conforming to a precisely articulated regime of behavior. The action of the story revolves around the search for a way out of the cylinder. The discourse, however, never presents a more specifically articulated purpose of the great game that consumes the energy of the occupants than what appears in the opening lines: "Abode where lost bodies roam each searching for its lost one" (7).

The discourse implicitly invites us to share the roles of lost ones, searching for a way out (or a way in), with the occupants of the cylinder. We operate, however, like visitors to a country where the inhabitants speak a language that we do not comprehend. We have a heightened sense of the movement before us while we retain an acute awareness of our ignorance as to its significance. Consequently, actions unfold without a clear sense of the motivation behind them, and one is left with a tremendous amount of freedom for development. As in earlier works, any immediate response to this does not strictly constitute interpretation. Rather, we step in as game players with the predetermined pieces of the fiction arranged before us, because of the ambiguity of motivation, in a relatively neutral condition. We then replicate the act of initial reading by a rereading, attentive to the motivations for action that our imaginations supply for us. From this rereading, this explanation of events, we move to critique or interpretation. We have projected what we have seen onto a matrix of motivations—the why. From that gesture we can then move to the derivation of meaning—the whatness of it all. Like Stephen Dedalus we are acutely aware of the provisionality and the artifice of our actions, but as with Stephen we have come to distrust certitude and so welcome the ambiguity inherent in our response.

In his final pieces of fiction, Beckett foregrounds the impulse for gaming inherent in all art—the playful interaction between artist and audience. The starkness, even the apparent randomness, of the discourse stand as necessary for overcoming habits of reading that unconsciously suppress our inclination to play. The spareness of Beckett's writing augmented, not contrasted, by the preciseness of his detail does not announce his abdication of artistic responsibility but rather affirms our own role in the aesthetic experience. Beckett's work remains overtly incomplete, but this does not stand as a flaw in his creative process but rather as a strategy for engaging us as a vital element in the artistic experience.

As you have noticed, I have not attempted to act as arbiter in these games. The whole thrust of my essay has been to foreground the act of making rules for the games and not to apply the rules themselves. As readers we must base our evaluations on a number of variables: our sense of the characters, our reading of the social ambiance in which they exist, and our appreciation of the verbal play of the language of the discourse. In any discrete encounter with the chapter, the pre-eminence given to each of these factors will vary and more likely than not will parallel the mixture of satisfaction and frustration that Stephen himself feels at the end of the episode in *Ulysses*. This, of course, impels us to further game playing.

WORKS CITED

Bakhtin, Mikhail. *Rabelais and His World*. Cambridge: The MIT Press, 1968.

Barthes, Roland. *S/Z*. Trans. Richard Miller. New York: Hill & Wang, 1974.

Hutchinson, Peter. *Games Authors Play*. London: Methuen, 1983.

Iser, Wolfgang. *The Act of Reading*. Baltimore: The Johns Hopkins University Press, 1978.

Jauss, Hans Robert. *Aesthetic Experience and Literary Hermeneutics*. Trans. Michael Shaw. Minneapolis: University of Minnesota Press, 1982.

Lotman, Jorij. *The Structure of the Artistic Text*. Trans. G. Lenhoff and R. Vroon. Ann Arbor: University of Michigan Press, 1977.

8

Stephen Dedalus, Belacqua Shuah, and Dante's *Pietà*

Phyllis Carey

"QUI VIVE LA PIETÀ QUANDO È BEN MORTA," one of Dante's paradoxical puns from the *Inferno* (xx:28), provides not only a concise condensation of the Dantean cosmos but also—because of their respective appropriation of Dantean *pietà*—some fascinating insights into the artistic worlds of James Joyce and Samuel Beckett, distant literary heirs of the Italian poet. In their diverse approaches to *pietà*, Dante, Joyce, and Beckett reveal the shapes of their individual art.

In the *Inferno* Dante's Virgil reprimands Dante the pilgrim for his compassion for the damned: "Here pity/piety lives when it is dead" or, as Wallace Fowlie (132) translates it, "Here piety (to God) lives when pity (to man) is dead." The Latin root for both piety and pity is *pietas*; the Italian word *pietà* refers to either pity or piety or, as in Dante, to both. For Dante in *The Divine Comedy*, true Christian piety and true Christian pity can be seen as one and the same. Dante has transformed the notion of *pietas* that he received from his own artist-father, Virgil. For Virgil, writing from a pagan, Roman perspective, *pietà* meant the subordination of personal compassion to a political duty that served a national destiny decreed by the gods.[1] For Dante, writing from a Roman and a Catholic perspective, true *pietà* involves a synthesis of morality and devotion. Dante's God is just and holy; in humans, "morality opposes evil; piety aids the good" (Vossler I 78).

In the *Inferno*, where moral evil is explicit, piety is seen as a moral stance; in the *Paradiso*, opposition to evil being no longer

---

1. Virgil's depiction of *pietas* in *pius Aeneas* was not without its own paradoxes (see Johnson 360–64).

necessary, the moral will is indistinguishable from piety (Vossler I 78). In Dante, human piety evinces varying degrees of participation in the holiness of God. Dante's all-pervasive metaphor for God is the clear light that extends from the dazzling *claritas* of Paradise to the dark wood that opens the *Inferno* and defines Hell as the place cursed by God's absence. When Dante weeps in Hell for the terrible sufferings of the damned, he is rebuked by Dante's Virgil, the voice of reason from a spiritual perspective: "Here piety to God lives when pity to man is dead." In Dante's cosmos, natural pity is out of place where humans have freely chosen their destiny in opposition to God. For Dante personal compassion is not subordinated to a "higher" duty; rather, it must be transformed entirely if one is to see from a spiritual perspective. True pity in the world of *The Divine Comedy* is the piety that conforms action and will with the divine. Virgil counsels Dante to see more clearly that his kinetic pity must die in order for true piety/pity— *pietà*—to live.

While Dante's *pietà* spiritually synthesizes action and will with the divine, Joyce's artist as a young man aesthetically synthesizes body and spirit in the poetic word. To accomplish this synthesis, Stephen Dedalus incorporates his own version of Aristotelian pity into an aesthetic homage to the union of flesh and spirit; he essentially displaces Dantean piety from a spiritual union with God to an aesthetic union with beauty. In *Portrait*, Stephen delineates his aesthetic philosophy to Lynch. He defines Aristotelian pity as "the feeling which arrests the mind in the presence of whatsoever is grave and constant in human sufferings and unites it with the human sufferer" (204).

Borrowing from Thomas Aquinas, whom Dante had also appropriated in the *Comedy*, Stephen goes on to say that in apprehending the wholeness (*integritas*), harmony (*consonantia*), and radiance (*claritas*) of an aesthetic image, the mind is arrested in the contemplation of beauty. Aesthetic apprehension for Stephen is a progression from simple perception to recognition to satisfaction, a process whereby the reality of experience is revealed aesthetically. The divergence from Aquinas—and Dante—here is significant; Stephen substitutes a psychological progression from simple perception to epiphany for an ontological unfolding of the thing in itself (see Eco 20–24, 27). In Thomas, *claritas* is "the solid, clear, almost tangible display of formal harmony" (Eco 22), the "immanence of beauty in the objects of perception" (Took 13). For Dante, God is perfect *claritas*, perfect light and splendor (Took 15–16); the *claritas* of God is predicated of him from "empirical form, with its endless interplay of line and shadow" (Took 51). Stephen shifts the emphasis to the artistic phases of apprehension, which the artist, in turn, re-creates in the text. In appropriating Thomas and Dante for his own aesthetic, he is interested more in the "profoundly analogical drama of existence as it is mirrored in the cognitive powers in act" than in the object in itself (McLuhan 7). In Stephen's aesthetic the process of apprehension and its replication in words are paramount: the artist in transforming the objects of perception into an aesthetic image performs an aesthetic rite that produces artistic life; he becomes in Stephen's words "a priest of eternal imagination, transmuting the daily bread of experience into the radiant body of everliving life" (221).

Joyce forges his own link between piety and pity in two episodes of the *Portrait*. When Cranly appeals to Stephen's pity to receive the Eucharist for the sake of his mother because, as Cranly says, she has "gone through a good deal of suffering" (241), Stephen rejects the request and argues from an aesthetic stance: "I fear . . . the chemical action which would be set up in my soul by a false homage to a symbol behind which are massed twenty centuries of authority and veneration" (243). Stephen has already dismissed the idea that receiving communion for his mother would in any way alleviate her suffering (241). Moreover, to Cranly's proposition that the Eucharist "is a form: nothing else" (241), Stephen has substituted the words "symbol" and "homage." But since he has already vowed "to fly by those nets" of nationality, language, and religion (203), why is he concerned here with religious tradition?

A possible explanation lies in the dialogue between Stephen and Cranly as it is recorded in *Stephen Hero*. There, Stephen asks Cranly, "—But what is the Church? It is not Jesus. . . . The Church is made by me and my like—her services, legends, practices, paintings, music, traditions. These her artists gave her. They made her what she is. They accepted Aquinas' commentary on Aristotle as the Word of God and made her what she is" (SH 142–43). From the perspective of these words, Stephen's "I will not serve" (P 239) and his refusal to receive the Eucharist, rather than negations of religious belief or callousness toward his mother, become affirmations of a unique aesthetic stance.

Stephen respects the Church as a work of art but refuses to merge his artistic talents with the religious artistic fathers. He equates the piety of the Church, moreover, with a veneration of art. He will not sully his own piety to art by a false piety to religion out of a domestic piety to or pity for his mother. Like Dante's conception that pity must die for piety to live, Stephen's aesthetic piety implies the death of a natural pity, which he terms "kinetic pity" (an emotion generated by improper art [205–206]) in order for true pity/piety to live. But unlike Dante's piety, Stephen's *pietà* is not a union of the will with the divine but, rather, a union of the human mind and the emotions through an aesthetic image.

A Portrait as a whole shows the dynamic development of Stephen's aesthetic implicitly: the novel's structure illustrates the steps of his artistic apprehension. Chapter 4, however, serves as the immediate dynamic process that illustrates the theory Stephen elaborates in Chapter 5. At the beginning of Chapter 4, Stephen is piously following the rites and liturgy of an external religious form. His pieties are described as both "intricate" (151) and "burdensome" (150). The sterility of the experience derives from the dichotomy of body and spirit, the spirit denying the flesh. It is "instinct" "stronger than education or piety" (161) that drives him away from the priesthood of the Church to the priesthood of the artist.

After renouncing "the inhuman voice that had called him to the pale service of the altar" (169), Stephen experiences an integration of the physical and spiritual that transforms his view of the "pitiable nakedness" of the swimming boys and the "dread" of his own body (168) into an ecstasy of pious aesthetic adoration: "the body he knew was purified in a breath and delivered of incertitude and made radiant and commingled with the element of the spirit" (169). The much-celebrated bird-girl becomes the analogical image of his inner experience, the projected image of the union of flesh and spirit that he now worships. The silent outburst of profane joy in his soul, "Heavenly God," provides the climax of the aesthetic ritual, the stasis where flesh and spirit, human and divine are epiphanized in art. The use of religious words in the aesthetic context—"angel," "holy," "ecstasy," "worship"—suggests a reversal of the servitude of art to religion.

Stephen's kinetic pity for his own body has been transformed into what he calls aesthetic pleasure, a state of arrest, which sounds very much, among other things, like an aesthetic piety, "a spiritual state . . . called . . . the enchantment of the heart" (213). Like Dante dazzled by the light of Paradise and the revelation of the celestial rose, Stephen feels himself "swooning into some new world . . . a world, a glimmer, a flower? Glimmering and trembling, trembling and unfolding, a breaking light, an opening flower . . . wave of light by wave of light, flooding all the heavens with its soft flushes" (172). Dante's divine *claritas*, the summation of religious piety, is transformed by Stephen Dedalus into the radiance of human experience transmuted into artistic expression. Just as Joyce through Stephen displaces the notion of epiphany from a religious to an aesthetic context, so he displaces the interrelationship of pity/piety from a spiritual/moral perspective to an aesthetic perspective.

In the *Portrait*, Joyce as a young writer begins the process of appropriating Dante's religious piety/pity into his own developing vision of the artist. Stephen Dedalus in *Portrait* has yet to be led by his more earthy Virgilian father, Leopold Bloom, in *Ulysses*. By *Finnegans Wake*, Joyce's aesthetic "piety" will be personified in the "alshemist," the "*poeta*," writing "over every square inch of the only foolscap available, his own body" (185), transmuting in a ritual of aesthetic piety his own flesh into everliving art.

In contrast to Joyce's appropriation of Dante's *pietà* for aesthetic ends, Samuel Beckett in "Dante and the Lobster" both detranslates Dante's *pietà* line from the *Inferno* back to the underlying, hellish experience that it would transcend and demystifies Joyce's "priest of eternal imagination." Beckett's own aesthetic approach in this story emphasizes the transparent fictivity of artistic attempts to translate the inexpressible anguish of being into language. Beckett shapes the complex structure and the imagery of "Dante and the Lobster" to provide the contours for his own artistic *pietà*.

Like the external tripartite form of hell, purgatory, and heaven in *The Divine Comedy* and its internal tercets, the overt structure of Beckett's short story is based on a trinity of "obligations" that Belacqua Shuah[2] has before him on a particular day: "First lunch, then the lobster, then the Italian lesson" (MPTK 10), the story itself being printed in three sections. The fact that the narrative focuses on lunch, then the Italian lesson, then the lobster serves both to undercut the protagonist's obsession with order and to draw attention to the complex sub-text of the story. From the perspective of the narrative, the three sections of Beckett's story are analogous to Dante's schema in reverse order: Paradise, Purgatory, Hell.

The first section begins with Belacqua "stuck in the first of the canti in the moon" as though he were actually there with "Blissful Beatrice" and Dante (9). It also includes Belacqua's preparation and eating of his lunch, during which, as is mentioned later, "his teeth and jaws had been in heaven" (17); the second section centers in the Italian lesson and loosely parallels Beatrice's undertaking of Dante's guidance in the Earthly Paradise of the *Purgatorio* (cantos 30–33). Belacqua's tutor, whom "he had set . . . on a pedestal in his mind, apart from other women" (16) comments on his "rapid progress" (18), but in contrast to Dante's Beatrice, the Italian tutor defers or refuses to answer Belacqua's questions. To Belacqua's query "Where were we?" that echoes Dante's frequent questions about his location, the tutor replies, "Where are we ever? . . . where we were, as we were" (20); the third section of Beckett's story echoes the *Inferno* when Belacqua refers to earthly existence as "down below," and he goes further down "into the bowels of the earth" (21) with his aunt for the preparation of the lobster in the basement kitchen. Moreover, it is Belacqua's expression of pity for the lobster that brings the final narrative rejoinder, which, as we shall see below, parallels and contrasts Virgil's rebuke to Dante for his pity of the damned in the *Inferno* and, at the same time, suggests the shaping of Beckett's own artistic *pietà*.

2. Belacqua reappears in many Beckettian works and derives from Dante's *Purgatorio* iv: 112ff. In the Dantean context, Belacqua is an indolent lute maker who must repeat the span of his earthly life in ante-Purgatory because of his late repentance. "Shuah" echoes the epithet of one of Job's comforters, Bildad of Shuah. Bildad applies the authority of tradition and God's retributive justice to Job's sufferings, translating Job's agony into the clichés of orthodoxy. For the fascinating role Belacqua plays in Beckett's oeuvre, see my "Samuel Beckett's *Coup de Grâce*."

Underlying the external structure of the story, moreover, is an ironic, tripartite repetitive eucharistic motif, replicating the liturgy of the word, the offering of the sacrifice, and the communion meal. Belacqua's reading of the moon-spots passage from the *Paradiso* parallels the liturgical reading of the gospel. When the clock strikes twelve, Belacqua raises "the *Divine Comedy* face upward on the lectern of his palms" (10). He muses on the mark of Cain, the "man in the moon," while he prepares his lunch, a ritual described in terms of offering a sacrifice: the bread is "spongy and warm, alive" (11); Belacqua goes down "on his knees before the flame" of his toaster where "he had burnt his offering" (12–13). The "sacrifice" seemingly complete when he procures his "cadaverous tablet of cheese" (14), he devours the sandwich in a pub, completing the "communion meal" by washing his lunch down with "the precious stout" (17).

But the eucharistic symbolism does not end there. Belacqua's Italian lesson where he again attempts to translate the word of Dante—the *pietà* passage from the *Inferno*—and the preparation of the lobster repeat the eucharistic motif. As Belacqua had pondered the spots-on-the-moon passage while preparing his lunch, he later muses on the *pietà* passage from the *Inferno* as he goes home for supper:

> Why not piety and pity both, even down below? Why not mercy and Godliness together? A little mercy in the stress of sacrifice, a little mercy to rejoice against judgment. He thought of Jonah and the gourd and the pity of a jealous God on Nineveh. And poor McCabe, he would get it in the neck at dawn. What was he doing now, how was he feeling? He would relish one more meal, one more night [21].

Belacqua's interior monologue alludes to the problem of reconciling divine mercy and justice, a dilemma seen by Ruby Cohn as the underlying theme of the story (Cohn 18). But the references to the "sacrifice" as the ongoing experience "down below" and to the "last supper" of McCabe (a condemned murderer) reinforce the notion that judgment is already "a given"; what seems to be the central issue is the minimal possibility of pity—"a little mercy . . . a little mercy."

The musing on the "Word" of Dante's *Inferno* precedes "the

sacrifice" at the end of the story. Previously in the story, the lobster is associated with Christ when Belacqua, alluding to Christ's usage of the generic term, refers to it in French as a "fish" (19), the word also suggesting the Greek symbol for Christ. Prior to its boiling, moreover, it lies in a "cruciform position" (21). According to a pre-determined ritual, it will be boiled alive: "They must be. . . . It had to" (22). The story ends with Belacqua's aunt about to boil the lobster for yet another *communion* meal—"then lash into it for your dinner" (22). Belacqua's attempt to translate the image of the lobster into a pious cliché of pity becomes an unconscious dismissal from the ritual he has unknowingly partic-ipated in: "Go, the Mass is ended, thanks be to God" becomes "Well, thought Belacqua, it's a quick death, God help us all." Seen as an editorial comment, the final line "It is not" becomes an implicitly tripartite, inverse "Amen": It is not well; it is not a quick death; it does not appear that God will help us all.

The eucharistic motif in "Dante and the Lobster" suggests among other things an allusion to Stephen's priest of eternal imagination. Stephen wants to transmute daily experience into everliving life, but Belacqua habitually attempts to translate the suffering of existence into rational concepts and clichés. His internal monologue is punctuated with clichés, which lead up to his final inanity, "it's a quick death, God help us all." Appropri-ately, it is his mistranslating of the word "lepping"—he "supposed the man to mean that the lobster had very recently been killed" (18)—that forces him to confront at least momentarily the brute fact that lobsters are boiled alive.

Belacqua's repeated failures in translation and his unconscious participation in the eucharistic ritual provide an ironic response to Joyce's artist as a young man. Belacqua is not simply an *artiste manqué*; he is an anti-artist, a technician of the word, who would substitute his own rational categories and worn-out phrases for aesthetic apprehension. He becomes a type for the reader "too decadent" to receive the Joycean vision (*Disjecta* 26). His dismissal of his "epiphanic moment" through cliché, however, alerts the reader to what may be called the Beckettian "anti-epiphany" (cf. Jewinski 167), which attempts to strip away artistic expression to its underlying image.

The imminent boiling of the lobster becomes the "epiphanic

moment" of the short story with the eucharistic symbolism underscoring the sacrifice of the innocent victim. "In the depths of the sea it had crept into the cruel pot. For hours, in the midst of its enemies, it had breathed secretly. It had survived the Frenchwoman's cat and his witless clutch. Now it was going alive into scalding water. It had to. Take into the air my quiet breath" (22). The repetition of the eucharistic motif and the descending progression of the story merge in this passage to provide a response to the Dantean text from the *Inferno*.

Beckett responds to Dante's *pietà* both in image and in language. The following diagram illustrates Beckett's re-shaping of the Dantean *pietà*:

Dante:	*qui vive*	*la pietà*	*quando è ben morta*
Beckett:	sea	lobster	pot
	it's a quick death	God help us all	it is not

The contemplation of the lobster going from sea to pot—from womb to tomb—mirrors the shape of the *pietà* line from Dante's *Inferno: vive–la pietà–morta*. Just as the spots on the moon are traditionally associated with the mark of Cain, the word *pietà* is traditionally associated with the figure of the dead Christ—presumably between human death and divine resurrection but also suggesting Christ on the cross between the two thieves, the one saved, the other damned.[3] In Beckett's story, the lobster becomes an objective correlative of the *Pietà,* its very existence counterpoised between the womb (sea)—*vive*—and the tomb (pot)—*morta*—in the shape of a cruciform victim. Whereas in the *Inferno*, the *pietà* line is Virgil's reminder to Dante of the spiritual basis of pity, in Beckett's story the *pietà* becomes a concrete image of the suffering of being between birth and death "down below."

In Beckett's shaping, the lobster mirrors both Christ and Virgil's line from the *Inferno*. While the sea–lobster–pot serves as the ironic imaging of the *pietà* line from the *Inferno*, the final line of

3. The story also juxtaposes the lobster with Cain and McCabe (son of Cain? son of Abel?), two murderers. Cain is "saved" by the "stigma of God's pity" (12) while McCabe is condemned by the absence of human pity (17). The lobster, on the other hand, is clearly an innocent victim, analogous to Christ crucified between two thieves.

the story becomes a narrative rebuke paralleling Virgil's rebuke of Dante in the *Inferno*. Whereas Virgil's rebuke of Dante separates the observer (Dante the character) from the observed (the damned), Beckett's concretizing of the *pietà* in the lobster subsumes earthly existence into the living–dying "down below." The "It is not" undermines Belacqua's pity as a form of self-comforting that would separate the observer from the object pitied. Belacqua is reprimanded as much for his failure to see his own reflection in the lobster as for the hollowness of his pity. Pity must die in Beckett's hell not because the observer must reflect a spiritual order as in Dante's *Comedy* but because the observer is identified in the natural order of the lobster; the lobster is a concrete manifestation of "the stress of sacrifice" (21) that is a part of everyday existence. When all who exist are damned by virtue of their very existence, human pity becomes both presumptuous and blind.

In Beckett's complex shaping, the final line of "Dante and the Lobster" also becomes the *tertium quid* of his own tripartite verbal paradox that mirrors the shape of the line from the *Inferno:* Dante's "*vive–pietà–morta*" becomes "It's a quick death, God help us all. It is not." The lack of quotation marks allows us to see the final lines of the story as a counter-shape—Beckett's own paradoxical pun—for the *pietà* line from the *Inferno*. "It" is both a *quick* death (a living death) and a not *quick* (fast) death. Seen from this perspective, Beckett's *pietà* becomes a plea for divine mercy— "God help us all"—at the center of the paradoxical living–dying of being.

Aesthetically, the "It is not," furthermore, constitutes an "anti-epiphany" in negating its own context as artifice. Beckett's narrator, unlike Joyce's artist refining himself out of existence, foregrounds the narrative voice and the artifice in order to undermine them. Although the text opens as presumably within Belacqua's consciousness, the narrator increasingly distances himself from the protagonist, finally opening the third part of the story as a transparent *deus ex machina,* reflecting ironically the God of Creation. In contrast to the Genesis account where God calls all of creation into being with his "Let there be light" (Gen. 1:3), Dante's fictive cosmos where *claritas* is the prime cause, and Stephen's homage to "the clear radiance of the esthetic image" (P

213), Beckett's narrator calls for dusk to make the artifice of his fiction transparent: "Let us call it Winter, that dusk may fall now and a moon rise" (20). By a narrative *fiat* we are back with the man in the moon, the mark of Cain, but from the morning's reading of Dante, we have been moved into a winter twilight in Beckett's transparently fictive universe. The dim light of ambiguity has displaced Dante's *claritas* and Stephen's "radiance."

The narrator moves from a recounting of Belacqua's inner state at the beginning of the story to an obtrusive manipulator at the end. Belacqua, in turn, moves from trying to translate an actual text initially to trying to translate the "old parchment" of his aunt's face (22) as she prepares to boil the lobster. The movement is, however, illusory. The spots on the moon, Cain, McCabe, the lobster—even Belacqua's unwitting use of the word "fish"—are all forms of repetition, the particular in the universal, the universal in the particular. The narrator gradually reveals himself as he always was: a fictional device for detranslating an abstract intellectual question into its sensible embodiment in experience. Belacqua and the reader, in turn, have unwittingly been contextualized into the *Inferno*, both Dante's and its Beckettian gloss. Belacqua is not stuck in the first canti of the moon, as he thought himself initially; rather, like the lobster, he is among the damned. He is not the priest of the eucharistic sacrament as appeared to be the case in the preparation of his lunch; rather, he is a fellow victim in an impersonal sacrifice. We are, as the Italian tutor puts it, "where we were, as we were" (20). It is not a question of "get[ting] on" (9);[4] it seems to be a question of opening one's eyes to where one already is.

4. Belacqua, who was bored at the beginning of the story with the spots-on-the-moon text and anxious to "get on" to Piccarda (9) has unwittingly witnessed the concretization of the spots on the moon in Piccarda and, correspondingly, the reflection of Piccarda in the lobster. As Beatrice explains to Dante, the spots on the moon are the effect of the differing degrees by which entities reflect divine *claritas*. Piccarda, in turn, exemplifies the cosmic principle of the differing degrees of divine *claritas*. Like the lobster, an innocent victim of earthly violence, Piccarda explains to Dante that although she is perfectly happy, she is among the least blessed in heaven because her will was not totally in accord with God's. While Piccarda explains to Dante the workings of divine will, Belacqua's "lousy old bitch of an aunt" (16) tells him "how it is" down below: "Have sense . . . lobsters are always boiled alive. They must be" (22). Beckett's short story serves as an

In shaping his own *pietà*, Beckett detranslates Dante back to the *Inferno* and the uncertainty of ultimacy. It is the human inability to know for certain the meaning—if any—of existence that defines that existence as Hell. Seen from this perspective, Beckett's aesthetic *pietà* is a commitment to a continual reshaping of fundamental paradox, the inability either to hope or despair, to affirm or deny, within the confines of the only two "givens": birth and death.

Beckett's art over the fifty some years following "Dante and the Lobster" has explored the hell of human wasting and pining (WG 29) for ultimacy in the womb–tomb of existence. The Unnamable's "I can't go on, I'll go on" (TN 414), Moran's "It is midnight. . . . It was not midnight" (TN 92, 176), Gogo's "Yes, let's go" followed by the stage direction *"They do not move"* (WG 35, 60), the final word of *Company*—*"Alone"* (63)—are a few of Beckett's more explicit reshapings of the paradoxical dilemma of the human in a world where ambiguity seems to be the only absolute: "Haze sole/[soul] certitude" (ISIS 48).

From the spiritual perspective of *pietà* that would see experience from a divine point of view in *The Divine Comedy*, to an aesthetic worship of beauty that transmutes experience into aesthetic stasis in Joyce, to the concretization of *pietà* in the suffering, cruciform victim whose hope and despair is always in abeyance, the *pietà* of each artist defines the contours of his art. For Dante, the *pietà* lies in translating the transcendent meaning of the divine mysteries into images; for Joyce the *pietà* lies in transmuting daily experience into artistic words whose meanings stretch and reverberate in ever-richer resonance; for Beckett the *pietà* lies in detranslating the illusionary words into images and echoes of the underlying, inexpressible quandary of human existence.

In their individual piety to perhaps their primary artist-father, finally, Joyce and Beckett have been attracted to different segments of the Dantean metaphorical cosmos. Beckett described Joyce's work as a spherical "purgatory" with "endless verbal germination, maturation, putrefaction, the cyclic dynamism of the intermedi-

implicit, ironic gloss on Piccarda's words, which are among the most famous in the *Comedy:* "In his will is our peace" (*Par.* iii: 85). Beckett appropriates the mirroring technique of Dante as a form of repetition.

ate" (*Disjecta* 33, 29). Beckett himself, on the other hand, has excavated the hellish ambiguity of "how it is" "down below." In the artistic trinity of Dante, Joyce, and Beckett, the imaginative realms of the Christian afterlife become mirrors of the shapes of their respective art. And their art, in turn, allows us, their readers, to glimpse in divergent modes the heaven–purgatory–hell that both is—and is not—our earthly existence.

Works Cited

Carey, Phyllis. "Samuel Beckett's *Coup de Grâce.*" *Notes on Modern Irish Literature* 1 (1989): 23–26.

Cohn, Ruby. *Samuel Beckett: The Comic Gamut.* New Brunswick: Rutgers University Press, 1962.

Eco, Umberto. *The Aesthetics of Chaosmos: The Middle Ages of James Joyce.* Tulsa: University of Tulsa Press, 1982.

Fowlie, Wallace. *A Reading of Dante's Inferno.* Chicago: The University of Chicago Press, 1981.

Jewinski, Ed. "James Joyce and Samuel Beckett: From Epiphany to Anti-Epiphany." *Re: Joyce'n Beckett.* Ed. Phyllis Carey and Ed Jewinski. New York: Fordham University Press, 1992. 160–74.

Johnson, W. R. "Aeneas and the Ironies of *Pietas.*" *Classical Journal* 60 (1965): 360–64.

McLuhan, Marshall. "Joyce, Aquinas, and the Poetic Process," *Renascence* 4 (Autumn 1951): 3–11.

Took, J. F. "*L'etterno piacer*": *Aesthetic Ideas in Dante.* Oxford: Clarendon, 1984.

Vossler, Karl. *Mediaeval Culture: An Introduction to Dante and His Times.* Trans. William C. Lawton. 2 vols. New York: Harcourt, Brace, 1929.

9

Krapping Out: Images of Flow and Elimination as Creation in Joyce and Beckett

Susan Brienza

I can scarcely detail for you all the things that resolve themselves into—excrement for me (a new Midas!)
—Sigmund Freud to Wilhelm Fliess, December 1897

[Shem] winged away . . . across the kathartic ocean and made synthetic ink and sensitive paper for his own end out of his wit's waste.

Finnegans Wake

What matters is to eat and excrete. Dish and pot, dish and pot, these are the poles.

Malone Dies

BOTH JAMES JOYCE AND SAMUEL BECKETT repeatedly use images and metaphors of bodily fluids and elimination; and both authors—writing in post-Freudian times—link these images of urination and defecation to the process of artistic creation. But here the similarity ends, for in Joyce the mind flows on as the body does, while obsessively in Beckett characters are thwarted, stuck, or constipated: literally and figuratively they cannot move. For Joyce, the body operates in accord with Nature, and thus natural processes provide metaphors for creative fluidity. Joyce routinely spelled "rear" as "rere," a form of the Latin for matter, *res*, implying virtually an identity between feces and all of the cosmos (Brivic 139). For Beckett, bodies and birth are unnatural, and writing becomes a painful but necessary (sometimes extorted) activity. "Constipation is a sign of good health in pomeranians," says Molloy (TN 12), and it also seems to be a sign of normalcy in Beckett protagonists. For both authors, we can trace a complex cluster of images—fluids, bodily processes, eating and excreting, sexuality (or lack of it), and natural cycles—together representing or paralleling the creative process, but with diametrically different, as it were, outcomes.

Of course, much has been written about Stephen and the body, Bloom and his bowel movement, Molly and water, and Biddy the hen's letter; I would like to blend all these ideas and more to show that images of flow become a controlling metaphor for Joyce's whole fictional cosmos—and for Beckett's world, images of constriction function similarly. One is tempted to begin an analysis of Joyce's fluid metaphors with *Portrait*, but, in fact, as early as "The Dead," Gabriel, the would-be artist, uses ocean imagery to describe passion—in the context of the natural processes of snow and rain. Gabriel in his love and lust feels "a sudden *tide* of joy"; "a *wave* of yet more tender joy . . . went coursing in warm *flood* along his arteries"; and memories of his past with Gretta "broke like waves in his mind" (D 212–13; emphasis added). These images lead stylistically to what most critics describe as the *liquid* l's and s's of the famous final paragraph. Though the ending of "The Dead" contains an ambiguous merging of positive and negative associations of waves, snow, sleep, and death, in *Portrait* the image of a tide—often the "sordid tide" of life—threatens to overwhelm the young artist. Thus the ending of "The Dead" suggests the notion that water can be either dangerous and dirty or redemptive and creative and that streams of water are bodily fluids, are words themselves—the stuff of life—which by *Finnegans Wake* is Joyce's reigning metaphor (Splitter 194).

Joyce's specific conflation of fluids and verbal production begins as early as *Portrait*. In the first sections of the novel, argues Vincent Cheng, dirty or cold water represents the ugliness of the physical world that the sensitive writer needs to escape.[1] In the later sections, Stephen's sensibilities are further offended by "wet rubbish" and "mouldering offal" (177), rendered by Joyce the stuff of the artistic world as well as the material one when he follows the phrase "as odour assailed him of cheerless cellardamp and decay"

---

1. Vincent Cheng, " 'Goddinpotty': James Joyce and the Literature of Excrement," paper given at the Joyce Symposium in Venice, June 1988 (unpublished).

Meet Lenny Kravitz, and pencil games too!!!
Starts 8:30 P.M.   no PASS no ENTRANCE!!

Wait

Content

→

(178) with "he walked on . . . among heaps of *dead* language" (178; emphasis added). (Of course in *Finnegans Wake* the huge creative enterprise of the novel itself will spring from a heap of dead language, the midden heap where the dung-fouled letter is found.) Stephen's phrasing "tides of filth" links the aversion to dirty water to fear of the mother—which will recur at the beginning of *Ulysses,* and which in both novels impedes Stephen's relation to his own body and to his art.

Simultaneously, Joyce develops a parallel between language and bodily fluids that is sometimes positive (and certainly productive for Stephen by the middle of *Ulysses*), but can be mired in the "shit" of sin. When the shamed young boy tells his sins in the confession box, his words pour forth like diarrhea in one of Joyce's more graphic passages: "His sins trickled from his lips, one by one, trickled in shameful drops from his soul festering and oozing like a sore, a squalid stream of vice. The last sins oozed forth, sluggish, filthy" (144). Yet in a different mode, when the young artist composes his wet dream villanelle (sexual fluid fused with poetic creation as his soul gets "all dewy wet"), language itself becomes a liquid: "and like a cloud of vapour or like waters circumfluent in space the liquid letters of speech, symbols of the element of mystery flowed forth over his brain" (223). Because of Stephen's precise religious imagery, argues Sheldon Brivic ("O! In the virgin womb of the imagination the word was made flesh"), it is clear that "the main subject of the dream and the villanelle is the roselight of the female heart" (70). Artistic creation combines associations of women, sex (signaled above by the ejaculation "O!"—Joyce's euphemistic way for both Gerty and Molly to express sexual climax), and fluids. Later in the novel the very phonemes of words exist in an ocean of sound: "A soft liquid joy flowed through the words where the soft long vowels hurtled noiselessly and fell away, lapping and flowing back and ever shaking the white bells of their waves . . ." (225–26), where "soft long vowels" exactly parallels "soft liquid joy." These associations culminate in Stephen's creation of an artistic muse out of the bird-girl seen on the shore, where names, nature, words, water, and feminine beauty form a cluster of images suggesting creation. Significantly, both of Stephen's creative breakthroughs, this one and his walking and urinating along the shore in "Proteus," take place by the sea—in metaphorical and psychological proximation to a Molly.

However, words can still be a dirty or squalid flow, especially when Stephen is depressed and seeks literature not as an analogue to water but as an escape from the watery tea of the Dedalus household. In an explicit simile near the end of *Portrait,* again a flow is negative: "The gross name had passed over it like foul water poured over an old stone image" (232). One of Stephen's favorite phrases, "tides of filth," links his hatred of dirty water to dread of the mother. It makes sense, moreover, that the immature, potential artist would often display an aversion to water (again, related to his fear of women; woman is the stranger, Marilyn French shows [69], bearing "tides, myriadislanded, within her, blood not mine"), while the artistic Bloom and the creative Molly are not merely comfortable in and with fluids but are fascinated by them. Bloom, for example, is a "waterlover, drawer of water, watercarrier" (U 17.183) and, combining his scientific, artistic, and humanistic traits, he often thinks of existence as a stream of life. Bloom turns on the tap and feels one with all mankind.

In "Telemachus" Stephen's phobia of water and aversion to dirty water continue, but by the middle of "Proteus" he submits himself to Nature and thereby becomes more creative and organic with words: "Pan's hour, the faunal noon. Among gumheavy serpentplants, milkoozing fruits, where on the tawny waters leaves lie wide. Pain is far" (U 3.442–44). Right after this, during Stephen's urination, the sounds, the water, the weeds, all "evoke a profound sense of the eternal recurrence of nature" (French 80). Even more important for his development as an artist (and for the argument of this article), the very act of micturating, with Stephen's playful mind playing on the sounds of peeing, produces the young writer's best poetry thus far:

> In long lassoes from the Cock lake the water flowed full, covering greengoldenly lagoons of sand, rising, flowing. . . . Better get this job over quick. Listen: A fourworded wavespeech: seesoo, hrss, rsseeiss, ooos. Vehement breath of waters amid seasnakes, rearing horses, rocks. In cups of rocks it slops: flop, slop, slap: bounded in barrels. And, spent, its speech ceases. It flows purling, widely flowing, floating foampool, flower unfurling [U 3.453–60].

Stephen reinvents the penis as a lake holding water, so that the body becomes a small earth; and by the end of the passage the pool of pee evolves into a flower, resonant with Molly as flower and Bloom's penis as flower, with a pun on "flow-er." Between these two images Stephen experiments with alliteration, assonance, internal rhyme, parallel construction, and more metaphors (e.g., a "spent," post-orgasmic feeling) to make his flow indeed— and self-reflexively—a "fourworded wavespeech." As Vincent Cheng argues, Stephen here, unlike his earlier blocked artistic self, "is not only now at ease with his own urination, he seems to understand its analogical link with art, to understand that urination is—like writing poetry or printing books—just another mode of production" (6). Stephen gradually learns, in part through osmosis from Bloom, that elimination means creation rather than sin. Later, in "Ithaca," when he and Bloom urinate together, the more cerebral Stephen re-creates religious dogma while Bloom's thoughts remain on the physical, but in each case body and mind are simultaneously productive.

Stephen begins to share Bloom's knowledge of the natural cycle when, like the older man, he meditates on dying bodies, on decaying and being eaten. When he remembers that a drowned corpse may wash ashore that day, Stephen imagines the disintegration and transformation of the dead body with metaphors similar to Bloom's—with a vision of the foul gases inside, with a verbal echo to *Titbits* (the newspaper that transmutes Bloom's defecation into creation), and with an echo of Bloom's story of cannibals eating the missionary's genitals and thus gaining potency: "Bag of corpsegas sopping in foul brine. A quiver of minnows, fat of a spongy *titbit*, flash through the slits of his buttoned trouserfly. God becomes man becomes fish becomes barnacle goose becomes featherbed mountain" (U 3.476–79; emphasis added). And by the end of this cycle of transformations, Stephen—unbeknownst to himself but known to the reader—has introduced Joyce's muse, Nora Barnacle, and Bloom's main artistic inspiration second only to bodily processes, his featherbed mountain, Molly.

Bloom, like Stephen, is fascinated with the processes of eating and eliminating. Lindsey Tucker, by documenting Joyce's depiction of Bloom's responses to bodily functions contrasted with Stephen's, describes the two different approaches to creativity (2).

Tucker agrees with Mark Shechner's conclusion that Stephen is "a closed character with a retentive temper," while the open Bloom has an "eliminative temper" (quoted in Tucker 3). Bloom subconsciously expresses profound puns in words like "gestation" of an idea or "conception" of a plan when he thinks, "Never know whose thoughts you're chewing" (U 8.717–18). When he grows more creative with language, he puns on food images, whether for lively women, or dead men, like "Plumtree's potted meat" becoming "Dignam's potted meat"; and he imagines the whole world in terms of food (see Tucker 67; see also 50)—in this case, a candy image for the big bang theory: "Gas: then solid: then world: then cold: then dead shell drifting around, frozen rock, like that pineapple rock" (U 8.582–84). Even his literary theory is based on food—"you write what you eat" (Tucker 67), (a notion that Joyce later embodies in Shem, the artist preferring artificial to natural foods).

In "Calypso" Bloom is especially concerned with bodily processes, and Joyce structures the chapter to begin at the top of the body with the mouth and ingestion and in the later pages moves to expulsion and the anus (Tucker 47). Throughout *Ulysses*, fluids so preoccupy Bloom that he transforms everything he thinks about—smells, meat, and the horror of life—into liquids (Tucker 47–49). But even in the negative images of death in "Hades," Bloom is able to perceive the cycles of Nature, and through his depression in this chapter we can see some glimmers of redemption (Tucker 61): about a ritual murder he thinks, "It's the blood sinking in the earth gives new life" (U 6.771).

For Bloom, Sheldon Brivic notes, dung is positive, waste matter and desire are wonderfully linked, and his "excremental vision" acquires the power of a religion; even his pseudo-philosophical definition of time plays on the word "movement" and thus conflates passage or duration, yearning desire, and bowel movement (158). Obsessed with all types of excretions, "Bloom's literary life begins with the fact that he likes to eat kidneys, partly because they taste of urine, and ends with him kissing his wife's buttocks" (139). Bloom's fondness for excrement, combined with his feminine aspects ("the new womanly man," able to produce an off-

spring, i.e., a work of art), can be seen in Jungian terms, says
Lindsey Tucker, as evidence of his receptivity and his expressive,
artistic nature (5).

Bloom best fits the parallel between natural processes and
creation, as many critics have pointed out, when his reading of
Titbits and his fantasy of himself as a short-story writer coincide
with his morning "sit down" in the outhouse. As Bloom reads
the literary piece in the newspaper, "in Joyce's description it is
impossible to distinguish between a column of printed words and
a turd, a column of shit, and the very confusion suggests the
identification" (Cheng 7), while the repetition and ambiguity of
the word "quietly" to modify both activities further conflate them:
"Quietly he read, restraining himself, the first column and, yielding but resisting, began the second. Midway, his last resistance
yielding, he allowed his bowels to ease themselves quietly as he
read, reading still patiently that slight constipation of yesterday
quite gone" (U 4.506–509). Certainly any artistic constipation is
gone as well, as Bloom's confusion of the author Beaufoy and the
prolific Purefoy, and his blending of thought and bodily processes, testify. As he remembers the author's "masterstroke," he
wonders to himself "Did I pull the chain? Yes. The last act"
(U 8.279). "Act" conflates defecating and drama. Here and
throughout the novel, "he creates himself creating" (Tucker 51).

Defecation as creation has been recognized by many modern
writers and critics; for example, W. H. Auden links outhouse
activity with self-identity, self-creation, and intellectual production:

> A young man has discovered his true identity when he becomes
> able to call his thoughts and actions his own. . . . Luther [became]
> Luther when he heard in St. Paul's phrase *The Just shall live by Faith*
> the authentic voice of God. That this revelation should have come
> to him in a privy is fascinating but not, I think, surprising. There
> must be many people to whom religious, intellectual, or artistic
> insights have come in the same place, for excretion is . . . the
> primal creative act—every child is the mother of its own feces . . .
> [86].

It is thus significant that Joyce offers us no scene of Stephen
defecating: he has not reached the stage where he can mother
himself, not reached the artistic heights (that is to say, depths) of

Bloom, Molly, Shem, and HCE. Joyce himself (as evidenced by his obscene letters to Nora) linked excretion to pleasure and also to writing. Like a good Freudian's, his unconscious linked defecation to spending money, and then his conscious mind connected his father's " 'spendthrift habits' " to his own behavior and to " 'any creativity I may possess' " (quoted in Maddox 102).

Similar scenes of defecation as literary creation arise in *Finnegans Wake* for both Shem and HCE. Glugg, one of Shem's manifestations, sits on the toilet reading Aquinas and masturbating after his frustration at failing with the girls (240). During this experience, as Brivic suggests (204), Shem divides into an artist and his own censor/hunter: "He would split" (228). The implications of the phrasing, however, are much larger than might immediately be evident. "Sit down" may equally be understood as "writing down" and, therefore, be connected to the similar experiences of Bloom and HCE. The implication seems to be that composition takes place on the pot while decomposition comes out. To stress the point, Joyce describes Glugg's intention to expose his parents artistically with the punning sentence "He would jused sit it all write down . . ." (229); you just set it down while you sit down in the outhouse.

HCE spends even more time than Bloom in the privy, sometimes smoking—with its obvious phallic and erotic associations. John Gordon suggests that while there (like Bloom) HCE is reading and that his reading matter (as it were) is Aubrey Beardsley's pornographic but classy, illustrated edition of *Lysistrata,* over which the master of the house masturbates (another masterstroke?); further, argues Gordon, HCE's famous sin combines the motifs of the privy—voyeurism, exhibitionism, sexual indiscretion, and scatology (16–17). He suggests that the incident with the girls in Phoenix Park—which also involves voyeurism and scatology, peeping on girls peeing—might have originated from pictures in HCE's dirty book. If his original sin was defecating in public himself (we can never be sure), then once again defecation is creative since HCE's sin—that is, mankind's fall—provides the central plot for *Finnegans Wake*. Finally, the idea of reading matter associated with eating and feces, "eatwords" (569), brings us to the central metafictional incident of the *Wake*, the letter found in the litter, the dunghill. And apparently there is a literal or metaphorical road from HCE's outhouse to the letter: Kate remarks that the yard and path near the privy are full of rotten rubbish and the "droppings of biddies" (79–80), that is, the waste of Biddy the Hen, who finds the letter.

Since this letter is edged with manure, it seems a resurrection of the piece of *Titbits* Bloom used to wipe himself with. In general, its discovery implies that there is litter in literature, potty in poetry (Irish "pottery"), and thus shit in art. Ireland's sod must have soiled the letter, and this description alludes to the scene with the Russian general using the earth, Irish turf, to wipe himself: "Well, this freely is what must have occurred to our missive (there's a sod of a turb for you! please wisp off the grass!)" (111). And appropriately embedded in the turds are two literary titles: *A Tale of a Tub* and *Leaves of Grass*. For Joyce is suggesting here, in other scenes, and with other scatological puns that "what the poet writes is himself—his own ex-pressions, multitudinous products squeezed out of himself" (Cheng 15). Besides the littered letter as impetus for the novel, one major structural device of the *Wake*, the ten thunderclaps, also fits the fecal motif, for these represent the noises of HCE's defecation. As such, argues Sheldon Brivic, they show phallic power and fertility and are thus creative as well as apocalyptic—each one beginning as well as ending a cycle (213).

Significantly, the metaphor of eating and shitting as creativity operates for Joyce's so-called minor characters as well: in the "Eumaeus" chapter Murphy the sailor is continuously chewing on tobacco as he spins his yarns, making assimilation part of the creative process (see Tucker 130–35). When Murphy goes outside to urinate, he awakens a horse—as if there were some special kinship between Murphy and Horse or elimination and Horse— and horse imagery also figures in Stephen's urine speech and in the description of the litter/letter ("what you do get is, well, a positively grotesquely distorted macromass of all sorts of horse-happy values and masses of meltwhile horse," that is, horseshit). Another horse becomes an artist figure at the end of the chapter, producing three "globes" of turds, which link him to Shakespeare's Globe Theater and to the three sections of Joyce's epic novel. Murphy shares many characteristics with the horse (e.g., they both are said to distill poteen in their stomachs), and in my reading Murphy becomes the combination of horse and sweeper at the end of the chapter. (The horse with its "proud feathering tale" is an Icarus-like creator.) Even more similarities link Murphy with James Joyce himself, until he becomes the walking embodiment of the artist as assimilator of past writers' material.

In a long article presenting a new interpretation of "Eumaeus," I argue that Murphy's strange tattoo is a picture of the artist as part cannibal, that Murphy represents Joyce as the product of Homer and Shakespeare.[2] The tattoo artist Antonio depicted on Murphy's chest, said twice to be Greek, has a pictured face that can be made to smile or frown, which for me suggests the traditional masks of Greek comedy and tragedy, then implies a genre that transcends both, the epic, and thus (with other details) conjures up Homer. When asked what has become of Antonio, Murphy (Joyce) smiles slyly and says, "Ate by sharks after." This cryptic code can be broken by reading back to "Scylla and Charybdis" where Stephen thinks after giving his Hamlet theory, "One day in the national library we had a discussion. *Shakes. After.* His lub back: I followed" (U 9.1108–1109; emphasis added). Antonio (Homer) eaten by sharks means that Homer was assimilated by Shakespeare, who in turn was ingested and recreated by Joyce in *Ulysses* (alias Murphy, who is chewing all the while he is speaking). The artistic process is one of consuming, digesting, transforming, defecating, creating; and all this culminates in Shem's methodology.

Murphy's blue ink tattoo reappears as Shem's blue ink that he alchemically manufactures out of his own excrement and uses to write on his own body, tattoo-like:

> when the call comes, he shall produce nichthemerically from his unheavenly body a no uncertain quantity of obscene matter not protected by copriright in the United Stars of Ourania or bedeed and bedood and bedang and bedung to him, with this double dye, brought to blood heat, gallic acid on iron ore, through the bowels of his misery, flashly, faithly, nastily, appropriately, this Esuan Menschavik and the first till last alshemist wrote over every square inch of the only foolscap available, his own body . . . [185].

Justius (Shaun) criticizes his brother for defecating and calling it writing: "even extruding your strabismal apologia, when legibly

2. My essay *"Eumaeus'* Style and Murphy's Tattoo Means 2 + 2 . . . = 16: A New Reading of Chapter 16 of *Ulysses*," is under consideration.

depressed, upon defenceless paper" (189). It is because Shem makes his "indelible ink" from such a dirty, turdy substance that it is referred to as "inkenstink," that his work is termed "crap," and that he is actually identified with his own writing material: he is called "the shit" (179). He has "his penname SHUT sepia-scraped on the doorplate" (182). Several other associations between "Eumaeus" and Chapter 7 of the *Wake* suggest that Murphy was one precursor for Shem the penman.[3] In Father Boyle's eucharistic interpretation of Joyce's metaphor for creation, "Shem makes his ink from experience, here as in 'The Holy Office' imaged as defecation, mixed with artistic insight or skillful exercise of art, imaged as micturition" (9). For urine is part of the recipe as well, as is obvious with Father Boyle's translation of the Latin formula given in the *Wake* (185):

> First of all, the artificer, the old father [with echoes back to the end of *Portrait*], . . . defecated (literally: emptied) into his hand; and secondly, having unburdened himself of the black living thing . . . , he placed his own faeces, which he entitled his "purge" . . . in a once honorable vessel of sadness . . . and into the same . . . he pissed happily and melodiously [cf. Stephen and his "fourworded wavespeech"], continuously singing with a loud voice the psalm which begins, "My tongue is the reed of a scribe swiftly writing." Finally, from the vile crap mixed with the pleasantness of the divine Orion [whose myths and legends associate urine with birth], after the mixture had been cooked and exposed to the cold, he made for himself imperishable ink [3–4].

Thus Shem becomes the Joycean artist in the most literal way—not merely suggesting or imaging literary creation with bodily processes but flowing endlessly from one to the other. Shem finally transcends Stephen's fear of water by (Christ-like) turning urine into ink and thus water into words. Once again, child-like "making" is the making of literature, "imperishable" or immortal art, just as Molly's micturating and Issy's tinkling in *Finnegans Wake* mean making more than mere urine: "Lissom! lissom! I am doing it" (21); "Listen, listen! I am doing it" (571).

3. For more on Shem and his links back to Murphy (e.g., bogus and forged writing), see my article "Murphy, Shem, Morpheus, and Murphies: 'Eumaeus' Meets the *Wake*," *Joycean Occasions*, ed. Janet E. Dunleavy, Melvin J. Friedman, and Michael P. Gillespie.

Of course, it has become a commonplace of Joyce criticism to discuss woman as god-like creator, best exemplified by the creative fluidity of his women ALP and Molly (and we might recall too that Gerty McDowell has begun her period as her mind overflows with the rosy thoughts of romance magazine rhetoric). Bloom's adoring description of Molly's behind, calling her cheeks eastern and western hemispheres (U 17.2229), equates woman with the entire world, and earlier Bloom had addressed Cissy with "Speak, woman, sacred lifegiver" (see Brivic 160, 137). Molly, referred to as "= Spinning Earth" in Joyce's notesheets, uses a style where "the rhythms flow like water, which frequently in the novel is associated with sex, eternal recurrence, continuation" (French 245). Molly's almost audible stream-of-consciousness chapter, beginning and concluding with the word "Yes" (itself ending with the sibilant "s" that produces a continuous stream of sound) contains talk of her periodic flow, her flatulence, and her urination—as well as her reproductive powers; and each bodily function becomes a parallel for her fertile and fluid discourse. Thus Joyce's tendency "to take everything literally, to equate everything with words and words with bodily substances" that Randolph Splitter (199) finds in *Finnegans Wake,* began in the previous novel.

Molly's sexual words (which are also Joyce's chosen words to represent the female, specifically womb, breast, woman), "Yes," "because," and "O," are used as connectives, to keep the verbal flow going, often joined together in "yes because" or "O yes" as a transition to a new thought. "O," appearing 29 times, visually represents Molly's verbal description of women as "so round and white" (Card 128). It is significant that there is a cluster of four "yeses" during her creative interpretation of the Tarot cards. Professor Card (as it happens; Joyce would like this coincidence) has noticed how taken Molly is with prepositions, especially double prepositions like "down off" and "up into"—in particular "up" (87 times) and "down" (97 times)[4]—without, however, pointing out the sexual suggestiveness of up-and-down movement.

4. See Card 128, 132. Note also that Bloom plunges the spoon "up and down" in his egg (U 18.932), and Molly "washed up and down" (U 18.204).

Within Molly's associative logic, thought flows from one pseudo-sentence to the next, sometimes through simple repetition of the same words and phrases in different contexts and often through the very notion of fluids themselves, e.g., from oranges, to water, to urine, to the frozen canal, to using the outhouse. Even more explicitly linking continuity, power, water, and the sound of words, three passages start with the idea of Molly's period and shift from the sound of a train to a series of vowels, to (phallic) engines, to sex, to water, to songs and love and music, and then to making wind:

> frseeeeeeeefronnnng train somewhere whistling the strength those engines have in them like big giants and the water rolling all over and out of them all sides like the end of Loves old sweeeetsonnnng [U 18.596–98].

> Frseeeeeeeeeeeeeeeeeeeeefrong that train again weeping tone once in the dear deaead days beyondre call close my eyes breath my lips forward kiss sad look eyes open piano ere oer the world the mists began I hate that istsbeg comes loves sweet soooooooooooong [U 18.874–77]

> give us room even to let a fart God or do the least thing better yes hold them like that a bit on my side piano quietly sweeeee theres that train far away pianissimo eeeee one more tsong [U 18.906–908].

With "piano" the song's music and the body's music become one, just as earlier in the day Joyce had conflated Bloom's wind with the windy rhetoric he was reading. Molly certainly believes that the body has a language and syntax of its own: she could tell when Milly was sick from the look of her feces. Often it is a thought of a body part or a bodily process (e.g., breasts for nursing and then breasts for sexual attraction) that provides the transition from one paragraph to another. Molly's preoccupation with sex and fluids is manifested in the very terms of her ignorance: her transposition and reduction of the difficult word she wrestles with, "metempsychosis," is "met something with hoses in it" (U 18.565), "hoses" suggesting both the male and water.

Molly is continually concerned about whether or not something is "natural" and frequently uses "naturally" (three times on one page) and "of course" with the meaning of "naturally" (47 times)

(Card 128), as connectives or transitions. For her, sex, nature, and the sea all intertwine and overlap. Her urine is a river ("O how the waters come down at Lahore"), and her period is a natural event: she is "all in a swamp" or "its pouring out of me like the sea." As she urinates and flows, she repeats six times the word "easy," loosely a blend of "sea" and "yes." For Molly, genitals are nothing to blush at ("its only nature"); and sex is usually connected to nature's water. She daydreams about naked boys "plunging into the sea"; because of her early experience, she associates necking with "the Malta boat passing yes the sea" and "I was thinking of him on the sea all the time after." And "because the smell of the sea excited me of course" might be why one fantasy is to "pick up a sailor off the sea thatd be hot on for it." Molly is merely the best example of a larger pattern in Joyce: Stephen and his bird-girl at the shore, Bloom and Gerty at the shore, and ALP and HCE *becoming* a shore.

(Conversely, Beckett's characters usually manage only dry sex in a dry land; and even the few exceptions are significant. In the play *Embers* Henry and Ada used to make love by the sea in the past, but in the present the sea represents only death. In *Krapp's Last Tape* the fondest memory and most replayed tape is the scene with Krapp and his girl in a punt, being rocked sexually back and forth in the reeds; yet he repudiates this romantic relationship, and indeed it is by the sea one stormy night that he bids his farewell to love.)

For Molly, sexuality and Nature are one, and she sees this unity as being "round you": you "see it all round you like a new world." She herself, like the land, craves to be renewed each spring: "I'm always like that in the spring [sexual] Id like a new fellow every year." When Molly, explicitly and implicitly, compares herself to spring flowers by the end of the monologue, the identification between woman, Nature, creation is complete: artistic creation blended with cyclical Nature and natural processes. "I was a flower of the mountain yes so we are flowers all a womans body," but a man's body too is a flower. Explicitly, of course, Bloom's penis is a "languid floating flower," but also indirectly Bloom becomes a flower or plant in Lenehan's description: "He's not your common or garden [variety] . . . you know." Molly seems to realize this as she puns on Bloom's name and the suggestive garment "bloomers," and as she thinks "there is a flower that bloometh." Both male and female blossom in love. When Bloom links woman and nourishment in recalling the seedcake kiss from Molly, he remembers "Flowers her eyes were" (U 8.910).

Earlier in the novel, when "Mr. Henry Flower" receives a pressed flower from Martha included in her letter, Joyce experiments with a syntax of flowers, as Bloom creatively merges the visual of nature and the verbal of artifice: "Language of flowers. . . . Angry tulips with you darling manflower punish your cactus if you don't please poor forgetmenot how I long violets to dear roses when we soon anemone meet all naughty nightstalk . . ." (U 5.261–66). With these puns Joyce alludes to the idea of figures of speech in rhetoric as flowers of language, as Margot Norris shows, the tropes in "heliotrope." This word again appears in *Finnegans Wake* as the correct answer to the riddle that the girls tease Shem with; if he guesses the right answer—"heliotrope"— he wins the right to chase a girl (FW 224). As Sheldon Brivic in *Joyce Between Freud and Jung* emphasizes, two of the meanings of this flower in context are vagina and intercourse (203). As all language is creative, and all conversation is ultimately sexual, concludes Brivic, "Joyce portrays intercourse as intercourse" (126).

Since she is not confined to water and flowers but represents all of nature, Molly is also identified with the sun (as many critics have pointed out), with her "orange petticoat I had on with the sunray pleats." In this, and because of her lapsed sense of logical sequence and clock time ("I never know the time even that watch he gave me never seems to go properly"), she keeps biological and evolutionary time. (Just the opposite are Beckett's characters who are ignorant of the seasons and Earth's time, and who avoid the flow of emotions by counting the seconds or watching a second hand.) In fact, Molly feels that an act of love can stop time and that she herself is eternal. Molly is all for excess and abundance— "I always want to throw a handful of tea into the pot"—and is against "measuring and mincing." Her 81 yeses to life contrast with the repeated noes of Beckett's characters (recalling Beckett's line in the aborted novel *Texts for Nothing*, "No's knife in yes's wound"). Molly, who like Shakespeare is "all in all" and a filler of voids (French 245–48), is a world apart from Beckett's narrators trying desperately to subtract life, to create voids. In Molly's text the noun "all" is the most frequent (at least 120 occurrences), reinforced by 19 uses of "everything," showing her inclusiveness, expansiveness (Card 129).

Joyce celebrates the fluid world of nature in his last novel: the very river Liffey forms part of ALP's name, and it is her liquid monologue at the end that circles the novel back to its riverrun source. A stream of words renders the babbling of the river's flow synonymous with the strings of gossip from the washerwomen (Splitter 197); they "drink in" each other's phrases. The notion of Joycean words as liquid is most prominent with the women in *Finnegans Wake,* where they all flow, speak, and sing simultaneously. ALP as river looks back at her girlhood in Issy, the cloud, and looks ahead to becoming the older Kate with her chamberpot (each characterized by natural symbols or signs of water and elimination). All three watery women have a great many "liquids" in their speech, Anna Livia often beginning sentences with "well," and speaking in terms of "nonsery reams" (619), combining nursery and nonsense, rhymes and streams. While Issy is experiencing her first period, ALP is nearing her last one (Gordon 63–64). Thus do they continue the streams of speech of Gerty and Molly. Gordon speculates that Issy's name refers to both her lisp and cute euphemisms for urinating in her chamberpot, "siss" and "whiss," which in turn echo her whisperings and the drip of faucet water into the fireplace basin: "As Kate is well and washtub and ALP a river, Issy is rain and dew" (Gordon 77). For Issy, "making" is urinating, but she also uses "making" as pretending, as fictionalizing; in a footnote in the Lesson chapter she admits that the children are "Making it up as we goes along" (268, n. 2). At the end, when ALP relinquishes her "rain"/reign to Issy, Joyce's pun conflates natural and linguistic powers.

In an ever-continuing cycle, the water and sewage of the Liffey are said to provide nutriment (Gordon 231), just as Kate in her reincarnation as Biddy the Hen provides the nutriment for Shem the penman: he eats the hen's eggs, digests them, and thus produces the excrement he then transforms into ink for writing. In yet another way, the flowing women help to create the book we read, since they are all singers and their songs call forth the dreams of all the dreamers waking (Gordon 75). Says Shaun, "We just are upsidedown singing what ever the dimkims mummur allalilty she pulls inner out heads" (373). The phrasing here contains mom (mum) and ALP's lilting murmur of all—eternity—that she pulls out of our dreamers' heads. In fact, there is a direct link between flows of urine, the flowing water of the river, and the flow of speech from ALP that she pours into her husband's ear, thus motivating his novel-length dream. At the beginning of the story, for HCE "Words weigh no no more to him than raindrips to Rethfernhim" (74), but by the end it is not whiskey that wakes the corpse but the resurrecting murmurs of the maternal river when Anna Livia Plurabel (also called "Pourable") pours her rejuvenating and inspiring words/water/urine into her husband's ear (Splitter 197, 200). Indirectly and directly, then, woman as natural and metaphorical flow is responsible for the creation of *Finnegans Wake*. As her hair becomes the foliage on the river, Anna Livia is "leafy" and "Leafiest," and by the end her leaves—and the leaves of the book—diminish (see Gordon 274), as natural growth, decay, and renewal determine the development of the text.

For Samuel Beckett as well, mental processes, especially artistic ones, call up images of bodily processes and fluids. Hamm as the Chronicler in *Endgame* remembers "something dripping" in his head "ever since the fontanelles," that is, ever since infancy; this flow of water charts the flow of thought. In the radio play *Words and Music* the character Words describes language as if it were water passing through the faucet of his mouth; when he begins speaking he says "I turn on" and when he ends, "I turn off." Although these same terms could refer to a radio dial, the water imagery is enhanced by metaphors about sailing (e.g., "oars," "sea . . . louder . . . thunder . . . manes of foam," "heading nowhere . . . for the island"). But while in *Finnegans Wake* menstrual blood and the flow of language move from Kate to ALP to Issy, in Beckett flows of various sorts constantly threaten to stop, and Nature is usually on the verge of freezing or drying up.

In part, this paralysis and constipation might be explained by a difference in the attitude toward women in the two authors[5]—

5. The complicated issues involved, of course, have been treated in a variety

Beckett's fear and loathing vs. Joyce's eventual acceptance and embracing (after working through Stephen's fear and guilt)—and it is noteworthy that there are very few children in Beckett and no loving parental relationships. In Joyce, the artistic Bloom is the new womanly man, and indeed the ideal artist is an androgynous combination of passivity and power, child and god; the artist becomes the mother (Splitter 202). If women are the key to this stark contrast in metaphors for creativity, then Marilyn French's generalization about Joyce's world can be reversed for Beckett. Joyce defines mankind, she writes, as "a feeling, sexual animal cursed and blessed with intellect. . . . Feelings and sexuality are problems, true, but because of the 'unremitting' and 'hornmad' intellect" (French 53). For Beckett, man is an intellectual, philosophical being cursed with feelings and sexuality (always represented by Woman)—indeed, cursed with a physical body that he must tie down or quiet down in order to come alive in his head.

While Joyce's characters have fairly natural bodily functions as they eliminate and narrate ("There's a touch of the artist in old Bloom" even as he sits on the pot), Beckett's characters are warped or stalled in various ways. Yet what else would we expect in a fictional cosmos where, as Molloy explains, people are born from the arse? Molloy himself produces an enormous number of farts (which he counts with Beckettian precision); yet no "globe" of art, no coherent report or story is produced from them. In *How It Is* the narrator admits that his phrases make up only "a fart fraught with meaning issuing through the mouth no sound" (26). Beckett has written that his work "is a matter of fundamental sounds, made as fully as possible," and we can hear a pun in both "matter" and "fundament."

Krapp in *Krapp's Last Tape* has renounced romantic love in order to produce his "Magnum Opus" which sells all of 17 copies; he is literally a constipated artist who cannot crap (he delights in the word "spool" which, of course, echoes "stool") and worsens his problem by compulsively eating bananas (the cure for just the

of ways. For the Beckettian side, see my "Clods, Whores, and Bitches: Misogyny in Beckett's Early Fiction," in Linda Ben-Zvi, ed., *Women in Beckett: Gender and Genre*. For the Joyce side, see Suzette Henke and Elaine Unkeless, *Women in Joyce* or Bonnie Kime Scott, *Joyce and Feminism*.

opposite condition). The Mouth in "Not I" seems to alternate between streams of verbal diarrhea and the constipation of long periods of silence. In this she resembles the author himself, argues H. Porter Abbott (219–38), for Beckett, like his female protagonist Mouth, was "coming up to seventy" as he was writing the play, and, thus, the work reveals Beckett's sense of alternating between inexplicable verbal paralysis and unbearable and almost involuntary spurts of writing. Beckett apparently felt constrained by fits of silence disturbed when unsummoned voices (like the mysterious and clamoring "they" of *The Unnamable*) would dictate in his ear and demand him to play scribe.

Malone Dies stands at about the midpoint of Beckett's fiction and is self-consciously yet not incomprehensibly metafictional; lying abed, partially paralyzed, writing a monologue, and trying hard to die—to stop all bodily processes—Malone presents a parodic reversal of the life-affirming Molly Bloom, who does *move* to and from her chamberpot. For these and other reasons *Malone Dies* serves as a useful contrast to Joyce's middle and late fiction. Malone writes about himself as writer and experiments with different protagonists and stories. In the process, he discusses his own bodily fluids and demonstrates the lack of flow of his creative efforts with periodic false starts, dead ends, and white spaces on the page. *Malone Dies* thus provides a revealing counterpart to *Finnegans Wake*: both heroes are in bed for the entire fiction, dreaming or creating. But, again here, the comparison ends since Malone is mostly alone while HCE is surrounded by family, patrons, and the whole family of Man; Joyce's linguistically rich narrative never ends while Beckett's stark and staccato story never really begins. Malone's false starts and frustrated musings echo Joycean concerns about Nature and the body—but permeated with Beckettian negativity and infertility.

Both novels are set in March,[6] the first month of spring, conventionally—and for Joyce—a time of rebirth, but for Beckett a time of eager yearning toward death. *Malone Dies* begins with a spring setting but a wintry resignation:

---

6. John Gordon documents this for *Finnegans Wake*, and indeed shows that it is set on Nora's birthday.

> I shall soon be quite dead at last in spite of all. Perhaps next month.
> Then it will be the month of April. . . . Perhaps I am wrong,
> perhaps I shall survive Saint John the Baptist's Day and even the
> Fourteenth of July, festival of freedom. Indeed I would not put it
> past me to pant on to the Transfiguration, not to speak of the
> Assumption [MD 1].

By the midpoint of the novel, Malone has lasted until the height
of spring, but this brings hellish thoughts and only ironic fertility:
"For I believe I have now reached what is called the month of
May, I don't know why, I mean why I believe that, for May
comes from Maia, hell, I remember that too, goddess of increase
and plenty . . ." (60). (May is also used ironically and sarcastically
at the beginning of the play *Words and Music:* "Opener [*Cold.*] It is
the month of May . . . for me. . . . Yes, correct the month of
May. You know, the reawakening.") By the end of *Malone Dies*,
again trying to place himself in time, the narrator describes even
the sun as negative, and once more associates springtime with
hell: "The sun was dragging itself up, dispatching on its way what
perhaps would be, thanks to it, a glorious May or April day, April
more likely, it is doubtless the Easter week-end, spent by Jesus in
hell" (111). On the last pages Lady Pedal (an old and ironic flower
petal?) encourages the inmates to sing a song celebrating spring,
hope, and the resurrection of Christ, yet the only response is that
one patient vomits.

For HCE, springtime and dreaming of the past hold death at
bay. Both staying vigorous—and thus preventing a takeover by
his sons—and fantasizing about his young and lively daughter are
rejuvenating activities, but for Malone, in the Beckettian reversal
of natural processes, it is dying that is difficult and diligent work—
partially expressed through the difficulty of writing. This agony
is shown in sentences that Beckett critics like to describe as self-
canceling: "I could die to-day, if I wished, merely by making a
little effort, if I could wish, if I could make an effort" (1). Just the
opposite of a Wakian sentence that builds, accumulates, layers,
extends, expands, or explodes, the Malonian sentence implodes (a
favorite Beckett concept) and often gropes to say nothing as the
hero strives for his own absence—stories "lifeless, like the teller"
(2). Later Malone observes that "my notes have a curious ten-

dency, as I realize at last, to annihilate all they purport to record"
(88).

When he does achieve death, it will imply neither a fertile burial
in an embracing earth nor a cyclical rebirth but rather a final
expulsion from his mother the earth: Malone is "far already from
the world that parts at last its labia and lets me go" (12). Like
other Beckett characters, Malone is far also from the world of
Nature—distanced from the physical world and from his own
physical body. Sapo, one projection of Malone, rather than being
affected by natural cycles, experiences a dislocation from Nature,
even though he is the son of a farmer: "He confused the birds with
one another, and the trees, and could not tell one crop from
another crop. He did not associate the crocus with the spring nor
the chrysanthemum with Michaelmas. The sun, the moon, the
planets and the stars did not fill him with wonder" (14). By
contrast, of course, each character in *Finnegans Wake* is not merely
identified with, but virtually *identical* to, a natural feature: Howth
Head, River Liffey, rainbow, land, water, stone, tree, etc. While
Joyce's world is more awakening than funereally waking, filled
with the eternal cycles of weather—thunder, rain, river, sea—
Malone's cosmos, like *Endgame*'s environment of "gray" and
"zero" is stopped, stilled, dry: "Dead world, airless, waterless.
That's it, reminisce. Here and there, in the bed of a crater, the
shadow of a withered lichen" (MD 26). Similarly, Malone is also
estranged from the liturgical cycle—"Can it be Easter Week?"—
and neither spring nor resurrection brings renewal. Only absolute
death affords hope and joy: "The end of a life is always vivifying"
(37).

For both Sapo and Malone a favorite element of Nature is the
gull, perhaps because it lives off death—"swoop ravening about
the offal" (56). Death becomes a distorted, grotesque, macabre
parody of birth: "I am being given, if I may venture the expression, birth to into death, such is my impression. The feet are clear
already, of the great cunt of existence. Favorable presentation I
trust. My head will be the last to die" (114). Earlier in his
(mythic?) life, Malone had the power to consume the hours: "I
was time, I devoured the world" (26). Shem as the cad might
argue the same, and he would demonstrate this by his victory over
the father through time, essentially beginning a new cycle by

warning HCE that it is twelve o'clock; his time is up. But (not split into son *and* father; not creating his own renewal) a Beckettian man changes for the worse as he ages, Malone laments, and (similar here to ALP, but with no ricorso) suggests an image of man as a water drop drying and vanishing: "you have all old age before you, and then the lingers of evaporation, a drop in the ocean" (59). While ALP even in old age is still a flowing river, in *Malone Dies* the fluids harden, and time is strictly linear and terminal. Malone sees the world as a huge hourglass with time diminishing—"I feel at last that the sands are running out"—and later senses that he himself is petrifying into a speck of sand: "To speak for example of the times when I go liquid and become like mud, what good would that do? Or of the others when I would be lost in the eye of a needle, I am so hard and contracted? No, those are well-meaning squirms that get me nowhere" (51).

If the Joycean artist is God-like, powerful, the Beckettian artist is god-damned and pathetic; the prose and the body, corpus and corpse, wear down and dry up simultaneously. Malone's method of composition is to capitalize on weakness—"I gave rein to my pains, my impotence" (35)—and like Beckett, reveling in his impotence as writer, he touts his own ineffectiveness: "My body is what is called, unadvisedly perhaps, impotent. There is virtually nothing it can do" (8). In general, Malone is literally out of touch with his own body—he cannot feel his feet, cannot see his penis— and finally stops eating altogether when the bowls of soup no longer arrive: "Now that I have stopped eating I produce less waste and so eliminate less" (80). He concomitantly produces, expresses, less prose. Soon after this he loses his stick, escalates and rushes the story of Macmann, one of his projections, and then finishes him off. But while Macmann was still with us, he was not with himself; he does not realize, "any more than if he had been a crate of tomatoes," that parts of the body are "intimately and even indissolubly bound up together" (66). Predictably, Macmann too is impotent, infertile, and childless: "his semen had never done any harm to anyone" (68).

While both old men are strangers to their phalluses now, Malone is even distanced from that most intimate of activities, his own defecating: "if my arse suddenly started to shit at the present moment, which God forbid, I firmly believe the lumps would fall out in Australia" (61–62). A similar dislocation warps Malone's prose: "my fingers too write in other latitudes . . . so that the subject falls far from the verb and the object lands somewhere in the void . . ." (61). Since he cannot reach his pot, he is forced to urinate in bed like a baby (83) and now the body feeds on itself: "Water, for pity's sake! How is it I am not thirsty. There must be drinking going on inside me, my secretions" (104). The body has become a self-contained biological system (like Joseph Heller's darkly comic Soldier in White in *Catch-22* whose nourishment and elimination bottles are daily reversed) parallel to Beckett's linguistically and narratively self-contained systems in the late fiction, like *The Lost Ones* and *Fizzles*. By the end of *Malone Dies* we meet a reincarnation of Murphy, who was yet another example of a closed system (or one who aspired to be, like the solipsistic Mr. Endon, meaning "within"): this patient neither eats nor defecates; he is "dead young" (MD 112), as static and impotent as Malone.

For Joyce as well as for many other writers the pen is phallic, yet in Malone's case it is a minuscule and dwindling pencil—and not even a male one. His stick—sometimes confused with his pencil—seems a castrated eunuch: "What my stick lacks is a little prehensile proboscis like the nocturnal tapir's." His "little" pencil, too stub-like to have any length, becomes a small bosom for a grown infant, since it has a point at either end and "I use the two points turn and turn about [like two nipples], sucking them frequently, I love to suck." Specifically, it is a "Venus" pencil, yet neither the goddess of love nor any other goddess serves as Muse or inspiration for his writing. Indeed, Malone has trouble with every aspect of the novel—characterization, plot, setting: for example, "A stream at long intervals bestrid—but to hell with all this fucking scenery" (108). Just as important (and un-Joycean), Malone has never experienced, therefore does not recognize, and therefore cannot dramatize, one of the staples of the narrative, romantic love:

> Perhaps they are cold, that they rub against each other so. . . . It is all very pretty and strange, this big complicated shape made up of more than one, for perhaps there are three of them and how it sways and totters, but rather poor in colour. . . . So it is not cold

they are, standing so lightly clad by the open window. Ah how
stupid I am, I see what it is, they must be loving each other, that
must be how it is done [65].

Reclining in his lonely bed, recalling his pseudo-erotic episodes
with the unappealing Moll, Malone appears even more as a comic
mirror image of Molly Bloom as she daydreams of Boylan—and
spins out her own world. Molly cannot seem to stop flowing,
creating, while Malone cannot begin; he produces not exuberantly
but reluctantly: "I did not want to write, but had to resign myself
to it in the end" (32). And the body evinces a similar lack of
production: his "sex" no longer spouts the fluid of procreation
and can barely urinate, whereas Molly flows from every possible
aperture and plans to make (potentially fertile) eggs in the morning. Opposite of the eternally young Molly, Malone is "an old
foetus . . . hoar and impotent . . . [remembering] all the stories
I've told myself, clinging to the putrid mucus" (51).

His love interest, Moll (a stunted Molly? a tough moll?), is as
"impotent" as Macmann and Malone, and their lovemaking is
described as not exactly fluid and fertile: "they finally succeeded,
summoning to their aid all the resources of the skin, the mucus
and the imagination, in striking from their dry and feeble clips a
kind of sombre gratification" (89). As Moll writes in one of her
famous love letters, "It's all these bones that makes it awkward,
that I grant you" (91). Macmann in his turn composes several
romantic lyrics, "all remarkable for their exaltation of love regarded as a kind of *lethal glue*" (92; emphasis added). What is truly
lethal, however, is not their love (although something does termi-
nate Moll at the height of their affair), but Malone's mock phallic
pencil, which at the end of Macmann's saga transforms itself into
a hatchet, used to kill off most of the characters. Just the opposite
of the continually potent pen and the endlessly proliferating and
eternally recycling personages of the *Wake*, *Malone Dies* ends with
Lemuel (cf. Samuel Beckett) raising the hatchet/hammer/stick
while Malone fades out in jagged phrases like a broken radio. The
artist, after silencing the body, has silenced himself.

The dying natural world of the Beckett protagonist/narrator is
matched by a shrinking, condensed linguistic universe. Unlike the
artist as a portrait of Shem, borrowing words, stealing phrases,

ingesting ideas, creating ink from decreation/defecation, and writing in epic proportions ("an epical forged cheque"), the Beckettian artist strives for fewer and fewer words, for lessness (echoing the title of one of Beckett's later fictions). We might recall one of Beckett's explanations for switching to the French language: because, he said, English is too rich, whereas in French it is possible to write "sans style." Since the ultimate goal is absence and silence (pure thought), then the minimum number of words with the minimum meaning must be sought. Malone guards against any verbal excess: "I know those little phrases that seem so innocuous and, once you let them in, pollute the whole of speech. *Nothing is more real than nothing*" (16). Of course, in Joyce that "pollutant" is prolific and positive, and in the *Wake* even a single properly placed letter or syllable can multiply meanings. Despairing about the pollution of language, the nameless hero of *Texts for Nothing* accepts the verbal inevitability: "wordshit, bury me," he laments. If words are shit, they are not the stuff of creation as in Joyce, but crap to transcend. Traditional fiction in *Malone Dies* is "all this ballsaching poppycock about life and death" (51) and must be avoided if the true self is to be uncovered.

With the next stage in Beckett's trilogy of novels, *The Unnamable*, characters do not even pretend to be fictionalized people but instead are "mannikins." Deprived of physical movement and narrative action, The Unnamable himself is stuck in a jar and psychologically stuck in a catch-22 paradox: he cannot die properly because he was never fully born. Not part of the natural cycle since they live either in the pre-natal or the post-mortem state (like the curled, fetal corpses of *Imagination Dead Imagine*), Beckett's later characters are totally divorced from normal physical, bodily processes as well. The Unnamable and Mouth (in *Not I*) almost succeed in becoming pure voice, but no one achieves the complete stoppage of mental flow.

The last work that at all resembles a novel, *How It Is*, presents an intriguing example of Beckett's use of bodily fluids, for here, as in Joyce's "Lestrygonians" chapter, the structure is peristaltic; the "primeval mud" of the setting is actually feces. As William Hutchings argues, "the narrator (and by extension every human being) is a turd in the cosmic digestive process of time" (65). If we take one of Malone's comments literally, we can view *How It*

Is as an extreme state of *Malone Dies*: he interrupts a digression with "In any case here I am back in the shit" (MD 98). Although Malone says that to be "buried in lava" is a blessing, he also argues that the head is "the seat of all the shit and misery" (97) and that is why it must be clubbed to death. In *How It Is* the muddy, intestinal decay is both food and elimination, and thus body and cosmos become one (Hutchings 73). If fecal matter is a metaphor for all existence for both Beckett and Joyce, the Beckettian artist must write despite the shit, whereas Shem writes *with* it. While Shem is a "shit" in a positive sense, that is, an artist, all men are simply worthless turds in Beckett's fiction. Malone asks about Macmann (mankind), "Who is this shite anyhow, he said, any of you poor buggers happen to know?" (115). The muckheap of life from *Waiting for Godot* does not provide the inspiration of a letter, the beginnings of literature, as in the *Wake*'s middenheap, but is rather an obstacle that must be crawled around or through— especially in *How It Is* where movement and syntax are both "piecemeal"—since writing for Beckett is analogous to groping through a difficult terrain.

In Beckett's late prose fragments, Nature has disappeared from the face of the fiction, replaced by highly artificial structures like cylinders, domes, and, in his penultimate story, *Ill Seen Ill Said* (1982), "a zone of stones," perhaps representing the sterility of metafiction. The metaphor of bodily processes for artistic output becomes most precise when Beckett has the narrator of *Ill Seen Ill Said* explain that his words are produced "strangury," an unusual condition of the urinary tract whereby urine is emitted only drop by drop and with great pain. Sentences accrue here only hesitantly, word by tortured word. By the last paragraph, if the narrator does carry on the metaphorical functions of eating and eliminating, it is certainly not to create an overflowing Joycean world but, rather, a dessicated, static Beckettian void: "Grant only enough remain to devour all. Moment by glutton moment. Sky earth the whole kit and boodle. Not another crumb of carrion left. Lick chops and basta" (59).

In *Worstward Ho*, the last fiction, the flow of better words is impossible, and only sparse and "worse" ones are desired so that all verbal movement may cease to "go on." Here the language of fluids recedes to the "ooze" of the brain; and, in a parody of literary fullness, an ooze of minimal phrases remains after narrative no longer flows. Beckett's metafiction spurts out, no verbal flow, risking only single, discrete adjectives to describe—not a character—but merely a fleeting shade:

> Somehow again on back to the bowed back alone. Nothing to show a woman's and yet a woman's. Oozed from softening soft the word woman's. The words old woman's. The words nothing to show bowed back alone a woman's and yet a woman's. So better worse from now that shade a woman's. An old woman's [35].

By the end of *Worstward Ho* even the mental ooze threatens to dry up, like the desert environment of *The Lost Ones* where baked mucous membranes make the act of love an act of painful assault:

> Ooze back try worsen blanks. Those then when nohow on. Unsay then all gone. All not gone. Only nohow on. All not gone and nohow on. All there as now when somehow on. The dim. The void. The shades. Only words gone. Ooze gone. Till ooze again and on. Somehow ooze on [WH 39].

Finally the cosmos of the Beckettian fiction is reduced to pinholes, first "two black holes in foreskull," the two eyes leading from the outside world (what is left of it) to the gray matter of the brain: "Dim black. In through skull to soft. Out from soft through skull" (44). Then even this is too much, so two eyes give way to one Cyclops-like orb: "Or one. Try better still worse one. One dim black hole mid-foreskull. Into the hell of all. Out from the hell of all." Reminiscent of the dot of ink at the end of "Ithaca," Beckett's hole, unlike Molly's asshole (as some critics have interpreted the inky spot) does not lead to any flow of language or creativity. These "black holes" echo the "white dwarfs" in his "For to End Yet Again" from *Fizzles*, astronomical metaphors suggesting the implosion of stars leading to the heat death of the universe, a realm of cold. While the narrator of *Worstward Ho* concludes with "Back hole agape on all. Inletting all. Outletting all" (45), there *is* no "all"; with his verbs of "inletting" and "outletting" he gives the illusion of flow—of blood, of perception, of expression—but this is a cruel hoax on the reader. Beckett has constricted his world from ill-seen and ill-said details to nothing seen and nothing said. Beckett's black hole presents an endpoint while Joyce's represents the inked opening into Molly's (and later ALP's) flow.

Especially in Beckett's later prose, the breakdown of bodily processes parallels a diminishment of the artistic function, a reduction signaled best in the titles of these ever more condensed and impacted fictions from *Texts for Nothing* to *Worstward Ho.* In particular, *Fizzles* is the English version of the French "*foirades,*" which can mean false starts, but which Beckett defines as "little farts"—not a fully formed "globe" of a turd as in *Ulysses* but a fizzled-out precursor of a novel. Conversely, in Joyce's last and fullest fiction, *Finnegans Wake,* an elaborate story is drawn out of a letter found on a muckheap, and the artist-figure Shem writes prolifically with an ink made from his own crap. Beckett himself contrasted the two writers and their methods: Joyce was a can-er, the more he produced the more he was able to produce (until his fictional cosmos subsumed all language into a riverrun, then into mother/father sea) while he, by contrast, was a non–can-er, working out of ignorance and incompetence. With the American slang in mind of "can" as "pot" as, so to speak, "crapper," Beckett's depiction of himself as a non-can-er takes us back to constipation as a metaphor for his constricted writing.

Beckett's non–movement has a philosophical impetus and stylistic consequences, and the real starting point is his first novel, *Murphy*. Here characters have an interest not in fertile turds but in sterile surds (irrational numbers). Rather than bodily processes integrated with the larger world of natural processes (Bloom's world and Molly's), Murphy strives for an ideal of "Belacqua bliss," away from the distractions of human emotion, best achieved when he is motionless in his rocking chair:

> neither elements nor states, nothing but forms becoming and crumbling into the fragments of a new becoming, without love or hate or any intelligible principle of change. . . . He did *not move*, he was a point in the ceaseless unconditioned generation and passing away of line.
>
> Matrix of surds [112; emphasis added].

Beckett characters from Murphy on have been stuck in thought, constipated through excessive meditation and not enough narrative. They cannot move their legs, their bowels, or their mental positions; they are stymied by Cartesian doubt, by all the hesitations and hiatuses between body and mind. Afflicted (much more strongly than the young Stephen Dedalus was) by the full range of classic writer's block, simple stalling, and profound philosophical misgiving about the nature of the self and about the power of language, Beckett's narrators can neither create character nor move from creatures to story. Their constipated productions come out "piecemeal," like the prose in *How It Is*. And their style both embodies and prolongs constriction: a style of repetition (to paraphrase a line from Beckett's first poem, "Whoroscope," that's not moving; that's *not moving*), of paradox and self-destruction (which can block or kill a sentence), and of punning (which suspends the reader between two different meanings).[7] Features of impossibility, paradox, and constraint can be seen most clearly in *Imagination Dead Imagine* from the title on; and in *The Lost Ones* physical, syntactic, and critical paths become dead ends with "no way out"—no pun where none intended.

These substantive and stylistic paradoxes lead to the larger paradox that Beckett saw as the predicament of the modern artist: he is left with the "expression that there is nothing to express, nothing with which to express, nothing from which to express, no power to express, no desire to express, together with the obligation to express" (*Disjecta* 139). No wonder, then, that the Beckettian narrator/protagonist can neither defecate nor create, neither purge nor ex-press.

Works Cited

Abbott, H. Porter. "A Poetics of Radical Diplacement: Samuel Beckett Coming Up to Seventy." *Texas Studies in Literature and Language* 17 (Spring 1975): 219–38.

Auden, W. H. *Forewords and Afterwords.* Ed. Edward Mendelson. New York: Random House, 1973.

Boyle, Robert, s.j. *"Finnegans Wake,* Page 185: An Explication." *James Joyce Quarterly* 4 (Fall 1966): 3–16.

7. For more on the piecemeal style of Beckett's later fictions, see my *Samuel Beckett's New Worlds: Style in Metafiction.*

Brienza, Susan. "Clods, Whores, and Bitches: Misogyny in Beckett's Early Fiction." *Women in Beckett: Gender and Genre*. Ed. Linda Ben-Zvi. Urbana: University of Illinois Press, 1991. 91–105.

———. "Murphy, Shem, Morpheus, and Murphies: 'Eumaeus' Meets the *Wake*," *Joycean Occasions*. Ed. Janet E. Dunleavy, Melvin J. Friedman, and Michael P. Gillespie. Newark: University of Delaware Press, 1991. 80–94.

———. *Samuel Beckett's New Worlds: Style in Metafiction*. Norman: University of Oklahoma Press, 1987.

Brivic, Sheldon. *Joyce Between Freud and Jung*. Port Washington, N.Y.: Kennikat Press, 1980.

Card, James Van Dyck. "The Ups and Downs, Ins and Outs of Molly Bloom: Patterns of Words in 'Penelope.' " *James Joyce Quarterly* 19 (Winter 1982): 127–39.

Cheng, Vincent. " 'Goddinpotty': James Joyce and the Literature of Excrement." Paper given at the James Joyce Symposium in Venice, June 1988.

French, Marilyn. *The Book as World: James Joyce's "Ulysses."* Cambridge: Harvard University Press, 1976.

Gordon, John. *Finnegans Wake: A Plot Summary*. Syracuse: Syracuse University Press, 1986.

Henke, Suzette, and Elaine Unkeless, eds. *Women in Joyce*. Urbana: University of Illinois Press, 1982.

Hutchings, William. " 'Shat into Grace,' Or A Tale of a Turd: Why It Is How It Is in Samuel Beckett's *How It Is*." *Papers on Language and Literature* 21 (Winter 1985): 64–87.

Maddox, Brenda. *Nora: The Real Life of Molly Bloom*. Boston: Houghton Mifflin, 1988.

Norris, Margot. "Joyce's Heliotrope." *Coping with Joyce*. Ed. Morris Beja and Shari Berstock. Columbus: Ohio State University Press, 1989.

Scott, Bonnie Kime. *Joyce and Feminism*. Bloomington: Indiana University Press, 1984.

Splitter, Randolph. "Water Words: Language, Sexuality, and Motherhood in Joyce's Fiction." *ELH* 49 (Spring 1982): 190–213.

Tucker, Lindsey. *Stephen and Bloom at Life's Feast: Alimentary Symbolism and the Creative Process in James Joyce's "Ulysses."* Columbus: Ohio State University Press, 1984.

10

Authorship, Authority, and Self-Reference in Joyce and Beckett

Steven Connor

MANY ACCOUNTS OF THE RELATIONSHIP between Joyce and Beckett stress the curious interweaving in it of dependence and resentment, similarity and divergence, some seeing it as an exemplification of the operations of an artistic Oedipal struggle. As Alan Astro suggests, the issues of control and freedom that this raises are replicated in the relationship of each writer to his language and the political history that it seems to embody.[1] But the issues of control and freedom, authority and responsibility involve more than just language; they are important in accounting for the writer's relationship to his work and to the interpretations of his work, the question of control being extended for both writers outside and beyond the act of writing itself. This relates in turn to the issue of self-reflexiveness, which has become so important in Joyce and Beckett studies, for it enables us to ask what sort of attitude toward the work of art and its authority and influence does the self-reflection of Joyce's and Beckett's work embody? In the end, the work of both writers seems to provoke questions of the literary–critical activity that constitutes it, suggesting the nature and limits of the authority that criticism in its turn exercises.

The stress on the individual relationship of Joyce and Beckett sometimes means that the particular artistic and cultural context in which they came together is forgotten. The Paris of the late 1920s, though it had passed through its most vigorously avant-garde phase, was still a center of new and challenging artistic

---

1. Alan Astro, in his unpublished paper "The Language of the Master and the Mastery of Language in Joyce and Beckett" draws upon Hegel's master/slave dialectic to discuss Beckett's relationship to his native and adopted languages.

activity and production, providing a meeting-place for Anglo-American and Continental traditions. The work of Joyce and Beckett is framed interestingly by the avant-garde aesthetics of these years and in particular by the aesthetics of Dada and surrealism. The particular feature of these aesthetics upon which I want to focus is the tension maintained in them between control and freedom. For the surrealists, the artist needed to escape from the constraints of logic or rationality not in order merely to destroy them but in order to reconstitute their authority at a different level, the level of dream, symbol, or the unconscious. For André Breton in particular, the dissolution of conscious control was intended to allow the authority of the Freudian unconscious to assert itself. And what is described repeatedly in surrealist writings is the way in which the loosing of one kind of power, the power of reason, by the foregrounding of randomness or change, actually brings to light a more profound unity or design in the work of art. Louis Aragon, as quoted in Maurice Nadeau's *The History of Surrealism* (88), describes the effect of the automatic writing of the Dadaists and surrealists:

> "What strikes them is a power that they did not know that they had, an incomparable freedom, a liberation of the mind, an unprecedented production of images, and the supernatural tone of their writings. They recognize, in everything they produce in this fashion, without feeling that they are responsible for it, the incomparable quality of the few books, the few words that still move them. They suddenly realize a great poetic unity that proceeds from the prophetic books of all peoples to *Les Illuminations* and *Les Chants de Maldoror*. Between the lines, they read the incomplete confessions of those who once *maintained the system*: in the light of their discovery, *Une Saison en Enfer* sheds its riddles, along with the Bible and several other confessions of man that lay hidden under their masks of images."

The conviction of an underlying basis of control in chance or randomness is stated neatly in the phrase from Hume that Paul Eluard adapted for the definition of "hasard" in his surrealist dictionary—"equivalent de l'ignorance dans laquelle nous nous trouvons par rapport aux causes réelles des évenements"[2]—and in Tristan Tzara's famous formula for writing a poem:

2. This definition was not incorporated in the published form of the diction-

"Take a newspaper. Take a pair of scissors. Choose an article as long as you are planning to make your poem. Cut out the article. Then cut out each of the words that make up this article and put them in a bag. Shake it gently. Then take out the scraps one after the other in the order in which they left the bag. Copy conscientiously. The poem will be like you" [quoted in Rosemont 78].

Joyce's method, with the inclusiveness of its parodic and citational modes, seems to exemplify something like this withdrawal of artistic authority. Of course, all the time there is a balancing-act taking place, as Joyce effaces himself as an authorial presence and yet silently cooperates with and ratifies every element of the text. This is surely what is suggested most strongly by the famous story, first told by Richard Ellmann, of Joyce's incorporation of the words "come in" in the text of *Finnegans Wake* after being interrupted by a knock on the door. Here, in what seems to be a typical sequence, Joyce surrenders himself to the contingent, only to re-establish artistic control by licensing it. It is this dialectic between release and control that makes Joyce's works representative of their period, and explains, for example, the attraction that *Work in Progress* had for Eugene Jolas. In his "Revolution of the Word" manifesto, Jolas sees the destruction of " 'the hegemony of the banal word' " as leading to a different kind of autonomy, the autonomy of the imagination (quoted in Ellmann 588), and, like Aragon, looks to mystical writing as a precedent for this inspired unconscious writing. In his essay on Joyce in *Our Exagmination Round His Factification for Incamination of Work in Progress*, Jolas expresses a similar duality, arguing, on the one hand, that Joyce is a revolutionary artist in "exploding the antique logic of words," but claiming, on the other, that he is really a traditional writer since this is what all writers have always sought to do anyway. So, again, the revolutionary dissolution of control only uncovers another binding structure in the idea of the continuing tradition of literature.

Beckett's early critical writing makes similar claims for the

ary, the *Dictionnaire abregé du surréalisme* (Paris: Galerie Beaux-Arts, 1938), but is to be found in Eluard's manuscript drafts for it, held by the Humanities Research Center in Austin, Texas. I am grateful to Lynn Nead for bringing my attention to this entry and for interesting and helpful discussions of the material of this paper.

necessity of breaking down language. For Beckett, language is part of the carapace of habit, which insulates us from the condition of our real being. As such it must either be destroyed or be transformed. In his essay on *Work in Progress*, Beckett stresses Joyce's achievement in the latter: "Here is the savage economy of hieroglyphics. Here words are not the polite contortions of 20th century printer's ink. They are alive. They elbow their way on to the page, and glow and blaze and fade and disappear" (*Disjecta* 28).

Beckett's emphasis here is on the return to the primitive fullness of language and as such has something in common with the contemporary avant-garde aesthetics, which proclaimed that language was to be both destroyed and surrendered to in order to produce the energetic autonomy of the word, which is evoked here. Beckett tends to lay stress on the surrender of artistic control, but the tension between freedom and authority persists. The Shenker "interview" explores this tension: " 'The kind of work I do is one in which I'm not master of my material. The more Joyce knew the more he could. He's tending toward omniscience and omnipotence as an artist. I'm working with impotence, ignorance. I don't think impotence has been exploited in the past' " (Shenker 3). As Alan Astro has observed, the interesting thing about the formulation here is that it simultaneously involves passivity and struggle; Beckett is both working with ignorance (in the sense of working *in* ignorance) and working *with* it, turning impotence to account by exploiting it (see Astro, note 1 above). The dialectic between control and surrender can be found elsewhere in Beckett's sparse critical writings, as in the first dialogue with Georges Duthuit about Tal Coat, in which Beckett speaks (dismissively) of the "submission" or "mastery" in the painter's representation of nature or when he praises Jack B. Yeats for his "final mastery which submits in trembling to the unmasterable" (*Disjecta* 138, 149).

What changes in Beckett's writing—and what may be seen as a mark of his move away from Joyce's influence—is the sense of what kind of freedom might be obtainable from the surrender or destruction of conventional forms of language and experience. For Joyce, as for the young Beckett, familiar structures of authority are experienced as a limitation on the freedom of the individual self, epitomized in the Romantic figure of the lone artist, in Stephen Dedalus as, in the dominant reading of *A Portrait of the Artist as a Young Man*, he struggles to free himself from the clinging nets of Irish cultural, religious, and political life. The young Beckett sees that what is necessary is not just the destruction of habitual forms of existence, but also the surrender of rational control. Beckett's Proust is characterized by the "Romantic" humility with which he surrenders himself to the disintegrating flux of time, as opposed to classicist attempts to control time:

> The classical artist assumes omniscience and omnipotence. He raises himself artificially out of Time in order to give relief to his chronology and causality to his development. Proust's chronology is extremely difficult to follow, the succession of events spasmodic and his characters and themes, although they seem to obey an almost insane inward necessity, are presented and developed with a fine Dostoievskian contempt for the vulgarity of a plausible con-catenation [PR 62].

We should note, once again, that the relinquishment of control actually produces or reveals a different, underlying control, the "almost insane inward necessity" of Proust's writing. Beckett seems to be predicting here the movement of his own later work, in which the collapse of control and the dissolution of narrative superstructure reveal the obsessive "inward necessity" of the mon-ologue. But there is also an important distinction already apparent between Joyce's and Beckett's attitudes to authority and freedom. Where Joyce's early works seem to promise the gradual attainment of a free, or potentially free, selfhood, the escape from authority in Beckett's works seems to allow little hope of such an attain-ment. *Murphy* may be seen as a kind of inverted *Künstlerroman* or *Bildungsroman*, and so almost a reply to *A Portrait of the Artist as a Young Man*; far from surmounting and transmuting the impedi-ments that the external world ranges against him, Murphy merely withdraws into the indefinite freedom of his mind, which offers no resistance against the authority of the external except the consolation of dissolution. Similarly, Victor Krap, in Beckett's unpublished play *Eleuthéria,* finds freedom from the constrictive apparatus of bourgeois life only in death.

Correspondingly, where Beckett seeks to undermine literary

language, it is not, like Joyce, in order to rediscover its secret vitality but simply to dissolve the tyranny of language *tout court*. Beckett's assaults on convention lack the liberating ambitions of Joyce's rejection of conventional narrative and linguistic structure and therefore lack the political focus of Joyce's project. When he describes his desire to undermine language in his 1937 letter to Axel Kaun, the process does not seem designed to reveal some higher reality or imaginative synthesis of reality: "As we cannot eliminate language all at once, we should at least leave nothing undone that might contribute to its falling into disrepute. To bore one hole after another in it, until what lurks behind it—be it something or nothing—begins to seep through; I cannot imagine a higher goal for a writer today" (*Disjecta* 172)

For all the aggressive clarity of the destructive project outlined here, Beckett's view of the relationship between artist and work is much less certain and confident than Joyce's. In Joyce's formulation, the artist's relation to his works can be imaged and set forth in a regular and consistent metaphorical topography; the artist first "prolongs and broods upon himself as the centre of an epical event," then moves further away from it, so that "the centre of emotional gravity is equidistant from the artist himself and from others," and then, finally, retreats into complete invisibility (although this produces a multiple positioning of the artist "within or behind or beyond or above his handiwork" [P 214–15]). Beckett seems to be replying to and complicating these positionalities of artist and work in a dense passage from his unpublished novel *Dream of Fair to Middling Women*:

> The tense passional intelligence, when arithmetic abates, tunnels, skymole, surely and blindly (if we only thought so!) through the interstellar coalsacks of its firmament in genesis, it twists through the stars of its creation in a network of loci that shall never be co-ordinate. The inviolable criterion of poetry and music, the non-principle of their punctuation is figured in the demented perforation of the night colander. The ecstatic mind, the mind achieving creation, take ours for example, rises to the shaft-heads of its statement, its recondite relations of emergal, from a labour and a weariness of deep castings that brook no schema. The mind suddenly entombed, then active in an anger and a rhapsody of energy, in a scurrying and plunging towards exitus, such is the ultimate

mode and factor of the creative integrity, its proton, incommunicable; but there, insistent, invisible rat, fidgeting behind the astral incoherence of the art surface [*Disjecta* 44–45].

Here the relationship of the artist to his work resists spatialization. The mind of the artist "tunnels" in two directions, ratlike into the ground and mystically toward the sky, and is diffused among its "loci." All, one might say, following Beckett's account of the third zone of Murphy's mind, is "commotion, and the pure forms of commotion" (MU 79). Though he plunges toward "exitus," the artist abides invisibly in his work, not in the mode of immanence but as a verminous residue, the "insistent, invisible rat," which is no guarantee of the text's coherence but the reflex of its incoherence.

In the cases of both Joyce and Beckett, such questions of selfhood, authorship, and authority are crucially identified with the question of the self-referential autonomy of the text. The modernist assertion of autonomy is perhaps an effect of and compensation for an actual marginalization of artistic practice, an attempt to reclaim the artwork from its condition as commodity by, as it were, raising the stakes on alienation to assert the unconditioned priority of its own poetic and linguistic substance. The presence/absence dialectic of the Joycean aesthetic of authorial immanence connects with this. Necessarily abstracted from the production and distribution of his product and aware of the alienated nature of artistic production (and no author has ever felt more than Joyce the gap between the omnipotence of the creator and his humble dependence on the vicissitudes of book production), the modernist artist makes of that very exile a kind of authority. The work of art is therefore anonymously "itself" and yet also by that token signed through every syllable by the absent author.

Again, we need to make a distinction between Joyce and Beckett. Where Joyce's texts, and accounts of them, seem to claim the authority of autotelic self-reference, Beckett finds little consolation in this particular circularity. In a discussion of the painter Bram van Velde in the *Dialogues with Georges Duthuit,* Beckett argues that van Velde's work is utterly free of the intention to represent, free of any external "occasion." When Duthuit suggests that "the occasion of his painting is his predicament, and that it is expressive of the impossibility to express," Beckett rejects this neat alternative. Van Velde's work somehow negates even self-representation and so is deprived of—or set free from—even the temporary authority that this gives:

> Others have felt that art is not necessarily expression. But the numerous attempts made to make painting independent of its occasion have only succeeded in enlarging its repertory. I suggest that van Velde is the first whose passivity is bereft, rid if you prefer, of every occasion in every shape and form, ideal as well as material, and the first whose hands have not been tied by the certitude that expression is an impossible act [*Disjecta* 143].

For Beckett, then, the freedom from representation does not confer a necessary authority on the work of art in itself. If Beckett's self-referential works initiate the postmodern epoch, they do so by shifting the status of self-reference, making it connote poverty and paradox rather than the autonomy of the word.

This theme has been taken up with some alacrity by contemporary critics, who have used the Joyce/Beckett relationship as a metonymy for the whole shift from modernism to postmodernism. Hugh Kenner, whose sympathies lie primarily with the modernist tradition of artistic authority, was writing in these terms as long ago as 1962 when, in *The Stoic Comedians*, he charted the three different kinds of self-referential art associated with Flaubert, Joyce, and Beckett; Beckett, unlike the two other writers, is "the non-maestro, the anti-virtuoso, habitué of non-form and anti-matter, Euclid of the dark zone where all signs are negative, the comedian of utter disaster" (77). Theorists of postmodernity have taken up this theme but have shifted the evaluative priority so that postmodern strategies of decreation are accorded more authority than modernist creation. According to this account, literary works derive their value and authority not through the display and exploration of the specific conditions of their form but from an aesthetics of the sublime that, as set forth influentially by Jean-François Lyotard, "denies itself the solace of good forms . . . which searches for new presentations, not in order to enjoy them, but in order to impart a stronger sense of the unpresentable" (81).

Beckett's works can easily be induced to give exemplary authority to this aesthetic of non-mastery; indeed, such theory tends
increasingly to recruit Joyce's works to itself as when Ihab Hassan,
in *The Postmodern Turn*, argues that *Finnegans Wake* "is not only
supremely aware of itself as structure, it is also aware of the more
obscure need to de-structure itself" (107). These forms of critical
narrative may attempt to deny or wish away the principle of
aesthetic authority in the dimly articulated interest of a more
inclusive or pluralist art but may be blind to the ways in which
structures of authority persist or recur at different levels through
the whole repertory of abandonment. Jean–Michel Rabaté writes,
for example, of the ways in which Joyce's texts cede authority to
the reader, but in Rabaté's formulation, this is a reader who is
supposed always to be cannily aware in advance of his own
imminent discomfiture by the text: "Once I have become, thanks
to *Finnegans Wake*, the author of my reading, I can keep an
awareness of this recurring dissolution in the text, which, far from
comforting my own illusory mastery over texts and meanings,
underlines the fact that I am porous, open to alterity, read and
written in advance by other texts" (88).

Accounts of Beckett, in particular, tend to ignore the importance of his relationships to his texts in material and juridical, as
well as aesthetic, terms; indeed, the analytic separation of the
"external" and "internal" realms of authority within the protocols
of the critical profession make this almost inevitable. The paradox
here is that Beckett visibly exercised a high degree of proprietary
concern and power over a body of texts which consistently claim
the condition of being uncontrolled, unmastered, or without
origin in a responsible or authoritative "I." What focuses these
problems for Beckett in particular are, first, his turn to French,
with the resulting requirement to become his own translator, and,
second, his turn to drama. In both cases, Beckett found himself
no longer able simply to separate himself from his works after
their completion but continued to work with them (and against
them) in various ways. Having to translate prose texts and having
to translate dramatic texts into productions seem to crystallize the
problems of ownership, responsibility, and control that authorship involves. It is interesting to note the ambiguities in Beckett's
attitude to these activities. It is clear that he regarded self-transla-

tion as a weary chore, and indeed one can imagine no better illustration of the kind of alienation from oneself that language can bring about than having to translate one's own words as though they were the words of another. And yet, as self-translator, Beckett allowed himself kinds of freedom that a translator of another could never allow. Where early accounts of Beckett's self-translation stressed his brilliant conservatism in finding equivalents for jokes and wordplay and in maintaining the economy between comedy and pathos, more recent studies have begun to stress the extraordinary differences and variations that Beckett introduced in translating his own work and the complex patterns of authority and insubordination that this forms (see Beer 35–75; see also Connor chap. 4).

There is a similar tension between subservience and independence in Beckett's work as a director. Though extremely faithful to his texts and fiercely demanding of his actors, he was also capable of introducing changes where necessary. His authorial control over interpretation also showed a striking duality; he would sometimes allow, or collaborate with, extraordinary modifications of his work (as with the stitching together of different fragments from various texts for Jack MacGowran's performance of *Beginning to End*), but at other times he would seek to exert the most intense control over the interpretation of a single text (as in the production by the American Repertory Theatre in Cambridge, Massachusetts, of *Endgame,* which he publicly disowned and attempted to suppress).[3]

Beckett's stature in the literary world even put him in an ambiguous position with regard to his own corpus. His career was littered with abandoned, unfinished, and variously unsatisfactory works that endlessly came back to haunt him. Beckett in his later years was in the position of custodian of all those drafts and early works that have ended up in research libraries and are as well known to scholars as his published works. There was no way for Beckett to disown these works, except, perhaps, to exercise continuously vigilant control over them, nowhere to abandon them,

---

3. See the accounts in "Playwright–Director Conflict: Whose Play Is It Anyway?" *New York Law Journal* 193.123 (28 December 1984) and *The Beckett Circle: Newsletter of the Samuel Beckett Society* 6.2 (Spring 1985): 1–3.

except to the care of a critical profession that must endlessly restore them to life.

All this is to suggest that the conditions of production and circulation have become unavoidably implicated in the nature of the works themselves. The metaphors that self-translation and self-direction provide clearly interact with more abstrusely psychological or philosophical themes of self-possession and self-loss in Beckett's work, allowing for a different form of self-reflexivity. Plays like *What Where*, for example, or *Catastrophe* seem to concern the very business of staging a play and to connect the issues of control and authority, which are raised by that staging, with themes of isolation and epistemological uncertainty, while *Ohio Impromptu*, written as an "occasional" piece for an international academic conference on Beckett's work, seems to reflect on the ironies of this very enunciative situation.[4]

This tension between submission and control partially repeats that found in Joyce's texts and his relations to them. As with Beckett, there is an extraordinary contradiction between Joyce's withdrawal from the surface of his text as conspicuous or authoritative narrator and the energy that he devoted to his texts as literary commodities in writing to patrons, arguing with printers, and supervising critical work, like Stuart Gilbert's study of *Ulysses* or the *Exagmination* of *Finnegans Wake*. For Joyce, as for Beckett, withdrawal from the text and the achievement of irresponsibility for it prove impossible.

Nor is this the end of the spiral in which authority is relinquished and regenerated. The work of both Joyce and Beckett has encountered and contributed significantly to the increasingly centralized power of critical institutions and languages in the Western academies. Joyce realized early on, if only in an intuitive way, that his audience was likely to be a professional or semi-professional one and attempted to maintain authority for his texts by monitoring and influencing interpretation. Beckett's strategy for maintaining such authority has been to keep himself entirely aloof from matters of interpretation while holding jealously to the actual

---

4. This is particularly clear in the early drafts of the play which have been reprinted (see Beja appendix). See, too, the account given by Pierre Astier (331–41).

verbal and dramatic substance of his texts. But Beckett's fame,
unlike Joyce's, has been achieved almost entirely under the eye of
the critical institutions that he at first attempted to ignore. It is not
that avant-garde strategies of withdrawal or the eschewal of authority have no longer been possible since the Second World War;
it is that these gestures take place in a critical space that has
become practiced at assimilating them to its own authoritative
procedures. In this respect Beckett's own work and attitudes
toward the question of authority in it may be less important than
we have thought. For the discursive fields that encompass, admin-
ister, publicize, and accredit cultural practice (these include education and the media as well as the institutions of criticism and
research) admit, like Freud's unconscious, of no negativity. Every
gesture of renunciation can become a positive unit of currency to
be discursively circulated and reinvested. In this situation, the
question of the movement from an aesthetic of authority (Joyce)
to an aesthetic of impotence (Beckett) becomes a secondary effect
of the consolidation of disciplines and cultural discourses. The
question, increasingly, may not be whether one lines up behind a
modernist aesthetic of authority or a postmodernist aesthetic of
sublime incompetence but how one may read the question in such
a way as to include reference to all the conditions of discursive
authority under which it is framed in the academy and the interests
that its framing embodies. This would be to discover a way of
resisting the mere instrumentalization of the authority/irresponsi-
bility problematic in the further widening of critical–professional
authority.

WORKS CITED

Astier, Pierre. "Beckett's *Ohio Impromptu*: A View From the Isle of
    Swans." *Modern Drama* 25 (Fall 1982): 331–41.
Astro, Alan. "The Language of the Master and the Mastery of Language
    in Joyce and Beckett." Paper presented at the James Joyce International
    Symposium, Copenhagen, 16 June 1986.
Beer, Ann. "Watt, Knott and Beckett's Bilingualism." *Journal of Beckett
    Studies* 10 (1985): 35–75.
Beja, Morris, S. E. Gontarski, and Pierre Astier, eds. *Samuel Beckett:
    Humanistic Perspectives*. Columbus: Ohio State University Press, 1982.

Connor, Steven. *Samuel Beckett: Repetition, Theory, and Text*. Oxford: Basil Blackwell, 1988.

Ellmann, Richard. *James Joyce*. Rev. ed. New York: Oxford University Press, 1982.

Hassan, Ihab. *The Postmodern Turn: Essays in Postmodern Theory and Culture*. Columbus: Ohio State University Press, 1987.

Kenner, Hugh. *Flaubert, Joyce, and Beckett: The Stoic Comedians*. London: Allen, 1964.

Lyotard, Jean-François. *The Postmodern Condition: A Report on Knowledge*. Trans. Geoff Bennington and Brian Massumi. Manchester: Manchester University Press, 1984.

Nadeau, Maurice. *The History of Surrealism*. Trans. Roger Shattuck. Harmondsworth: Penguin, 1973.

Rabaté, Jean-Michel. "A Portrait of the Artist as a Bogeyman." *Oxford Literary Review* 7.1–2 (1985): 62–90.

Rosemont, Franklin. *André Breton and the First Principles of Surrealism*. London: Pluto, 1978.

Shenker, Israel. "Moody Man of Letters." *The New York Times* 6 May 1956: sec. 2; 1–3.

11

James Joyce and Samuel Beckett: From Epiphany to Anti-Epiphany

Ed Jewinski

SEVERAL YEARS AGO, Harold Bloom created a minor sensation with his argument that great writing, writing of magnitude, consists of rewriting the past: sons turning themselves into fathers, Blake rewriting Milton, Eliot attempting to show that all previous literature imitated him. Bloom, in *The Anxiety of Influence*, wanted to demonstrate that great writing was strong *misreading*. At the same time, thinkers like Derrida, Foucault, Lacan, de Man, and others began to be hailed as the articulators of the contemporary impulse to unwrite, un-invent, even "erase" the past, to write as if literary texts did not exist or had never existed, to create (if such a paradox is possible) a non-criticism criticism. The tendency became to speak of literature in terms of incompleteness, fabrication, irresolution. While readers like Geoffrey Hartman wanted to "save" the text, the majority of "post-modernists" wanted to jettison the whole notion of "literature."

Although it is not my purpose to rehearse cultural history, I believe the "influence" of Joyce on Beckett can best be understood by studying how these two writers have helped to "author" the postmodern desire to "rewrite" the very notion of "literature." I use the words "authored" and "authors" with trepidation because, since Joyce and Beckett (and partly because of them), the terms have become problematic. On the one hand, for example, a rather tempered critic like Wayne C. Booth, in his *The Rhetoric of Fiction*, argues that such a novel as *A Portrait of the Artist as a Young Man* is flawed beyond repair, "unless we make the *absurd* assumption that Joyce had in reality purged himself of all judgement by the time he completed his final draft . . ." (335; emphasis added). While Booth found himself confounded by the possible alteration of the sense of "author," Michel Foucault embraced the contradictory notion of "unauthored" art and began his seminal essay "What is an Author?" with Beckett's statement: "What matter who's speaking, what matter who's speaking" (115). For Foucault, Beckett's work affirms that "authors" do not "exist," that language has freed itself of any individual's effort of "expression" (116).

To some readers, Foucault's argument may be more ingenious than insightful, but it is important to note that Joyce, Beckett's precursor, is one of the writers who forces us to reconsider what an "author" is. In the *Portrait,* for example, Stephen presents the problem of the artist's godlike presence "within or behind or beyond or above his handiwork, invisible, refined out of existence, indifferent, paring his fingernails" (215). Beckett, aware of Joyce's disruption of the notion of "author," seems, initially, to go further than Joyce—now the "author" is not even an issue. The narrator of a Beckett work disclaims "author"-ity: "I seem to speak, it is not I, about me, it is not about me" (TN 291).

It seems a curious paradox that in an age that supposedly acknowledges—even espouses—the "death of the author," more is being said and written about the "author" than ever before. Moreover, writers seem to have become obsessed with what Linda Hutcheon calls "narcissistic narrative" (Hutcheon). Even the "author" as an "idea" or a "concept"—as an "implied" author rather than a "real" author—has become an added point of debate. Yet, no matter how often readers wish to throw their hands up in despair, the curious mind returns to the problem of authorship and "who is speaking." What, in effect, constitutes an author's writing? How might that writing be understood, analyzed, and made comprehensible? More important, how could one indisputably demonstrate that one "author" influenced another, particularly in an age that has lost its confidence and certainty about the role of an author?

The matter of "influence" is a difficult one. No one has ever satisfactorily defined the term; nor has anyone precisely demonstrated what kind of "evidence" unequivocally proves "influence." The problem often resembles the efforts of Beckett's Mr. Kelly who, in *Murphy,* attempts to reconcile the seen and the unseen by flying a kite to the point where the two intersect. Of course, like so many of Beckett's characters, Mr. Kelly fails brilliantly. A critic dealing with the problem of how far influence can be "seen" might equally fail. The exercise, however, could have benefits. Facing the difficulties, particularly the gaps in our knowledge about the nature of "influence," can illuminate the structure of assumptions underlying our notion of not only "authors" like Beckett and Joyce, but the concept of "influence" itself.

One possible approach to the topic rests in Harold Bloom's suggestive books *The Anxiety of Influence* and *A Map of Misreading*. For Bloom, neither Joyce nor Beckett is simply "expressing" an idea or view; rather, each is "rewriting" an older battle, one that Joyce had struggled with in *Finnegans Wake*: ". . . why, pray, sign anything as long as every word, letter, penstroke, paperspace is a perfect signature of its own?" (115). Why, in other words, be an "author" when language itself does the "writing"?

Clearly, Joyce's question is rhetorical; authors do "sign" their works, and with that signature comes the sense of one writer's having completed an "original" work, even if that writer is "influenced" by a tradition, by another writer, or by language itself. In *The Anxiety of Influence* Bloom argues that every serious writer recognizes the burden of the past, the "great tradition" as Leavis liked to call it, and that the task of all authors is to find a way of writing which makes them part of that tradition yet does not reduce them to being disciples of some previous "greater" writer. The goal is achieved, argues Bloom, because every writer "reorders" and "reshapes" the past for us. To be an "author," furthermore, *means* to be a rewriter of the past, to be a creative misreader, to be an individual who places the past into the perspective which will reveal the "new" author's "unique" contribution. By stressing *misreading* and *miswriting* Bloom hopes to offer a practical manner of dealing with the problem of how individuals "reconstruct" the tradition to open "imaginative space" for themselves (5).

For my purposes, Bloom's invitation to approach criticism from a "mythic" (13) perspective is worth accepting because it helps clarify why Joyce's "influence" on Beckett has been such a difficult and debatable issue. Part of the difficulty in studying this topic rests in the fact that Joyce and Beckett not only read each other but they directly "influenced" each other's works. Joyce, presumably, had a greater effect on Beckett than the reverse, but Beckett did affect Joyce's later writing, particularly the composition of portions of *Finnegans Wake*. We do know that Beckett provided Irish lore, helped with references that Joyce needed checked, and, finally, provided inspiration at moments when Joyce found himself searching for specific solutions. The now well-known origin of the phrase "Another insult to Ireland" has been recorded by Ellmann (398), Gluck (12), and Bair. Here is Bair's account: "Another time Joyce wanted to insert a story about a kindhearted Irish soldier in the Crimean War who could not bring himself to shoot a defecating Russian general until he picked up a chunk of turf to finish the act. 'Another insult to Ireland,' Beckett remarked dryly. Joyce used his exact words, as they were what he needed to nationalize the story" (70).

Since Beckett's early career overlapped with Joyce's later period, it is not surprising that the younger writer's possible influence upon the older writer would be considered "minor." By the time they met, Joyce's style had been fully developed. However, as Derrida, Lacan, Foucault and other postmodernists repeatedly argue, the "meaning" of a term like "style" must always be considered as a problem of "discourse" in general, rather than a problem of a particular text or writer. "Style" is a vague and troublesome notion. A general sense of style as "the right words in the right order" promises a basis of coherence and order for an understanding of any style, but by the time the revisions and corrections and alterations are completed, the end product of a text is often elusive and nebulous, a fact of "style" that Joyce exploits for comic effect in *Finnegans Wake*: "and look at this prepronominal *funferal,* engraved and retouched and edgewiped and puddenpadded, very like a whale's egg farced with pemmican, as were it sentenced to be nuzzled over a full trillion times for ever and a night till his noddle sink or swim by that ideal reader suffering from an ideal insomnia" (120). Joyce's deliberate exploration of a style that borders on "incomprehensibility" has, for better or worse, utterly changed many readers' sense of "language." Jacques Derrida, for example, even goes so far as to claim that "every time [he] write[s], and even in the most academic pieces of prose, Joyce's ghost is always coming on board" (Derrida 149). In any case, not only were Joycean sentences to be "nuzzled" over, but the very act of reading them also became an enterprise for "ideal insomnia." Joyce, in other words, recognized the difficulty his texts posed for his readers, and although he maintained a public pose of silence, he privately orchestrated the reception of his texts so that a "reading" could occur. Joyce's involvement with Stuart Gilbert's *James Joyce's 'Ulysses'* may be the most well-known example, but Joyce equally expended energy on the right preparation of the audience for *Finnegans Wake*. More important, Joyce also asked Beckett to assist in clarifying the aims of the *Wake*. Deirdre Bair may be overstating the case when she suggests that Joyce was "eager to guide his protegé [Beckett] to the correct" (76) reading of the *Wake,* but there is little exaggeration in noting that Joyce carefully planned *Our Exagmination Round His Factification for Incamination of Work in Progress.*

By contributing to Joyce's enterprise, by accepting Joyce's direct guidance, Beckett gained an insight not only into what Joyce hoped to project, but also into the methods whereby Joyce hoped to have his aims projected for him. Of course, the immediate impact of the essay, on Beckett's own career, was the charge of "over-influence" (see the Introduction of this book). However, Beckett had been "influenced" by Joyce in a more subtle way than might be immediately obvious: Beckett had learned the need to prepare one's audience. It will probably always be a matter of conjecture to estimate the degree to which Beckett prepared his own audience, but the carefully groomed and polished image projected for and by Israel Shenker seems too deliberately forged to be merely accidental. To what degree is it a vision shaped by Beckett's determination to present (or even have presented for him) the right image? Has the supposed disciple elected to use the supposed "influence" of Joyce to set the stage for his own particular presentation of himself? Partially because he had been charged with "over-influence," Beckett speaks out and explicitly denies the importance of Joyce's "influence." To avoid being the "disciple," to assert "imaginative space" (Bloom 5), to free himself of the specter of Joyce (at least in the portrait of him by Israel Shenker), Beckett resorts to the strategy of "lowering" himself, of deliberately positioning himself "below" the "master's" level: " 'the difference is that Joyce was a superb manipulator of material—perhaps the greatest. He was making words do the absolute maximum of work. There isn't a syllable that's superfluous. The kind of work I do is one in which I'm not master of my material.

The more Joyce knew the more he could. He's tending toward omniscience and omnipotence as an artist. I'm working with impotence, ignorance' " (3). Once Beckett has established a clear and sharp gulf between the "superb manipulator" and the manager of "impotence," he can emphasize his own "little exploration" (Shenker 3). Bloom's analysis of influence suggests that Beckett's reaction is not uncommon when a writer feels pressured by the "anxiety of influence." Bloom calls this stage or pose "[k]enosis, which is a breaking-device similar to the defense mechanisms our psyches employ; . . . kenosis then is a movement towards discontinuity with the precursor" (14). Bloom expands by suggesting that the writer who might be viewed as overly "influenced" may choose to accept a "reduction from the divine to human status" (14). Not being the "master," Beckett "seems to humble himself as though he were ceasing to be a poet" (15). Of course, concludes Bloom, someone like Beckett adopts such a strategy to draw attention to himself, to emphasize the newness and the importance and the originality of his own works: " 'My little exploration is that whole zone of being that has always been set aside by artists as something unuseable—as something by definition incompatible with art' " (Shenker 3). Beckett's divesting himself of "divine" status, of asserting himself to be of a "lower" order than the "master," has worked convincingly enough to lull critics themselves into asserting that Joyce is the encyclopedist, and Beckett the minimalist. At times the myth has such sway that Beckett's achievement stands in danger of being diminished; at these moments critics like Ruby Cohn remind readers that both Joyce and Beckett are "cosmopolitan" writers, and not simply either "divine" or "human," who differ only because Joyce attempts to "embrace all knowledge, all experience, all language" while Beckett "doubts all knowledge, all experience, all language" (390).

The very need for an accomplished critic like Ruby Cohn to "defend" Beckett without tarnishing or reducing the general estimate of Joyce's accomplishment explains why Bloom has a crucial corollary to poetic miswriting: just as poets "misread" literary history, so do critics. "Poets' misinterpretations or poems are more drastic than critics' misinterpretations or criticism, but this is only a difference in degree and not at all in kind. There are no interpretations but only misinterpretations, and so all criticism is prose poetry" (Bloom 94–95). Critics too participate in the rewriting of tradition, and if Shenker assisted Beckett (be it knowingly or unknowingly) to orchestrate a reading of the Beckettian vision, a stronger "misreading" may be required to trace the force of Joyce's influence on Beckett. The title I have selected for this essay proposes such a *misinterpretation* of the events: "James Joyce and Samuel Beckett: From Epiphany to Anti-Epiphany." The argument involved is this: Joyce taught Beckett how to orchestrate the reception of an author's work, and Beckett learned his lesson well. To achieve his goal, Beckett repeatedly insisted that Joyce was the consummate master of "omniscience and omnipotence" (Shenker 3). Beckett insists on this point of difference. In so doing, he (knowingly or unknowingly) directs the appropriate reception of Joyce's work, one which grants an achievement that in no way endangers Beckett's own work. Joyce, according to Beckett, is the author whose writing is, above all, a writing of "epiphanies," a writing that implies language can be constructed, syllable by syllable, to penetrate the welter of immediate experience and, thereby, reveal the "reality" underlying it. " 'Joyce believed in words. All you had to do was rearrange them,' " Beckett is quoted as saying, " 'and [the words] would express what you wanted' " (Harvey 249–50). Whether being interviewed by Shenker or explaining his views privately to Axel Kaun, Beckett repeatedly insists on Joyce's ability to control every word. When writing to Axel Kaun on "9/7/37," for example, Beckett stresses the point: "Mit einem solchen Programm hat meiner Absicht nach die allerletzte Arbeit von Joyce gar nichts zu tun. Dort scheint es sich vielmehr um eine Apotheose des Wortes zu handeln. Es sei denn, Himmelfahrt und Höllensturz sind eins und dasselbe. Wie schön wäre es . . . ." (*Disjecta* 53). However difficult the nuances of the passage are to translate, Beckett here asserts that "There [in Joyce's later work] it appears to be a matter of the apotheosis of the word. It gives the appearance that the ascension and the fall to the pits of hell are one and the same. How wonderful if it were so. . . ." The notion that Joyce's later work, presumably *Finnegans Wake*, represents that "apotheosis of the word" is crucial to Beckett, for it grants him the power to assert the view that Joyce's art is limited: "It would be wonderful if it were so"—if language had that capacity—but clearly, for Beckett, it does not. For that reason, his work has nothing to do ("gar nichts zu tun") with such a "program."

In Bloom's terms, Beckett is carefully *misreading* his precursor so that Joyce, as has so often been the case since Beckett, is seen as the writer who uses language to transcend the immediate. Beckett, in effect, is implying that Joyce belongs to the tradition of Hegelian "Aufhebung"—a moving above or beyond the immediate world of phenomena to a higher level of understanding and insight, a moment that transcends the everyday to give entry into the enduring and eternally "real."

By placing Joyce into the context of the "epiphany" (a "sudden spiritual manifestation" [SH 211]), Beckett can place himself at the center of the search for the new materials "always" (Shenker 3) discarded and overlooked. He asserts, in this way, his "originality." Moreover, he carefully places Joyce into a clearly antithetical position, one which allows Beckett to seize for himself the "mastery" of what, for the purposes of this argument, I shall call "anti-epiphany." For Beckett, language is not capable of an "apotheosis." Beckettian language—especially the word—will remain opaque, impenetrable, unredeeming. No transcendence is allowed with or through or by language. In part, the handling of language to achieve this effect remains consistent throughout much of Beckett's career. In *The Unnamable* he writes "what I best see I see ill" (TN 297), and in later years he titles a novelette *Ill Seen Ill Said*.

By articulating a clearly distinct and antithetical theory of the "word," Beckett "rewrites" Joyce—in effect, Bloom would argue, Beckett becomes an "author" of *Finnegans Wake* by guiding us into a particular way of "reading" it. No matter how complicated the Joycean text of *Finnegans Wake*, readers will search for, even see, a language that meets Beckett's guidelines: "if you don't understand it [the language], . . . it is because you are too decadent to receive it. You are not satisfied unless form is so strictly divorced from content that you can comprehend the one almost without bothering to read the other" (*Disjecta* 26). The implication of Beckett's argument is, in part, that when the form and the content are "united," the "meaning" can and will "come" through. The "author's" job is to force readers beyond that "scant cream of sense" (*Disjecta* 26).

I earlier placed the issue of the "influence" of Joyce on Beckett into the center of the recent controversy about "language" to demonstrate that Beckett's strategy is a form of *misinterpreting* Joyce that is neither unique nor unusual, but one largely initiated by Joyce's own effort to stress "the apotheosis of the word." The now famous scene of Beckett's "surprise" when Joyce is willing to incorporate an accidental phrase into *Finnegans Wake* merely functions as an apocalyptic story that underscores Joyce's control of all language—even the accidental, chance phrases that can and do "enter" a text. Ellmann records the scene for us:

> Once or twice [Joyce] dictated a bit of *Finnegans Wake* to Beckett, though dictation did not work well for him; in the middle of one such session there was a knock at the door which Beckett didn't hear. Joyce said, "Come in," and Beckett wrote it down. Afterwards he read back what he had written and Joyce said, "What's that 'Come in'?" "Yes, you said that," said Beckett. Joyce thought for a moment, then said, "Let it stand." He was quite willing to accept coincidence as his collaborator [649].

The importance of the anecdote is that it emphasizes a confident control of language—nothing need disturb the "master's" handling of it; even "coincidence" has its appropriate place in Joyce's view of language. The notion, in fact, has been so powerfully projected that readers are still offering skeleton keys or prose paraphrases of the *Wake* to clarify the "vision" which underlies it. Michael Begnal, for example, bluntly states what underlies every effort to summarize or paraphrase or condense Joyce's *Wake*: "The language is a kind of linguistic shell that surrounds the text" (633). Every desire for a skeleton key for *Finnegans Wake*, I would suggest, accepts Beckett's particular form of *misreading*. Read "properly," the "text" will become visible, the "apotheosis of the word" will occur, the shell will open to reveal its contents.

When Ellmann writes that "Beckett was fascinated and thwarted by Joyce's singular method" (649) of incorporating the phrase "Come in," the biographer is reinforcing the image of a Beckett who cannot accept the convergence of word and accident. The myth of recalcitrant language that will not crack open to offer a specific epiphany implicitly becomes firmly tied to Beckett.

Ironies, however, exist in all *misreadings* of literary history, and probably the most crucial irony when dealing with the Joyce/Beckett relationship is that once Beckett's view of language becomes the dominant mode, both Beckett and Joyce are "re-read" and "re-written" again. By the time critics become accustomed to Beckett's "original" way of writing, the new "readings" of Joyce emphasize the troublesome burden of language rather than its power to create an apotheosis. As Beckett takes his place in the tradition, the changing view of what language can do leads critics to emphasize the utter separation of language and "expression." Even the theory of the appropriate "reading" of the *Wake* takes on a new form—the effort to break the "shell" of the words, in particular, is abandoned. Any reading must now take into account the fundamental impenetrability of the language. As Jean-Michel Rabaté put it so well: "As soon as we try to pinpoint the 'events' of a story [in the *Wake*], it trails off elsewhere, and we have to discover to our surprise that we are in the middle of another narrative. Nevertheless, we retain a constant sense that some kind of storytelling is going on . . ." (137). The question is, of course, what kind of storytelling?

Numerous critics have shifted from the emphasis on "understanding" the *Wake* in the terms Beckett suggested in *Exagmination* to an exploration of the infinite possibilities of the "text." In fact, like Derrida, readers have come to look at the *Wake* as "the greatest power of meanings buried in each syllabic fragment, subjecting each atom of writing to frission in order to overload the consciousness with the whole memory of man: mythologies, religion, philosophies, sciences, psychoanalysis, literatures" (Derrida 150). The emphasis is on the intractability of language and the "unreadability" of the text. By overloading consciousness, the mind comes to a stage Derrida calls "aporia," a stage of undecidability and indeterminacy, a stage of "impasses of meaning" (Eagleton 133–34). The increasing emphasis on the inability to "read" a text, interestingly enough, accompanies the growing reputation of Beckett as the "master" of the "unusable." That the two should follow in parallel lines, however, is no accident. Beckett, too, relies on the word "aporia," especially in the opening section of *The Unnamable*, a text that concentrates on the narrator's inability to clarify, explain, or "name" his experiences (TN 291). The end result of Beckett's fiction—its constant habit of placing its readers into the same state of "aporia" as the narrators—resembles in effect, although not in style or technique, Joyce's accomplishment in *Finnegans Wake*. What in Beckett's novels *Company* or *Ill Seen Ill Said* or *Imagination Dead Imagine* does constitute the "story"? Often Beckett's words are as much of a stumbling block as Joyce's, although few words are "twosome twiminds" (FW 188).

In other words, Beckett's "rewriting" of Joyce ends in a curious paradox: the more he separates himself from his precursor, the more he brings his writing closer to Joyce's. Incapable of evading or ignoring that Joyce's *Finnegans Wake* represents the "embarrassments of a tradition grown too wealthy to need anything more" (Bloom 21), Beckett seems to be the first writer to lead the way toward what John Barth will call the "literature of exhaustion," the literature that exploits the worn-out forms to reinvigorate them (Barth 62–76). The point might best be illustrated by Beckett's method of characterization, a technique of merging identities which seems, initially, extremely similar to that of Joyce. Beckett, with his penchant for M's (names like Molloy, Malone, Mercier, and so on), equally merges one character with another, often confounding the reader with the problem of the stability of identity (Coe 54–68). Beckett's hold on "originality" seems tenuous when one re-reads Joyce with Beckett's work in mind. The similarities, however, are fascinating examples of Beckett's rewriting of his predecessor, for the habit of drawing on the device of initials is used differently in each writer. Joyce, for example, creates characters like HCE and ALP or Shem and Shaun, figures who constantly flow into one another, often so smoothly that a reader fails to detect the exact moment of shifting from one figure to the other. The method, in fact, bears a strong resemblance to Stephen Dedalus' theory that in literature "We walk through ourselves, meeting robbers, ghosts, giants, old men, young men, wives, widows, brothers-in-love, but always meeting ourselves" (U 9.1044–46). In Beckett's world, however, the very opposite seems to happen—we are always outside ourselves, and the figures who may be part of us never come close enough to allow self-recognition. Beckett's "unnamable" explains the typical inversion of "walking through ourselves": "I am certainly not at the circumference. For if I were it would follow that Malone, wheeling about

me as he does, would issue from the enceinte at every revolution,
which is manifestly impossible. But does he in fact wheel, does he
not perhaps simply pass before me in a straight line" (TN 295)?
When Beckett does merge characters, when they do seem to
merge, they remain stubbornly other and different and unrecog-
nizable; they are what Moran, in *Molloy,* calls "a rabble in my
head, . . . a gallery of moribunds. Murphy, Watt, Yerk, Mercier
and all the others" (TN 137).

The methods of characterization, then, share some essential
features, although they differ in effect. Joyce's characters meet and
merge and flow; Beckett's remain separate, isolated, distinct, yet
strikingly incomplete for all their obsession with their inner
experiences. The same may be said of Joyce's and Beckett's
handling of words. Joyce, for example, often teases his readers
with their desire for a clear surface reading: "(Stoop) if you are
abcedminded, to this claybook, what curios of signs (please
stoop), in this allaphbed! Can you rede (Since We and Thou had it
out already) its world? It is the same told of all. . . . They lived
and laughed . . ." (FW 18). Beckett's originality lies in the very
fact that he "rewrites" Joyce by being painstakingly "literal" or
"abc" minded—he can be accused only of borrowing one of his
major techniques directly from Joyce in order to emphasize his
own vision. By making every passage exact, by keeping every
passage to the "abc," Beckett forces the reader to "stoop" in quite
a different way. Where Joyce uses a portmanteau word to describe
how the earth has always been our inheritance, Beckett extends
and protracts the insight: "And the poor old lousy old earth, my
earth and my father's and my mother's and my father's father's
and my mother's mother's and my father's mother's and my
mother's father's and my father's mother's father's and my mother's father's mother's and [so on for about a half page]" (W 46–
47). My very impatience with transcribing the passage, I believe,
illustrates what Beckett can do when he ruthlessly goes from "ed
to zed" (FW 123). In the *Wake* there is always the mystery of the
words which might, somehow, fall together, but in Beckett, there
is relentless repetition and unceasing drudgery of exact word after
exact word. The words do build up, but they "accumulate," not
"illuminate"; they tire out, they exhaust, they defeat—do any-

thing but grant a moment of insight that allows for a transcendent leap.

Where Joyce's style seems to continually overwhelm the intellect (how should the words be unpacked?), Beckett's constantly overwhelms the senses, almost as if they were objects in themselves. *Not I*, with the constant chatter pouring from a mouth, for example, illustrates how Beckett has, over the years, only refined this technique, not abandoned or altered it. In each case, be it Beckett's or Joyce's, the "meaning" slips away. In both cases, the familiar words become unfamiliar, and language itself becomes foreign, but in strikingly different ways.

Beckett, more importantly for this argument, is rewriting Joyce not simply by scrambling words, but by using the everyday words—he, I, we, you—the simple pronouns—to show us how their reverberating nuances are explored through visual techniques by Joyce, and not through their own, hard, stubborn recalcitrant forms. In our usual scheme of things, we distinguish between the "denotation" and the "connotation" of words, a process Joyce disrupts with "spelling" and a process that Beckett disrupts with endless repetition and reuse of the same word in a single passage. The technique is particularly noticeable when a character uses a pronoun that asserts what the character will do, while denying that the goal can actually be achieved:

> I shall never do anything any more from now on but play. No I must not begin with an exaggeration. But I shall play a great part of the time, from now on, the greater part, if I can. But perhaps I shall not succeed any better than hitherto. Perhaps as hitherto I shall find myself abandoned in the dark, without anything to play with. Then I shall play with myself. To be able to conceive of such a plan is encouraging [TN 180].

Once Beckett links the repetition of pronouns to juxtaposition, he often creates the striking effects he desires because, unlike Joyce, he puts multiple senses together simultaneously without disrupting conventional spelling. Passages like these illustrate the point:

> Yes, let's go. (*They do not move.*) [WG 60[b]].

> It is midnight. The rain is beating on the windows. It was not midnight. It was not raining [TN 176].

> I can't go on, I'll go on [TN 414].

The technique of juxtaposing two opposites forces the reader into Beckett's version of the Viconian *recursus*. In the first example, the first "go" initially puzzles in the light of the second phrase "(*They do not move*)." Estragon and Vladimir do "go on" in their paralysis, so in that sense they do "move" while going nowhere. In time they are not stationary, but they appear to be stationary, and so on. Even the effect of the language to explain such simple juxtapositions sounds like a parody of Beckett's style. Like Joyce's style, however, Beckett's constantly invites "multiple" readings—but without the use of portmanteau words.

The conclusions Bloom's method seems to lead toward are these: Beckett is pressured by "the anxiety of influence," and he relieves that anxiety by both *misreading* and *rewriting* Joyce. The process begins when Beckett first emphasizes that Joyce's words, unlike his own, can and do express what one might call the "greater realities." By initially emphasizing this point, Beckett can make room for his vision, for his portrayal of the word in all its stubborn "permanence." The *rewriting* allows Beckett to emphasize that man is constantly "en attendant" (waiting) for an apotheosis of the word. By emphasizing that Joyce's use of language is a promise of "redemption," Beckett can reveal that his "original" contribution is the insight that we cannot get past the first word. No wonder, then, that Beckett rewrites and misreads Joyce—to make room for himself he shows how language cannot be mastered because his subject is the rewriting of Joyce's mastery of it. Beckett, in other words, is *rewriting* a quarrel with Joyce that began the moment Joyce allowed coincidence to be his collaborator. For Joyce, there could always be the sudden entry of the appropriate word. Because the epiphany could occur at any moment, Joyce let the phrase "Come in" stand. Beckett, of course, rejects that vision. His characters are often in the closed rooms that resemble words which can be neither left (*The Lost Ones*) nor clearly entered (*Imagination Dead Imagine*). Ironically, of course, as Beckett is granted the stature of "master," his view of "language" begins to dominate, and the end result is that while Joyce is liberated from the tyranny of "omniscience and omnipotence," his writing becomes an extension of Beckett's ambiguous fictional voices—"what matter who's speaking, what matter who's speaking." Or as Joyce put it so poignantly: the "author was always constitutionally incapable of misappropriating the spoken words of others" (FW 108).

WORKS CITED

Bair, Deirdre. *Samuel Beckett: A Biography*. New York: Harcourt Brace Jovanovich, 1978.

Barth, John. *The Friday Book: Essays and Other Nonfiction*. New York: Putnam, 1984.

Begnal, Michael H. "The Language of *Finnegans Wake*." *A Companion to Joyce Studies*. Ed. Zack Bowen and James F. Carens. Westport: Greenwood, 1984. 633–45.

Bloom, Harold. *The Anxiety of Influence: A Theory of Poetry*. Oxford: Oxford University Press, 1973.

Booth, Wayne C. *The Rhetoric of Fiction*. Chicago: The University of Chicago Press, 1961.

Coe, Richard N. *Samuel Beckett*. New York: Grove, 1964.

Cohn, Ruby. "Joyce and Beckett, Irish Cosmopolitans." *James Joyce Quarterly* 8 (Summer 1971): 385–91.

Derrida, Jacques. "Two Words for Joyce." *Post-Structuralist Joyce: Essays from the French*. Ed. Derek Attridge and Daniel Ferrer. Cambridge: Cambridge University Press, 1984.

Eagleton, Terry. *Literary Theory: An Introduction*. Oxford: Blackwell, 1983.

Ellmann, Richard. *James Joyce*. Rev. ed. New York: Oxford University Press, 1982.

Foucault, Michel. *Language, Counter-Memory, Practice: Selected Essays and Interviews by Michel Foucault*. Ithaca: Cornell University Press, 1977.

Gluck, Barbara. *Beckett and Joyce: Friendship and Fiction*. Lewisburg, Pa.: Bucknell University Press, 1979.

Harvey, Lawrence. *Samuel Beckett: Poet and Critic*. Princeton: Princeton University Press, 1970.

Hutcheon, Linda. *Narcissistic Narrative: The Metafictional Paradox*. Waterloo: Wilfrid Laurier University Press, 1980.

Rabaté, Jean-Michel. "Narratology and the Subject of *Finnegans Wake*." *James Joyce: The Centennial Symposium*. Ed. Morris Beja, Phillip Herring, Maurice Harmon, David Norris. Urbana: University of Illinois Press, 1986. 137–148.

Shenker, Israel. "Moody Man of Letters." *The New York Times* 6 May 1956: sec 2; 1, 3.

12

Beckett et Joyce et Beckett-esque:
A One-Act Play

Denis Regan

The characters:

> Samuel Beckett
> Peggy Guggenheim
> James Joyce
> Lucia Joyce
> Hamm*
> Pozzo*
> Lucky*
> Prudence

*These are characters from Beckett's plays and are to be costumed as such.

The set:

> An ash can (of sorts). A table set with glasses, wine bottles, and a confused game of chess. Caricatures (approximately 4 ft. wide by 6 ft. high) of James Joyce standing, and Samuel Beckett sitting, with concentric circles surrounding each of them. Each face is cut out. A huge black-and-white photograph of two chimps playing chess.

The time:

> The afterlife mind of Samuel Beckett.
>
> (*The play begins with Joyce and Beckett behind the caricatures; their faces show through their respective drawings.*)

BECKETT: I wouldn't be doing this under normal circumstances. As a matter of fact this is really not I, not me . . . really speaking. It is . . . Me to Play. (*Pause.*) While I . . . well that is, before, in that other state, that state of agonies, and habits and

---

It should be noted that much of the material in this play paraphrases the writings of James Joyce, Samuel Beckett, and Peggy Guggenheim.

boredom . . . that state that affirms pain. I think you know it
. . . while there, before here, while enduring . . . waiting for
where I am now . . . where I'm not sure. . . . (*Beckett enters from
behind drawing.*) I rarely gave interviews. Why? I always believed
the work came before the person. (*Makes a gesture toward Joyce.*)
This was not an original notion, but it has become somewhat
. . . confused . . . bemused . . . infused. (*Pause.*) My name is
Sam Beckett. I was born somewhere outside of Dublin, Ireland,
in 1906, and died somewhere in Paris, France, in 1989. Those
are the facts outside somewhere, from where I am. . . . Consider
where I am sitting to be a tree. I am quite fond of trees,
especially ones I can sit in. I never thought while I was breathing, breath by precious breath, like the rest of you, that it would
have been best . . . if I were to be interviewed in a tree.

JOYCE: (*Joyce enters.*) Me to play.

BECKETT: Me to play? That's my line.

JOYCE: I must go on.

BECKETT: I can't go on. (*Beckett gestures that Joyce should carry on.*)

JOYCE: I must go on. . . . His lines. His cant. I can't go on. I must
go on. I can't go on, and so on and so on. It's the sort of push-
me/pull-me rhetoric Mr. Beckett made infamous.

BECKETT: This alleged infamy began sometime after I became part
of Mr. Joyce's . . . circle. Me to play. (*Pause.*) This is my
Imagination Dead Imagine. It is the precise position of two
immobile bodies in a sphere, plotted by geometrical coordi-
nates.

JOYCE: Remember, Mr. Beckett, there is no triangle, however
obtuse, but the circumference of some circle passes through its
wretched vertices. Remember also, one thief was saved.

BECKETT: (*Gesturing to the display.*) Our styles, however obtuse,
circle and intersect. I cartooned this as a homage to Mr. Joyce.

JOYCE: Ah . . . sordid Sam, a dour decent mathematics man.
Unwashed. Haunted. Perplexed, apostle of the absurd. Intoxi-
cated with words.

BECKETT: I was a bit bibaciously bibulous over Mr. Joyce's words,
and all the estranging humanity in those words. Words circling
upon words circling.

JOYCE: One thief was saved, whose circling words, circled with
fatal monotony about the Providential fulcrum.

BECKETT: A taciturn mollusk. . . . In Mr. Joyce's circle, I was being referred to as the New Stephen Dedalus incarnate. Mr. Joyce's personification. Himself as the young Irish intellectual in self-imposed exile. Me to play. I played the role. It was fitting. I'd stride languidly along the Seine in search of that nightmare I was trying to awake from.

JOYCE: (*Half laugh.*) He was always depressed. A mixture of self-denigration and conceit. A bothered wandering scholar.

BECKETT: (*Reciting one of his poems.*) Spend the years learning/ squandering/ courage for the years of wandering/ through the world politely turning/ from the loutishness of learning.

JOYCE: That constant disdain for academia. It was quite charming. He also had a disposition for ushering . . . and assuring . . . and rendering . . . silence. This I liked and respected. It came to my notice one evening when we were both attending a party.

BECKETT: The circle, and then some, gathered to celebrate the twenty-fifth anniversary of Bloomsday. That singular day in literature on which Mr. Joyce's novel *Ulysses* takes place. (*Enter party members with posters that have critical comments of the writing styles of J. and B. For example: "To Beckett boredom is the most durable of human evils." "Beckett's work is slapstick with a dash of bitter theology." "Beckett's bums are metaphors for . . . ?" "Mr. Joyce cannot be read. He can only be reread." "If Mr. Joyce is baroque, Beckett must be minimal." "Mr. Joyce uses cycles as a trellis."*) It was Joysous for a while. Mr. Joyce perhaps sang more than he should have.

JOYCE: Mr. Beckett perhaps drank more than he should have.

BECKETT: The road of excess leads to the palace of wisdom. (*Party-goers whisper.*)

JOYCE: There suddenly was an excess of prattle. I never minded prattle, as prattle goes, but literary prattle is intolerable prattle. I witnessed Beckett clam up like a saint being burned at the stake. He refused to betray his faith. I followed his inspiration. Our silence was possessive and forbidding. It vexed the prattling crowd. (*Party whispers grow louder.*)

BECKETT: At an opportune moment Mr. Joyce turned to me. . . .

JOYCE: If only they would talk about turnips?

BECKETT: Are you hungry? Do you care for a tuber?

JOYCE: A tuber?

BECKETT: That's all there is.

JOYCE: Then a turnip will do. (*B. rummages through all his pockets. Gives J. a carrot. J. bites. Party-goers watch, enraptured.*) It's a carrot.

BECKETT: Oh, pardon. I could have sworn it was a turnip. You must have eaten all the turnips. (*Rummages pockets again. Pulls out a carrot.*) Wait; I have it. There, dear fellow. Make it last; that's the end of them. (*Party-goers exit prattling—whispers.*)

JOYCE: My generous friend helped me with many a turn, and we shared our share of nips . . . and silences. Sam came to my home often to assist me with my work in progress, *Finnegans Wake.* But, as our interaction eased into friendship, his visits became more the stuff of conviviality. (*J. and B. sit in silence.*) (*Enter Peggy Guggenheim. She is well-dressed and gossipy.*)

P. GUGGENHEIM: Convivial . . . to say the least. Ha-ha. And they certainly did that. Here, two of the most imaginative minds of modern times would sit . . . saying nothing. Not only to each other, but to anyone else who would not listen. Wait, did I say that correctly? Some have said, including Mister I-never-give-interviews-Beckett, that I am prone toward hyperbole, and that gossip was my . . . penchant . . . if you will. But I am here to tell you . . . I was there. And they were boring. Boring. Boring. Boring.

BECKETT: Please, Miss Guggenheim.

P. GUGGENHEIM: Miss Guggenheim? He was always excessively polite. Well, both Sam and Mr. Joyce shared this perverse overindulgence with silence, and of all things, Numerology. Yes, the study of numbers, as if numbers had some arcane import. I one day, accidentally mind you, interrupted one of their Con-vivial exchanges. (*J. and B., sitting at opposite sides of the stage, with their backs to each other, raise their arms silently with various counts upon their fingers.*) I was at the Joyce home visiting when I walked in, and there they were soundless, speechless, carrying on some sort of numerological dialogue. Now who in his right mind would call this convivial? Not I. No, not I. No one. No one with any sort of social grace. And that's not all. Sam was . . . was less than . . .

LUCIA JOYCE: Me to play. (*Joyce's daughter enters wearing a shimmering fish costume. She dances a wild, sexy, brief dance.*)

JOYCE: (*After dance, stands, applauds.*) Nous reclamons l'Irelandaise! (*Exits.*)
(*Joyce's daughter waits for father to leave. Sits on Sam's lap. Kisses him passionately.*)

LUCIA JOYCE: Sam, I'm yours. Take me. Take me.

BECKETT: (*Fumbling for words.*) You . . . you don't seem to understand. . . . I . . . I come to be with your father. (*Joyce's daughter exits angrily.*)

P. GUGGENHEIM: (*In a brogue.*) Mrs. Joyce once said to me, "Sure, like St. Francis himself, that Sam had a queer way of charmin' the birds." Sam thought sex . . . grotesque. I can vouch for that. He was not your typical Irishman. He secretly told, and I vowed I'd tell no one . . . but you're special. (*Mimicking Beckett.*) "I am emotionally dead. I am unable to fall in love." (*Imitating Mae West.*) Thanks a heap, big boy. (*Pause.*) I don't think he was ever in love with me for more than twenty minutes at a time.

BECKETT: But twenty times twenty minutes amounts . . .

P. GUGGENHEIM: We never amounted to anything, that is, in regard to love. Oh, he did finally get involved with someone. She made drapes, while I made scenes.

BECKETT: Making love without being in love is like taking coffee without brandy.

P. GUGGENHEIM: Brandy and champagne nourished him. He was unpredictable and drunk. He could barely get out of bed. Which . . . there were times I didn't mind, but there's a limit. His bed was his cocoon . . . and his clothes, entirely too tight. I think they caused him to have a circulation problem, and thus he was tired all the time. And if you haven't discovered it through his writing, I'm here to tell you he was a fatalist. . . . It's true. He never thought he could alter anything. To say the least literature. But that's exactly what he did say . . . the least in literature. . . .

BECKETT: Really, Miss Guggenheim, I believe your part was . . . is . . . to expose the man, not the work.

P. GUGGENHEIM: Oh, so puns are reserved for you and your friend, Mr. Joyce.

BECKETT: Oh, go on.

P. GUGGENHEIM: I must go on. For Sam, love and friendship were not equal. And if you want my opinion, Sam's alleged friendship with Mr. Joyce was rather unequal. For Sam, Mr. Joyce

was no less than bliss, but Sam for Mr. Joyce was no less than
. . . chess. (*Pause.*) I would be the first to admit that I was
jealous. Sam was always leaving me to go see him. And when
Sam was in the hospital . . . well, Mr. Joyce . . . (*Beckett is
gesturing to her as if asking her not to continue.*) Oh so you don't
know about how he . . . Well, Sam and some friends had been
to see a movie and after the movie they . . . drank in a cafe till
the early morning hours. On their way home on the avenue
d'Orléans . . . (*Exit P. Guggenheim. Beckett stands and begins to
walk to her place. Man enters and confronts B. as they continue to
walk.*)

PRUDENCE: Hey, monsieur . . . Irish . . . money . . . money.

BECKETT: Prudence, I'm afraid I'm without . . .

PRUDENCE: You get no more damsels from me, no . . . no, you
don't pay.

BECKETT: I'll pay you as soon . . .

PRUDENCE: You pay me now. You Irish drunken cheater. No more.
(*Gestures obscenely.*)

BECKETT: This really isn't the prudent time to . . .

PRUDENCE: (*Suddenly pulls a knife and stabs Beckett. B. collapses across
easy chair. The easy chair becomes his hospital bed.*)

BECKETT: It was a moment without boundaries. Prudence, the
pimp, almost murdering me. My life was saved by a piano
student, who ended up being with me the rest of my days. I
rather enjoyed my stay in hospital. There was no guilt about
staying in bed. I began to write again. (*Pause.*) It was lovely
being there, even with a hole in my chest. My room was
brighter than the whole of Ireland in summer. I even felt
friendly towards visitors. How could I have malice towards this
man, Prudence, who had been virtually condemned to act in
the manner in which he did? I didn't want to prosecute. The
French government made me. And . . . there was that time
when Mr. Joyce . . . (*Joyce enters. Concerned.*)

JOYCE: Beckett, Beckett, you're better today? I can tell. Yesterday
you seemed groggy.

BECKETT: I was drunk. The Duncans brought me wine in the
morning.

JOYCE: I have read your novel *Murphy*. And, I admired it. You do have talent. But all those commas. It reads as if you and all your characters suffer from congenital hiccups.

BECKETT: Style is absolute.

JOYCE: But the vanity of style for style's sake is like a bow-tie around a cancerous throat.

BECKETT: I see what you're saying.

JOYCE: I'm not sure one can see spoken words, but then again you're only apperceiving what I said. Oh yes, I have something for you. I did find your bit about Murphy's wake amorally amusing . . . and let me see, that is, reflect. . . . Murphy has been cremated. His ashes put into a packet and carried by the character Cooper . . . till Cooper sits down at a bar for the first time in twenty years and drinks. . . . (*Joyce recites.*) "Some hours later Cooper took the packet of ash from his pocket, where earlier in the evening he had put it for greater security, and threw it angrily at a man who had given him great offence. It bounced, burst off the wall on to the floor, where at once it became the object of much dribbling, passing, trapping, shooting, punching, heading and even some recognition from the gentleman's code. By closing time the body, mind, and soul of Murphy were freely distributed over the floor of the saloon; and before another dayspring greyened the earth [Murphy] had been swept away with the sand, the beer, the butts, the glass, the matches, the spit, the vomit" (MU 275). Now that's a wake to remember.

BECKETT: And so I am resurrected. (*Reaches into his pockets.*) I have something for you.

JOYCE: Not another carrot? (*After a comical search, as in the old illusion of sleight of hand, Beckett picks up Joyce's hat and reveals a stone.*) A sucking stone?

BECKETT: A sucking stone? No, it's a stone I picked out of the river Liffey.

JOYCE: I see and you've engraved something here on the back. (*J. strains to read it while B. recites.*)

BECKETT: A way a lone a last a loved a long the "riverrun, past Eve and Adam's, from swerve of shore to bend of bay, brings us by a commodius vicus of recirculation . . ." (FW 1).

JOYCE: Ah, Sam, you were invaluable to my *Finnegans Wake*. Sit down, and share a glass of France's finest. Now tell me, who's reading my *Wake* in Dublin?

BECKETT: Jewish intellectuals.

JOYCE: Good, it is a sort of Talmud . . . but as for this German demigod who is making war and getting in the way of the celebration of my *Wake*, he didn't frighten you into returning from Ireland, the land of your unsuccessful abortion. (*They laugh and toast.*)

BECKETT: To Ireland.

JOYCE: To Ireland.

BECKETT: No, I preferred France at war with the Nazi menace than Ireland at peace with her menacing self.

JOYCE: (*B. and J. get up.*) Once an exile always an exile. (*J. sings "The Old Bog Road."*)

My feet are here on Broadway
this blessed harvest morn
And oh the achin' in my heart for the
place where I was born
My weary hands are blistered
from work in cold and heat
And oh to swing a scythe today
through fields of Irish wheat
Had I a chance to wander
or own a king's abode
'Tis then I'd see the hawthorn tree
by the old bog road. . . .
(*B. escorts him off stage.*)

BECKETT: I never really liked his singing. Mr. Joyce moved to Zurich and there died. (*B. recites from* Finnegans Wake *as he moves to chair.*) A way a lone a last a loved a long the "riverrun, past Eve and Adam's, from swerve of shore to bend of bay, brings us. . . ." Never have two thought so crooked as we. (*Pause.*) I worked for the French resistance during the war, not for the sake of France—I never believed in nations or governments—but because my friends were suddenly disappearing. I was also on a list of those to be disappeared, so I disappeared myself. One of my alleged disappearing tricks was to sit in a tree for two days as the Nazis bustled back and forth below me. It was a time of waiting. Waiting for the absurd to end. (*Lucky enters with a rope around his neck. He eats from a picnic basket. Drinks from various bottles. Moves a chess piece. Reaches into the ash can and drinks from bottle. Drops bottle back into can. Exits.*) I returned to Ireland. I felt a sense of pain and urgency that drove me to recklessness and excess. I was drinking and brawling and swimming in the Irish Sea . . . to regather my thoughts. . . . Then one night I found myself staring blankly at the black sky, at the black sea, freezing in the wind, at the end of a jetty in Dublin harbor. I was struck by an epiphany. What I had to do was to write. (*Pozzo enters tethered to the end of Lucky's taut rope.*)

POZZO: Monologues! (*Cracks whip.*) Senseless. Issueless. Sightless. Monologues. All those Murphys, Malones, Molloys, just love to rattle on . . . compulsively, bitterly, giving you a worm's eye view of words in a crazy man's voice, besieging sanity. But I'm not here to waste your time with his words. No. I won't be back. Malone won't be back. Molloy either . . . or Murphy or, well I can't really say for Godot, no one ever has, not even the novel assassinator himself. (*Gestures toward B. Pozzo moves like the blind man he is to the chess board. Moves a piece.*) But all things come to thems that wait. Checkmate. (*Exits.*)

BECKETT: Have I suffered for nothing speaking for them . . . the Molloys, the Malones, the Murphys . . . when in order to stop speaking . . . I was only speaking for myself. I always felt I was the only rider on a rusty old ferris wheel in a deserted amusement park. (*Hamm enters in wheel chair, peering through telescope.*)

HAMM: Ahh, behold the gloom and doom mammal. Nothing is funnier than unhappiness. (*Still peering through telescope.*) Furrowed brow. Tired eyes. He seems unhappy. (*B. steps into garbage can. Only head and shoulders can be seen.*) But what makes him unhappy? The utter isolation and depravity of man? (*Chuckles.*) I love the old questions . . . the questions . . . the old answers. There's nothing like them. (*Peers through telescope.*) What's happening? (*Peers at audience.*) Who's he with? Who are . . .

BECKETT: Something is taking its course.

HAMM: Wait, we're not beginning to . . . to mean something?

BECKETT: Mean something? You and me mean something?

HAMM: I wonder. . . . Imagine if a rational being came back to earth, wouldn't he be liable to get ideas into his head if he observed us long enough? (*In a rational voice.*) Ah, good, now I see what it is, yes, now I understand what they're at. (*Drops telescope.*) And without going so far as that, we ourselves . . . we ourselves at certain moments . . . To think for a moment it won't all have been for nothing. (*Hamm exits.*)

BECKETT: How in words does one speak of meaning, in this place, without putting an end to us? Shall I ever be able to go silent? Immaculate silence. I exist now only because of my imagination, and your imaginations, because of my words and yours. . . . (*Pause.*) My closing years were spent fittingly enough in a dull grey neighborhood of Paris, the buildings tucked tightly together, designed to encourage suicide. I often lounged in the St. Jacques Hotel. Thinking of Shakespeare's Jacques' "all the world's a stage." And sitting there sipping coffee, sans teeth, sans eyes, sans tastes, my ruination and ruminations wrapped in humorous sadness. (*Pause.*) The hotel reminded me of one of those motels one stays in outside of American airports. Lonely people are always there. It was a small daily pleasure for me . . . those last days. . . .

I trundled on used and reused feet.
my tattered shoes flush and livid
with the Liffey river.
A barge carrying a cargo of nails.

my mind annulled and wrecked,
yet to some,
a banner,
(a literary banner)
of meat bleeding on the silk of language seas.
I was an arctic flower. . . .
   (*Beckett closes garbage can lid on himself.*)

Finis.

13

Joyce and Beckett: A Preliminary Checklist of Publications

John P. Harrington

THE FOLLOWING BIBLIOGRAPHY is a first, provisional effort to document existing critical sources relevant to the literary relationship of James Joyce and Samuel Beckett. Rather than attempt a comprehensive essay in bibliography, this list identifies the most accessible publications of pertinent printed criticism without pursuing the publication history of secondary sources that have been reprinted with or without revision. Also, this list includes only those sources that evince substantial discussion of Joyce–Beckett literary relations: it omits critical works that refer to the Joyce–Beckett relationship only in passing or only as a matter of custom. No attempt has been made to abstract in annotation the very diverse approaches to this complex literary relationship.

This initial effort of collecting the major comparative studies of Joyce and Beckett is indebted to the contributors in this volume, especially James Acheson, Susan Brienza, Phyllis Carey, Ed Jewinski, and Melvin Friedman. Previous reference works that have proven most helpful include Cathleen Culotta Andonian, *Samuel Beckett: A Reference Guide* (Boston: Hall, 1989); Raymond Federman and John Fletcher, *Samuel Beckett: His Works and His Critics: An Essay in Bibliography* (Berkeley: University of California Press, 1970); Lawrence Graver and Raymond Federman, *Samuel Beckett: The Critical Heritage* (London: Routledge & Kegan Paul, 1979); *The James Joyce Quarterly* "JJ Checklist"; *The Modern Language Association Bibliography;* and Thomas Jackson Rice, *James Joyce: A Guide to Research* (New York: Garland, 1982).

Abel, Lionel. "Beckett and James Joyce in *Endgame.*" *Metatheater: A New View of Dramatic Form.* New York: Hill & Wang, 1963. 134–40.

Adams, Robert Martin. "Samuel Beckett." *Afterjoyce: Studies in Fiction After "Ulysses."* New York: Oxford University Press, 1977. 90–113.

Albright, Daniel. "Beckett." *Representations and the Imagination: Beckett, Kafka, Nabokov, Schoenberg.* Chicago: The University of Chicago Press, 1981. 150–208.

Allen, Michael. "A Note on Sex in Beckett." *Across a Roaring Hill: The Protestant Imagination in Modern Ireland.* Ed. Gerald Dawe and Edna Longley. Belfast: Blackstaff, 1985. 39–47.

Andonian, Cathleen Culotta. "Barbara Reich Gluck. *Joyce and Beckett: Friendship and Fiction.*" *l'esprit créateur* 21 (Fall 1980): 100.

Atlas, James. "The Prose of Samuel Beckett: Notes From the Terminal Ward." *Two Decades of Irish Writing: A Critical Survey.* Ed. Douglas Dunn. Chester Springs, Pa.: Dufour, 1975. 186–96.

Aubarède, Gabriel d'. "En Attendant . . . Beckett." *Nouvelles Littéraires* 16 February 1961: 1, 7.

Bair, Deirdre. *Samuel Beckett: A Biography.* New York: Harcourt Brace Jovanovich, 1978.

Barnard, G. C. *Samuel Beckett: A New Approach, A Study of the Novels and Plays.* New York: Dodd, Mead, 1970.

Barth, John. "The Literature of Exhaustion." *The Friday Book: Essays and Other Nonfiction.* New York: Putnam, 1984. 62–76.

Bataille, Georges. "Le Silence de Molloy." *Critique* 7 (15 May 1951): 387–96.

Beebe, Maurice. "Reflection and Reflexive Trends in Modern Fiction." *Bucknell Review* 22 (Fall 1976): 13–26.

Beigbeder, Marc. *Le Théâtre en France depuis la Libération.* Paris: Bordas, 1959.

Beja, Morris. "Recent Books on Modern Fiction." *Modern Fiction Studies* 26 (Summer 1980): 276–81.

Ben-Zvi, Linda. "Fritz Mauthner for Company." *Journal of Beckett Studies* 9 (1984): 65–88.

——. "Mauthner's *Critique of Language:* A Forgotten Book at the *Wake.*" *Comparative Literature Studies* 19 (Summer 1982): 143–63.

Bernal, Olga. "Samuel Beckett: l'écrivain et le savoir." *Journal of Beckett Studies* 2 (Summer 1977): 59–62.

Bernhart, Walter. " 'Human Nature's Intricacies' and 'Rigorous Truth': Joyce's 'Clay,' Beckett's 'Dante and the Lobster,' und die Individuation." *Arbeiten aus Anglistik und Amerikanstik* 1 (1976): 25–64; 2 (1977): 63–98.

Bernheimer, Charles. "Grammacentricity and Modernism." *Mosaic* 11 (Fall 1977): 103–16.

Boyd, Michael. "Joyce into Beckett: Prolegomena to Any Future Fictions." *The Reflexive Novel: Fiction as Critique*. Lewisburg, Pa.: Bucknell University Press, 1983. 118–45.

Brée, Germaine. "The Strange World of Beckett's 'Grands Articulés.' " *Samuel Beckett Now: Critical Approaches to His Novels, Poetry, and Plays*. Ed. Melvin J. Friedman. Chicago: The University of Chicago Press, 1970. 73–87.

Brick, Alan. "The Madman in His Cell: Joyce, Beckett, Nabokov, and the Stereotypes." *Massachusetts Review* 1 (October 1959): 40–55.

Brown, Terence. "Dublin in Twentieth-Century Writing: Metaphor and Subject." *Irish University Review* 8 (Spring 1978): 7–21.

Busi, Frederick. "Joycean Echoes in *Waiting for Godot*." *Research Studies* 43 (June 1975): 71–87.

———. *The Transformations of Godot*. Lexington: University Press of Kentucky, 1980.

Caramello, Charles. *Silverless Mirrors: Book, Self, and Postmodern American Fiction*. Tallahassee: University Presses of Florida, 1983.

Carey, Phyllis. "Beckett's Pim and Joyce's Shem." *James Joyce Quarterly* 26 (Spring 1989): 435–39.

Chalker, John. "The Satiric Shape of *Watt*." *Beckett the Shape Changer*. Ed. Katherine Worth. Boston: Routledge & Kegan Paul, 1975. 19–37.

Chaucer, Daniel. *"Waiting for Godot."* *Shenandoah* 6 (Spring 1955): 80–82.

Cohn, Ruby. "Joyce and Beckett, Irish Cosmopolitans." *James Joyce Quarterly* 8 (Summer 1971): 385–91.

———. *Samuel Beckett: The Comic Gamut*. New Brunswick: Rutgers University Press, 1962.

Cronin, Anthony. *A Question of Modernity*. London: Secker & Warburg, 1966.

Davie, Donald. "Kinds of Comedy." *Spectrum* 2 (Winter 1958): 25–31.

Deane, Seamus. "Heroic Styles: The Tradition of an Idea." *Ireland's Field Day*. Notre Dame: Notre Dame University Press, 1986. 45–58.

———. "Irish Poetry and Irish Nationalism." *Two Decades of Irish Writing*. Ed. Douglas Dunn. Cheshire: Carcanet, 1975. 4–22.

———. "Joyce and Beckett." *Celtic Revivals: Essays in Modern Irish Literature 1880–1980*. London: Faber & Faber, 1985. 123–34.

Dearlove, J. E. *Accommodating the Chaos: Samuel Beckett's Nonrelational Art*. Durham: Duke University Press, 1982.

———. "Allusion to Archetype." *Journal of Beckett Studies* 10 (1985): 121–33.

Doran, Eva. "Au seuil de Beckett: Quelques notes sur 'Dante . . . Bruno . Vico . . Joyce.' " *Stanford French Review* 5 (Spring 1981): 121–27.

Ehler, Sidney A. "Beckett: Irlandais déraciné." *Nouvelles Littéraires* 11 December 1969: 5.

Ellmann, Richard. *James Joyce*. Rev. ed. New York: Oxford University Press, 1982.

——. "Samuel Beckett: Nayman of Noland." *Four Dubliners: Oscar Wilde, William Butler Yeats, James Joyce, Samuel Beckett.* New York: Braziller, 1988. 91–116.

Fitch, Noel Riley. *Sylvia Beach and the Lost Generation: A History of Literary Paris in the Twenties and Thirties.* New York: Norton, 1983.

Fletcher, John. "Samuel Beckett as Critic." *The Listener* 74 (25 November 1965): 862–63.

Friedman, Melvin J. "Introductory Notes to Beckett's Poetry." *Samuel Beckett: The Art of Rhetoric.* Ed. Edouard Morot-Sir, Howard Harper, and Dougald McMillan. Chapel Hill: North Carolina Studies in the Romance Languages and Literatures, 1976. 143–49.

——. "The Novels of Samuel Beckett: An Amalgam of Joyce and Proust." *Comparative Literature* 12 (Winter 1960): 47–58.

——. "Prefatory Note." *The Seventh of Joyce.* Ed. Bernard Benstock. Bloomington: Indiana University Press, 1982. 27–28.

——. Review of *Beckett and Joyce: Friendship and Fiction* by Barbara Reich Gluck. *Journal of Beckett Studies* 6 (1980): 138–41.

Frye, Northrop. "The Nightmare Life in Death." *Hudson Review* 13 (Autumn 1960): 442–49.

Fujii, Kayo. "Joyce to Beckett." *Joyce Kara Joyce.* Ed. Yukio Suzuki. Tokyo: Tokyodo Shuppan, 1982. 231–41.

Furbank, P. N. "Beckett's Purgatory." *Encounter* 22 (June 1964): 69–72.

Gibson, Andrew. "One Kind of Ambiguity in Joyce, Beckett, and Robbe-Grillet." *Canadian Review of Comparative Literature* 12 (September 1985): 409–21.

Gluck, Barbara Reich. *Beckett and Joyce: Friendship and Fiction.* Lewisburg, Pa.: Bucknell University Press, 1979.

Golden, Sean. "Familiars in a Ruinstrewn Land: *Endgame* as Political Allegory." *Contemporary Literature* 22 (Fall 1981): 425–55.

Gontarski, S. E. Review of *Beckett and Joyce: Friendship and Fiction* by Barbara Reich Gluck. *James Joyce Quarterly* 17 (Spring 1980): 323–25.

——. "The Intent of Undoing." *The Intent of Undoing in Samuel Beckett's Dramatic Texts.* Bloomington: Indiana University Press, 1985. 1–21.

——. "Samuel Beckett, James Joyce's 'Illstarred Punster.'" *The Seventh of Joyce.* Ed. Bernard Benstock. Bloomington: Indiana University Press, 1982. 29–36.

Gruen, John. "Samuel Beckett Talks About Samuel Beckett." *Vogue* 154 (December 1969): 210.

Gullette, David. "Mon jour chez Sam." *Ploughshares* 1 (June 1972): 65–69.

Hassan, Ihab. "Beckett: Imagination Ending." *The Dismemberment of Orpheus: Toward a Postmodern Literature.* Rev. ed. Madison: University of Wisconsin Press, 1982. 210–46.

——. "( ): *Finnegans Wake* and the Post-Modern Imagination." *Paracriticisms: Seven Speculations of the Times*. Urbana: University of Illinois Press, 1975. 77–94.

——. "Joyce, Beckett, and the Postmodern Imagination." *Tri-Quarterly* 34 (Fall 1975): 179–200.

——. "Joyce–Beckett: A Scenario in Eight Scenes and a Voice." *Paracriticisms: Seven Speculations of the Times*. Urbana: University of Illinois Press, 1975. 63–73.

——. *The Literature of Silence: Henry Miller and Samuel Beckett*. New York: Knopf, 1967.

Hayman, David. "Joyce ♦ Beckett/Joyce." *The Seventh of Joyce*. Ed. Bernard Benstock. Bloomington: Indiana University Press, 1982. 37–43.

——. "A Meeting in the Park and a Meeting on the Bridge: Joyce and Beckett." *James Joyce Quarterly* 8 (Summer 1971): 372–84.

——. "Some Writers in the Wake of the *Wake*." *Tri-Quarterly* 38 (Winter 1977): 3–38.

Hibon, Bernard. "Samuel Beckett: Irish Traditions and Irish Creation." *Aspects of the Irish Theater*. Ed. Patrick Rafroidi, Ramonde Popot, and William Parker. Lille: Publications de l'Université de Lille, 1972. 225–41.

Hickman, Vera. "Waiting for Something: Samuel Beckett, Disciple of Joyce." *Ante* 2 (Summer 1966): 57–64.

Higgins, Aidan. "Tired Lines, or Tales My Mother Told Me." *A Bash in the Tunnel: James Joyce by the Irish*. Ed. John Ryan. London: Clifton, 1970. 55–60.

Hoffman, Frederick J. *Samuel Beckett: The Language of Self*. Carbondale: Southern Illinois University Press, 1962.

Hogan, Robert. "Trying to Like Beckett." *"Since O'Casey" and Other Essays on Irish Drama*. Totowa, N.J.: Barnes & Noble, 1983. 113–18.

Hunter, G. K. "English Drama, 1900–1960." *The Twentieth Century*. Ed. Bernard Bergonzi. London: Barrie and Jenkins, 1970. 310–35.

Hutchings, William. " 'Shat into Grace' Or, A Tale of a Turd: Why It is How It Is in Samuel Beckett's *How It Is*." *Papers on Language and Literature* 21 (Winter 1985): 64–87.

Janvier, Ludovic. "Sames: Joyce et Beckett." *L'arc* 36 (1968): 39–43.

Jennings, Paul. "Joyce à Beckett." *Oodles of Oddlies*. London: Reinhart, 1963. 15–18.

Johnston, Denis. "Waiting with Beckett." *Irish Writing* 34 (Spring 1956): 23–28.

Jolas, Maria. "A Bloomlein for Sam." *Beckett at 60: A Festschrift*. London: Calder and Boyars, 1967. 14–16.

Jude the Obscure [pseud.]. "The H. U. Business Section." *Honest Ulsterman* 30 (September–October 1971): 12–15.

Kearney, Richard. "Beckett: The Demythologizing Intellect." *The Irish Mind: Exploring Intellectual Traditions*. Ed. Richard Kearney. Dublin: Wolfhound, 1985. 267–93.

——. "Myth and Motherland." *Ireland's Field Day*. Notre Dame: Notre Dame University Press, 1986. 61–80.

——. *Transitions: Narratives in Modern Irish Culture*. Dublin: Wolfhound, 1988.

Kellman, Steven G. "Beckett's Trilogy." *The Self-Begetting Novel*. New York: Columbia University Press, 1980. 129–43.

Kennedy, Sighle. *Murphy's Bed: A Study of Real Sources and Surreal Associations in Samuel Beckett's First Novel*. Lewisburg, Pa.: Bucknell University Press, 1971.

——. "Spirals of Need: Irish Prototypes in Samuel Beckett's Fiction." *Yeats, Joyce, and Beckett: New Light on Three Modern Irish Writers*. Ed. Kathleen McGrory and John Unterecker. Lewisburg, Pa.: Bucknell University Press, 1976. 153–166.

Kenner, Hugh. *Flaubert, Joyce, and Beckett: The Stoic Comedians*. Boston: Beacon, 1962.

——. *The Mechanic Muse*. New York: Oxford University Press, 1987.

——. *A Reader's Guide to Samuel Beckett*. New York: Farrar, Straus & Giroux, 1973.

——. *Samuel Beckett: A Critical Study*. Berkeley: University of California Press, 1968.

——. "Shades of Syntax." *Samuel Beckett: A Collection of Criticism*. Ed. Ruby Cohn. New York: McGraw-Hill, 1975. 21–31.

——. "The Terminator." *A Colder Eye: The Modern Irish Writers*. New York: Knopf, 1983. 262–73.

Kern, Edith. "Beckett's Multi-Lingual Existence." *Centerpoint* 4 (Fall 1980): 133–35.

Klinkowitz, Jerome. *The Self-Apparent Word: Fiction as Language/Language as Fiction*. Carbondale: Southern Illinois University Press, 1984.

Knowlson, James. "Beckett and Joyce." *Samuel Beckett: An Exhibition*. London: Turret, 1971. 25–29.

——, and John Pilling. *Frescoes of the Skull: The Later Prose and Drama of Samuel Beckett*. New York: Grove, 1980.

Krause, David. "The Principle of Comic Disintegration." *James Joyce Quarterly* 8 (Fall 1970): 3–12.

Le Sage, Laurent. *The French New Novel: An Introduction and a Sampler*. University Park: Pennsylvania State University Press, 1962.

Lukács, Georg. "The Ideology of Modernism." *The Meaning of Contemporary Realism*. Trans. John and Necke Mander. London: Merlin, 1962. 17–46.

McGurk, Tom. "Remembering Mr. Joyce" [Samuel Beckett interview]. *Sunday Tribune* (Dublin) 13 June 1982: 17.

McMillan, Dougald. "Samuel Beckett." *Transition: The History of a Literary Era, 1927–1938*. London: Calder and Boyars, 1975. 148–56.

Mayoux, Jean-Jacques. "Beckett and Expressionism." Trans. Ruby Cohn. *Modern Drama* 9 (December 1960): 238–41.

——. "Beckett et l'humour." *Cahiers Renaud-Barrault* 53 (February 1966): 33–41.

Mays, J. C. C. "Young Beckett's Irish Roots." *Irish University Review* 14 (Spring 1984): 18–33.

Mercier, Vivian. *Beckett/Beckett*. New York: Oxford University Press, 1977.

——. "Samuel Beckett and the Sheela-na-gig." *Kenyon Review* 23 (Spring 1961): 299–324.

Montgomery, Niall. "No Symbols Where None Intended." *New World Writing* 5 (April 1954): 324–37.

Morris, Wright. "Being Conscious." *Voicelust: Eight Contemporary Fiction Writers on Style*. Ed. Allan Weir and Don Hendrie, Jr. Lincoln: University of Nebraska Press, 1985. 23–36.

Morse, J. Mitchell. "The Contemplative Life According to Samuel Beckett." *Hudson Review* 15 (Winter 1962–1963): 512–24.

Moses, Michael Valdez. "The Sadly Rejoycing Slave: Beckett, Joyce, and Destructive Parody." *Modern Fiction Studies* 31 (Winter 1985): 659–74.

Murray, Patrick. *The Tragic Comedian: A Study of Samuel Beckett*. Cork: Mercier, 1970.

Noon, William T. "Modern Literature and the Sense of Time." *Thought* 33 (Winter 1958–1959): 571–604.

O'Brien, Eoin. *The Beckett Country: Samuel Beckett's Ireland*. Monkstown, Co. Dublin: Black Cat, 1986.

O'Donoghue, Bernard. "Irish Humor and Verbal Logic." *Critical Quarterly* 24 (Spring 1982): 33–40.

Partridge, A. C. "A Trio of Innovators: Joyce, Beckett, and Flann O'Brien." *Language and Society in Anglo-Irish Literature*. Totowa, N.J.: Barnes & Noble, 1984. 284–327.

Pasquier, Marie-Claire. "Blanc, gris, noir, gris, blanc." *Cahiers Renaud-Barrault* 106 (1983): 61–79.

Pearce, Richard. "From Joyce to Beckett: The Tale that Wags the Telling." *The Seventh of Joyce*. Ed. Bernard Benstock. Bloomington: Indiana University Press, 1982. 44–49.

——. "Symmetry/Disruption: A Paradox in Modern Science and Literature." *One Culture: Essays in Science and Literature*. Ed. George Levine and Alan Rauch. Madison: University of Wisconsin Press, 1987. 164–79.

Poulet, Robert. "Samuel Beckett." *La Lanterne magique.* Paris: Nouvelles Éditions de Bresse, 1956. 236–42.

Pountney, Rosemary. "Samuel Beckett's Interest in Form: Structural Patterning in *Play*." *Modern Drama* 19 (September 1976): 237–44.

Power, Mary. "Samuel Beckett's 'Fingal' and the Irish Tradition." *Journal of Modern Literature* 9 (1981–1982) 151–56.

Rafroidi, Patrick. "Pas de Shamrocks pour Sam Beckett: La Dimension irlandaise de *Murphy*." *Études Irlandais* 7 (December 1982): 71–81.

Read, David. "Artistic Theory in the Work of Samuel Beckett." *Journal of Beckett Studies* 8 (Autumn 1982): 7–22.

Restivo, Guiseppina. "Pozzo e Joyce." *Studi Inglesi* 2 (1975): 275–82.

Rickels, Milton. "Existential Themes in Beckett's *Unnamable*." *Criticism* 4 (Spring 1962): 134–47.

Robinson, Fred Miller. *The Comedy of Language: Studies in Modern Comic Literature.* Amherst: University of Massachusetts Press, 1980.

Rose, Marilyn Gaddis. "Decadence and Modernism: Defining by Default." *Modernist Studies: Literature and Culture, 1920–1940* 4 (1982): 195–206.

Scholes, Robert. *Fabulation and Metafiction.* Urbana: University of Illinois Press, 1979.

Schulz, Hans-Joachim. *This Hell of Stories: A Hegelian Approach to the Novels of Samuel Beckett.* The Hague: Mouton, 1973.

Seaver, Richard. "Samuel Beckett: An Introduction." *Merlin* 1 (Autumn 1952): 73–79.

Shenker, Israel. "Moody Man of Letters." *The New York Times* 6 May 1956: sec. 2; 1, 3.

Smith, Michael. "Theater: Cafe Round-Up." *Village Voice* 23 (February 1961): 10.

Smith, Stan. "Historians and Magicians: Ireland Between Fantasy and History." *Literature and the Changing Ireland.* Ed. Peter Connolly. Buckinghamshire: Smythe, 1982. 133–56.

Spender, Stephen. "Lifelong Suffocation." *The New York Times Book Review* 12 October 1958: 5.

Stamirowska, Krystyna. "The Conception of a Character in the Works of Joyce and Beckett." *Kwartalnik Neofilologiczny* (Warsaw) 14 (1967): 443–47.

Staples, Hugh. "Beckett in the *Wake*." *James Joyce Quarterly* 8 (Summer 1971): 421–24.

Stevenson, Randall. "The Autonomy of Language: James Joyce and Samuel Beckett." *The British Novel Since the Thirties: An Introduction.* London: Batsford, 1986. 194–200.

Tagliferri, Aldo. "Beckett and Joyce." Trans. A. T. and Daphne Hughes.

Samuel Beckett: Modern Critical Views. Ed. Harold Bloom. New York: Chelsea House, 1985. 247–61.

——. "Mimésis et illusionisme: À propos de Joyce et Beckett." *Psychoanalyse et sémiotique*. Paris: Union Générale d'Éditions, 1975. 267–79.

Tindall, William York. "Beckett's Bums." *Critique* 2 (Spring–Summer 1958): 3–15.

Topsfield, Valerie. *The Humour of Samuel Beckett*. New York: St. Martin's, 1988.

Tynan, Kenneth. "Theatre—A Philosophy of Despair." *Observer* 7 April 1957: 15.

Updike, John. "Small Cheer for the Old Sod." *The New Yorker* 51 (1 September 1975): 62–66.

Verdicchio, Massimo. "Exagmination Round the Fictification of Vico and Joyce." *James Joyce Quarterly* 26 (Summer 1989): 531–39.

Warner, Francis. "The Absence of Nationalism in the Work of Samuel Beckett." *Theatre and Nationalism in Twentieth-Century Ireland*. Ed. Robert O'Driscoll. Toronto: University of Toronto Press, 1971. 179–204.

About the Contributors

JAMES ACHESON is Senior Lecturer in English at the University of Canterbury in Christchurch, New Zealand. He is co-editor of *Beckett's Later Fiction and Drama: Texts for Company*, editor of *The British and Irish Novel Since 1960* and *British and Irish Drama Since 1960*, and author of two forthcoming books—one on Beckett, the other on John Fowles. A member of the Editorial Board of the *Journal of Beckett Studies*, he has published articles on Beckett and other writers in various edited collections and journals.

SUSAN BRIENZA is the author of *Samuel Beckett's New Worlds: Style in Metafiction* as well as numerous articles on Joyce and Beckett in many leading journals. She has delivered papers on Joyce and/or Beckett in Paris, Scotland, and Venice as well as at several American conferences. She has served on the Executive Board of the Samuel Beckett Society and as co-editor of *The Beckett Circle*. While continuing her Joyce scholarship, she is completing her study of law at Stanford Law School.

PHYLLIS CAREY is Associate Professor of English at Mount Mary College, Milwaukee, Wisconsin. She has published on Joyce and Beckett in the *James Joyce Quarterly*, delivered papers on Joyce–Beckett panels in Frankfurt and Milwaukee, and published several essays on Beckett and Václav Havel. She is currently working on a book-length study of Beckett and Havel.

DAVID COHEN has taught at Washington College and the University of Minnesota–Twin Cities and is now Lecturer in English at the University of Miami. He has published on Flann O'Brien, Samuel Beckett, and James Joyce and has delivered conference papers in Philadelphia, Dublin, Copenhagen, and Stirling, Scotland. His doctoral dissertation is entitled "Conclusion of the Foregoing: James Joyce, Samuel Beckett, and Flann O'Brien."

STEVEN CONNOR is Reader in Modern English Literature at Birkbeck College, University of London. He has published articles on nineteenth- and twentieth-century literature, literary theory, and contemporary popular culture. He is also the author of *Charles Dickens*,

Samuel Beckett: Repetition, Theory, and Text, Postmodernist Culture: An Introduction to Theories of the Contemporary, and *Theory and Cultural Value.*

JOHN FLETCHER is Professor of Comparative Literature at the University of East Anglia. His books include *The Novels of Samuel Beckett, Samuel Beckett's Art, Claude Simon and Fiction Now, Novel and Reader,* and *Alain Robbe-Grillet.*

MELVIN J. FRIEDMAN is Professor of English and Comparative Literature at the University of Wisconsin-Milwaukee. He is author or editor of some fifteen books. His latest title is *Pound/The Little Review: The Letters of Ezra Pound to Margaret Anderson.* He serves on the editorial boards of the *Journal of Modern Literature, Contemporary Literature, Studies in the Novel, Studies in American Fiction, Journal of Beckett Studies, International Fiction Review, Fer de Lance, Yiddish, Journal of Popular Culture, Arete: The Journal of Sport Literature.* He is currently finishing a five-year term as president of the American Association of Professors of Yiddish. He serves on the selection committee for the Ritz Paris Hemingway Award.

MICHAEL PATRICK GILLESPIE is Associate Professor of English at Marquette University. He has published *Inverted Volumes Improperly Arranged: James Joyce and His Trieste Library, James Joyce's Trieste Library: A Catalogue of Materials at the Harry Ransom Humanities Research Center,* and *Reading the Book of Himself,* in addition to essays on Joyce, Wilde, Lawrence, and Modernism.

JOHN P. HARRINGTON is Associate Professor of Humanities at The Cooper Union, New York City. He is the author of *The Irish Beckett* and editor of *The English Traveller in Ireland* and *Modern Irish Drama.*

ED JEWINSKI is Associate Professor of English at Wilfrid Laurier University, Waterloo, Ontario. He is the co-editor of *Magic Realism in Canadian Literature* and has published articles on Beckett, Lawrence, and several Canadian writers including Leacock, Livesay, Birney, and Pratt. He has served on the editorial boards of *The English Quarterly, Jewish Dialogue,* and *The New Quarterly.*

ALAN SEARING LOXTERMAN is Professor of English at the University of Richmond, Virginia, where he has taught since 1970. He has published articles on Emily Brontë and James Joyce as well as interviews with Richmond writers and with Stanley Kunity, Donald Hall, and Marvin Bell. The most recent article is "Everyman His Own God: From *Ulysses* to *Finnegans Wake*" in *Finnegans Wake: A Casebook*, edited by John Harty.

DAVID REGAN is a poet and playwright who lives and works in Milwaukee, Wisconsin. His Play "Doublin Encounters" was performed at the Joyce in Milwaukee National Conference in June 1987, and he is currently working on a one-person play that uses many of Samuel Beckett's writings and is entitled "becketts of artifice." "Beckett et Joyce et Beckett-esque" premiered at Milwaukee's Irishfest in August 1990.

Index